Performance Appraisals & Phrases

2nd Edition

by Ken Lloyd, Ph.D.

A Wiley Brand

Performance Appraisals & Phrases For Dummies®, 2nd Edition

Published by: **John Wiley & Sons, Inc.**, 111 River Street, Hoboken, NJ 07030-5774, www.wiley.com

Copyright © 2025 by John Wiley & Sons, Inc., Hoboken, New Jersey

Published simultaneously in Canada

For general information on our other products and services, please contact our Customer Care Department within the U.S. at 877-762-2974, outside the U.S. at 317-572-3993, or fax 317-572-4002. For technical support, please visit https://hub.wiley.com/community/support/dummies.

Wiley publishes in a variety of print and electronic formats and by print-on-demand. Some material included with standard print versions of this book may not be included in e-books or in print-on-demand. If this book refers to media such as a CD or DVD that is not included in the version you purchased, you may download this material at http://booksupport.wiley.com. For more information about Wiley products, visit www.wiley.com.

Library of Congress Control Number is available from the publisher.

ISBN 978-1-394-27605-9 (pbk); ISBN 978-1-394-27606-6 (ebk); ISBN 978-1-394-27607-3 (ebk)

SKY10089731_110124

Contents at a Glance

Table of Contents

PART 2: WORKING YOUR WAY THROUGH THE PROCESS

CHAPTER 11: The Best Phrases for Planning, Administration, and Organization 245

Introduction

I n the past, many managers and their employees experienced significant levels of dissatisfaction and distress regarding performance appraisals. They often dreaded the appraisal sessions and questioned the value of the entire process. Fortunately, the performance appraisal process has undergone several major changes, and it's now a far more positive and productive experience for all of the participants.

These changes are thoroughly discussed in this book. They include continuous feedback, replacing annual appraisals with quarterly or biannual appraisals, focusing on employee growth and career development as well as performance improvement, all while maintaining open two-way communication at every point. This framework also includes jointly establishing performance goals as well as development goals, along with specific action plans that monitor progress and goal attainment. Today's performance appraisals have a strong forward-focus, and they incorporate managerial coaching as a central component of the process.

In light of these changes, performance appraisals are now more open and transparent, which leads to appraisal sessions that are two-way conversations and free of the angst, stress, and dissatisfaction that were hallmarks of such sessions in the past. Today's appraisals include constructive performance-based feedback that aligns with the information provided through continuous feedback during a given evaluation period, which eliminates any surprises during the appraisal sessions. In addition, these sessions include actual discussions that focus on plans, strategies, support, and coaching to improve performance, enhance employee learning and growth, strengthen career development, and build employee motivation, satisfaction, engagement, commitment, and productivity.

About This Book

I wrote this new edition to update the performance appraisal process and facilitate each step that is associated with it. Every chapter stands on its own, and you can read any that may be of particular interest to you and obtain practical information that you can immediately apply, while leaving other chapters for a later read.

If any specific aspect of performance appraisals is high on your list right now, you can easily go to the chapter that deals with it. For example, if you're interested in how to productively lead an appraisal session, there's a chapter on this exact topic. And the same applies if you're interested in knowing more about the widespread benefits of performance appraisals, building success with performance appraisals, or preparing for performance appraisal sessions — along with several other topics that are central to this process.

In addition, if you're interested in seeing the newest and best phrases to use in the appraisal process, you'll most likely be able to find some that work for you in nine separate chapters of phrases, more than 3,300 in all, followed by two chapters that deal with the top ten words to include and the top ten behaviors to recognize in this process.

Foolish Assumptions

As I wrote this book, I made a number of assumptions about you:

>> **You're responsible for appraising employees.** I assume that you're in a supervisory or managerial position, and that one of your responsibilities is to appraise the performance of each of your employees.

>> **You'd like to avoid the problems and issues that typically accompany performance appraisals.** At this point, you're seeking new, user-friendly, and productive ways to provide highly effective feedback and coaching for your employees.

>> **You want to build your effectiveness in carrying out performance appraisals.** Whether you're new to management or you're an experienced manager or supervisor, I assume that you would like to enhance your knowledge, proficiency, and skills in order to conduct performance appraisals that truly build productivity, contribute to employee development, and align with company goals.

If at least *one* of these assumptions sounds like you, then you've come to the right place.

Icons Used in This Book

Throughout this book, I use four different icons to highlight different points. Here's what they mean:

REMEMBER

I use the Remember icon to emphasize a point for you to keep in mind whenever you're conducting appraisals.

TIP

The Tip icon highlights particularly effective ways for you to carry out various performance appraisal steps.

TECHNICAL STUFF

The Technical Stuff icon flags information that focuses on various technical points associated with the appraisal process. These points can be easily skimmed without missing the major issues.

WARNING

When you see the Warning icon, it's a good idea to take heed. This icon identifies common mistakes or problems that can develop if key points are overlooked or if incorrect actions are taken.

Beyond the Book

In addition to what you're reading right now, this book also comes with a free, access-anywhere Cheat Sheet that discusses the most effective words and terms to use in appraisals and how best to conduct an appraisal session, including how to prepare for one and how to follow it up. To view the Cheat Sheet, simply go to www.dummies.com and type **Performance Appraisals and Phrases For Dummies Cheat Sheet** in the Search box.

In addition, three bonus chapters dealing with the types of performance appraisal feedback, gathering and analyzing performance data, and following up appraisal sessions are available online. They can be found at www.dummies.com/go/Performance Appraisals&PhrasesFD.

Where to Go from Here

Whether you're new to the process of performance appraisals or an experienced manager, the best way to proceed with this book is to start with Chapter 1, as the entire process has changed significantly. Chapter 1 provides you with an overview of the newest developments, along with key steps that you can implement right now to facilitate and enhance the performance appraisal process. This chapter also sets the stage for you to proceed with the chapters that follow.

At the same time, if you're interested in specific components of the performance appraisal process, there are chapters, headings, and subheadings that will take you wherever you want to go. In addition, if you're looking for phrases that are focused on your employees' levels of proficiency and effectiveness across a vast array of their work and related behaviors, you're likely to find them among more than 3,300 phrases in Chapters 5 through 13. If you're not sure where to go, the Table of Contents and the Index will point you in the right direction.

1

Getting Started with Performance Appraisals

Chapter **1**

Building Success with Performance Appraisals

Many managers still see the performance appraisal process as an administrative rite that consumes a lot of time while producing little more than frustration, confrontation, and a loss of valuable time. This reaction is totally understandable if you're relying on a performance appraisal system and related practices that are out of alignment with today's approach to performance management.

As I explain in this book, the performance appraisal process *can* play a remarkably powerful role in developing your employees and enhancing their performance and productivity — when it's done right.

In the past, a key source of the problems associated with the performance appraisal process has been the outmoded strategy in which managers treat appraisals as an isolated, annual set of steps that are separate and distinct from all other managerial responsibilities. Fast-forward to today and you'll find that performance appraisals can be highly useful and productive when they are part of your ongoing managerial functions on a year-round basis.

As a manager, a key part of your role is to maintain regular and frequent contact with your employees, whether remote, onsite, or a combination of the two, and to provide them with regular coaching, guidance, and feedback. These steps are key components of what is called *performance management*. As part of the performance management process, there used to be a specific time — typically once a year — when managers would gather performance data on their employees, analyze it, document it, and then provide employees with specific feedback. This piece of the performance management process is the *performance appraisal*.

However, this process has undergone some major changes, which have led to far more positive and productive outcomes for employees, managers, and organizations. The first major change is that the notion of once-a-year annual appraisals has dramatically changed. Because of the dissatisfaction noted above regarding the annual process, some companies have eliminated formal annual appraisals altogether. However, it turns out that taking this step is often an overreaction, because employees still want performance-related feedback and guidance. The more widely accepted approach now is to provide more frequent performance appraisals, such as twice a year or on a quarterly basis. At the same time, even for companies that still use annual appraisals, one key fact is clear: For these sessions to generate positive outcomes, they cannot be held in a vacuum.

Hence, a related development that has significantly enhanced the performance appraisal process is a practice called *continuous feedback*. This component of performance management calls on managers to meet regularly with employees, typically on a scheduled basis as frequently as once a week. These collaborative sessions focus on employee performance, status of goal attainment, professional growth and career development, health and wellness, new initiatives, and any questions or issues that may need attention.

In the past, managers typically viewed performance appraisal not only as an isolated annual event, but also as a feedback session focused primarily on evaluation and documentation of past events. Although both of these have a place in the process, today's performance appraisals can do much more, especially by focusing more on the employees' future goals and achievements. When collaborative sessions are conducted more frequently and supported by continuous feedback, they are likely to generate a significantly broader range of positive outcomes, especially in terms of the following:

- » Motivating employees
- » Improving performance and productivity
- » Increasing satisfaction and engagement
- » Establishing, updating, and tracking goals and career paths
- » Aiding overall administration

Laying the Foundation

In order to take full advantage of the wide range of measurable benefits associated with the newest approaches to performance appraisals, it's best to start with a few foundational steps.

Rethinking annual performance appraisals

Annual performance appraisals have often been found to generate significant levels of dissatisfaction and distress for managers and employees alike. For managers, they tend to be seen as a yearly interruption of questionable value. They are typically regarded as angst-inducing rituals based on events and behaviors throughout a given year, often taxing the memory while consuming hours of valuable time. When the planned feedback is less than positive, there tends to be a related increase in managers' anxiety and stress levels. The anticipation of forthcoming disagreements, arguments, or conflicts, which is not exactly uplifting for managers, often results in *grade inflation*, namely the practice of awarding high scores in order to avoid confrontation.

At the same time, employees who are about to receive their annual performance appraisals tend to experience a combination of fear, anxiety, and nervousness, especially if there was a problematic incident that occurred close to the date of the performance appraisal session. In many cases, employees believe that they're not being fairly or accurately evaluated on the basis of their performance during the entire year, but rather are likely to receive feedback that is skewed as a result of more recent events. In addition, employees today are interested in receiving coaching, guidance, and advice to further their professional growth and career development, and this need is largely left unmet in annual appraisals.

Recognizing the advantages of more frequent performance appraisals

Increasing the number of formal performance appraisals from once to twice a year or even quarterly offers numerous advantages to managers, employees, and the organization at large. In the first place, more frequent appraisal sessions allow the organization to tailor the process to its key cycles. For organizations that conduct quarterly financial analysis and reporting, aligning employee appraisals in accordance with this timeframe provides a logical and timely basis for this employee feedback. At the same time, for organizations that are more project oriented, more frequent performance appraisals can be aligned with the timing of other key benchmarks that are central to company operations during a given year.

More frequent performance appraisals also provide an opportunity to place the employees' goals in a more realistic timeframe. Although some goals can be a year-long pursuit, others can be pursued and met in a shorter period of time. More frequent performance appraisals provide employees with better opportunities to receive formal feedback and guidance on their goals while the achievement of those goals is still fresh in mind.

It's also important to recognize that many employees, especially Millennials (born 1981–1996) and Gen Z (born 1997–2012), are highly interested in sensing that their employer is truly committed to their growth, development, and career advancement. When employees are formally appraised quarterly or at least twice a year, they are more likely to sense this type of commitment from their managers and to thereby feel more valued, respected, satisfied, and energized.

These employees are not only highly interested in feedback, but they are also interested in *feedforward*: instruction and advice on the specific steps they can take to attain goals, improve performance, enhance growth, and guide their careers. More frequent formal performance appraisal sessions provide a meaningful and collaborative opportunity to address these interests.

Within this framework, an annual performance appraisal can still be provided at year-end, but it should not exist in isolation. Rather, if multiple appraisals are conducted during a given year, the year-end evaluation should encapsulate the formal feedback that was previously provided at the end of each evaluation period during that year. Handled in this way, the annual review is likely to be more accurate, useful, and forward-looking. However, to take the process to a higher and more productive level, a key element is the inclusion of continuous feedback.

Effectively incorporating continuous feedback

Continuous feedback is the managerial practice of providing regular feedback, feedforward, guidance, and coaching to individual employees on a regular basis, typically once a week or once every two weeks. These sessions can be held onsite or remotely, and they are not agenda-driven. Rather, these sessions provide an open forum to discuss topics of importance to each employee, the team, the department, and the organization at large. Premised on collaboration and two-way communication between managers and their employees on virtually any topic at work, the process of continuous feedback can include discussions that focus on an employee's progress and performance, concerns and suggestions, metrics associated with goals, adjustments of existing goals, frameworks for new goals, health and wellness, career coaching, and defining and refining additional steps for upskilling and career advancement.

Providing continuous feedback also helps meet the previously noted needs of many employees that are focused on receiving honest and accurate feedback and feeling that they are respected and valued by their manager and the organization at large. These employees want to sense that the company truly cares about them and seeks to partner with them as they move forward on their career path.

At the same time, continuous feedback has also been found to be directly related to a number of positive outcomes, including improved performance, higher levels of employee satisfaction, and greater levels of engagement. This type of feedback also further strengthens the working relationship between managers and their employees, hence reinforcing the levels of trust and support that are so important to employees today.

All these topics and more are discussed in greater detail in Chapter 2.

Utilizing additional sources of feedback

Many people think that the only source of feedback during the appraisal process is the manager. Although the manager's role in the process is central and essential, the quality and effectiveness of the entire process is significantly upgraded when two additional sources are included. These two sources — self-evaluations and 360-degree feedback — provide information and insight that lead to the continuation of excellent performance and improvement of subpar performance.

By including self-evaluations in the performance appraisal process, there is an increased opportunity for employees to generate a clearer picture of their past performance, as well as to further clarify their performance goals, development goals, and the near-term and longer-term steps required to meet them. In addition, it is quite revealing for employees to highlight the areas in which they feel positively about their performance, while simultaneously receiving feedback from their managers that can include recognition as well as suggestions for improvements. At the same time, it is equally important — and oftentimes uplifting — for employees to learn that some of the aspects of their own performance they regard as subpar are described and reviewed more favorably by their managers.

Another key component in gathering accurate and current performance-related information comes from 360-degree feedback, especially in terms of feedback from a given employee's peers and direct reports. This feedback provides an even wider perspective of the employee's performance and behaviors, thereby adding increased credibility, acceptability, and usability to the overall appraisal process.

Exploring the appraisal options

When conducting performance appraisals, it's important to have a clear understanding of the various methods you can utilize to provide performance feedback. This is particularly compelling information for each employee, not only because it is individually tailored to their performance, but also because it is directly related to the ways in which employees learn. Namely, there is an auditory aspect of learning that comes from discussing performance, along with a kinesthetic and visual aspect of learning that comes from providing each employee with a tangible and readable document regarding their performance.

As a result, it's quite useful to look at the main types of evaluation methods, along with the pros and cons of each. Taking this step helps you design and define the feedback that you are providing, while also enabling you to generate content that is more likely to be relevant and meaningful to each of your employees.

Some of today's most frequently used evaluation methods include:

>> Essays

>> Graphic rating scales

>> Checklists

>> Forced choice

>> Management by objectives

These appraisal options plus several more, along with hands-on information regarding the use of additional sources of feedback, are discussed in Bonus Chapter 1, "The Types of Performance Appraisal Feedback."

Successfully Navigating through the Appraisal Process

With this foundation in place, there are various preparatory steps that help set the stage for highly effective and productive performance appraisals, especially within the framework of multiple appraisal sessions and continuous feedback.

Generating the right mindset and the right plans

As your employees' manager, you play the central role in the performance appraisal process. You're the primary source of feedback regarding their performance, productivity, goal attainment, and overall actions on the job. It can be easy for managers to fall into a role that is closer to inspector or even disciplinarian when carrying out performance appraisals.

However, the entire process of performance appraisals will be significantly enhanced if you instead envision yourself as a coach. You'll certainly want to provide accurate, fair, timely, and useful feedback to each member of your team, but a coach does more than that. With this expanded mindset and orientation, your role in performance appraisals is focused on working collaboratively with each of your employees to develop areas in which their skills or performance were not up to par, guide their development, and jointly establish rewarding and fulfilling strategies that will help take their work and their careers to the next level.

At the same time, a key element of effective coaching is effective planning. For your appraisal sessions to generate the kinds of positive and productive outcomes you're seeking, some advance planning is essential. By approaching the logistics of these sessions within the framework of coaching, such as by including your employees in the planning side of these sessions, you increase employees' anticipation, involvement, and receptiveness.

On the one hand, the more you understand your employees as individuals, the more you'll be able to create positive and productive performance appraisal sessions. At the same time, even though a coaching approach to performance management will help you gain this insight, it is equally important to have a high degree of self-insight and personal understanding. Such insight plays a central role in the appraisal process. Some of the key formational steps include the following, all of which are discussed in more detail in Chapter 3:

>> Take a careful and honest look at yourself as a manager and coach.

>> Step back and look at the expectations that you've established for each of your employees and at the evaluation process itself.

>> Carefully consider the feedback that you've received regarding your managerial style and interactions with members of your team.

>> Delve inward and try to identify any fear or hesitation you may be harboring because of past negative experiences linked to performance appraisals.

TIP

By applying specific strategies to build your self-awareness, self-insight, and empathy, you greatly enhance your ability to understand your employees as well as your skills to appraise their performance and guide them toward future performance enhancement, growth, and development. By increasing your self-insight, you'll also be increasing your confidence and effectiveness in these sessions — and simultaneously reducing your own hesitation and anxiety.

Gathering and reviewing performance data from varied sources

For your feedback to have relevance and a lasting impact, it must be based on specific examples of employee performance. This type of information cannot be gleaned through quick and intermittent visits with your employees, nor is it accessible at the last minute.

Accurate appraisals require a real understanding of your employees' performance throughout the evaluation period, regardless of whether that period is one year, six months, or three months. In addition to data that you gather from self-evaluations and 360-degree feedback, you can generate current and useful performance-related information through direct one-on-one contact with your individual employees on a regular basis, onsite or remotely, through continuous feedback.

Essential performance data is generated by regularly communicating and collaborating with each employee, obtaining current and direct information regarding a given employee's performance and goal attainment, and by having ongoing discussions premised on feedback and feedforward. This approach clarifies and fortifies performance, upskilling, and growth on a continuous basis. At the same time, this type of interaction removes the unknown elements, surprises, and disagreements that typically have undermined so many performance appraisal sessions.

In addition to the approaches noted above, you can further enhance the quality, reliability, accuracy, and acceptability of your performance appraisals by familiarizing yourself upfront with other important pieces of job-related data. This includes a look at each employee's files, job description, prior appraisals, and any notes you've taken along the way. Additional performance-related data can also be generated and reviewed by using systems available through today's performance management software.

Marginal data gathering leads to useless feedback, which leads to employee resistance, dissatisfaction, and distress.

Preparing evaluations

After you've reviewed all the performance data from a variety of sources, the next step is to complete the evaluation form. These forms vary from one company to another, but some overarching tips can help you handle this step more easily and effectively. These tips include evaluating your best employees first, entering your written comments before the numerical ratings, and considering how your employees will feel when they read your comments.

Fortunately, if you provide your employees continuous feedback as well as more than one formal performance appraisal per year, many of the classical issues and problems associated with preparing evaluations cease to exist.

Your comments in the written appraisals will generate resistance if they're invalid, inaccurate, unsubstantiated, out of date, or focused on personality instead of performance.

I've included links to several companies that offer performance management software and apps in Bonus Chapter 2, "Gathering and Reviewing Performance Data."

Conducting highly effective appraisal sessions

After you've completed the individual evaluation forms with ratings that are based on current direct observations of your employees' performance, behaviors, goal attainment, and results during a given evaluation period, you're ready for face-to-face performance appraisal sessions.

Because you're providing your employees with feedback, coaching, and guidance throughout the evaluation period, your employees already have a clear understanding of how they've been performing on the job, and this means that you have all but eliminated the likelihood of resistance or defensiveness during this meeting. After all, these sessions are premised on two-way communication from start to finish. With this foundation in place, you'll be in an excellent position literally and figuratively to provide highly impactful feedback and feedforward.

Some of the key steps that will help make these meetings even more successful include:

» Identifying the key takeaways
» Jointly establishing the agenda
» Bringing relevant performance data
» Focusing on maintaining a dialogue

As you engage in the appraisal discussion with each employee, you can enhance the dialogue by opening the conversation positively, providing constructive feedback, reviewing goal attainment and future objectives, jointly analyzing critical incidents, honestly and candidly discussing strengths and areas needing improvement, setting the framework for additional growth and development, openly reviewing the various ratings, and properly concluding the sessions.

Actions that prevent the most common mistakes

As you navigate through the performance appraisal process and meet with each of your employees, note that all of your best efforts can be undermined by some common and easily preventable missteps. These types of errors contribute to the angst, frustration, and dissatisfaction that can accompany performance appraisals for managers as well as employees. Fortunately, these potential problems can be easily identified and preemptively avoided. Some of the most productive strategies to eliminate these disruptive issues include:

» Accurately weighing recent events
» Removing bias and stereotypes
» Blocking the halo and horns effects
» Avoiding skewed ratings
» Presenting facts rather than generalizations

There are also some common communication-related blockages that can easily disrupt and derail these sessions. Some of the most common sources of such blockages include labeling, mentioning other employees, getting defensive, and arguing. Along these lines, such behaviors as bargaining, talking too much, postponing sessions, and providing feedback that surprises your employees should also be avoided.

In Chapter 4, I cover all of the steps associated with effectively leading performance appraisal sessions, as well as identifying and avoiding the most common mistakes that can easily derail them.

Taking follow-up actions

Although some managers believe that the appraisal process ends when the performance appraisal session ends, the reality is that the end of the appraisal session is simply another step in the performance management process that includes ongoing contact and two-way communication, feedback, and feedforward with your employees. When the formal appraisal session has been completed, additional follow-up steps keep the process moving.

One central area that calls for such follow-up is centered upon the employees' goals. Depending upon an organization's operations and the nature of the work, projects, and business cycles, some prefer to include goal-setting during the individual performance appraisal sessions, whereas others focus these sessions on current goal attainment and drafting an overall framework for forthcoming goals. With the latter approach, the strategy is to set up a future meeting that will focus specifically on jointly establishing new goals.

Either way, as a result of the feedback and feedforward that you have provided to your employees in the performance appraisal sessions and throughout a given evaluation period, you and each of your employees will have plenty of data to use in jointly developing goals for the newest evaluation period and beyond, depending on the nature of the goals themselves.

For goals to be motivational and generate measurable value and productive results, they must be composed of more than general hopes, wishes, and visions, no matter how well-intentioned. To be meaningful, effective, and productive goals, goals must be clear, specific, prioritized, challenging, measurable, and supported by timelines, deadlines, and action plans. At the same time, your employees' goals should align with departmental and company goals with a clear focus on enhancing each employee's performance, productivity, and development.

Within this framework, I define two types of goals:

>> Performance goals: These goals focus on each employee's productivity, output, results, and the workplace behaviors associated with carrying out job responsibilities and pursuing objectives.

>> Development goals: These focus on enhancing each employee's effectiveness and personal growth through objectives that are centered on upskilling, training, and progress on their career path.

With these goals in place, your next step is to continue to maintain ongoing and open communications with your employees, such as through regular — if not continuous — feedback. Maintaining this level of contact clearly increases the likelihood that the employees' goals will be met or exceeded, while potential problems or glitches along the way can be managed. This contact also leads to increased agility when it comes to unforeseen circumstances that call for adjustments to existing goals or the creation of new ones.

With performance appraisals functioning as but one component in the performance management process, a cycle is developed. First, you and your employees jointly establish and agree upon specific performance and development goals. After this has been completed and finalized, you provide ongoing coaching, feedback, and feedforward throughout the evaluation period. As a result, when the time for performance appraisals arrives, both you and your employees know exactly how they've been doing. This means that you should have no difficulty creating the evaluation or conducting the face-to-face sessions, and your employees should have no difficulty understanding and accepting the feedback and working further with you to correct any existing performance problems as well as reaching and even exceeding the newest set of goals. After you've completed a given performance appraisal session, this goal-setting process starts anew.

Also, in terms of follow-up, the entire process is supported and enhanced through informal feedback. These unscheduled visits, whether in-person or virtual, provide excellent opportunities to learn more about how things are going for each employee. This type of contact further strengthens the relationship between employees and their managers.

However, as part of the follow-up process, there may be times when an employee needs more than coaching to improve performance. In such cases, a *performance improvement plan (PIP)* can be quite helpful, especially when provided in a supportive and constructive context with language that is more developmental than critical. With a solid and collaborative relationship between the manager and the employee already in place, the information that an employee receives in a PIP is more likely to resonate and positively impact future behavior. In most cases, PIPs also include a timeline related to the performance that warrants improvement. This timeline can specify a reevaluation meeting within 60 to 90 days, or it can indicate that employment will be terminated if the noted improvement or improvements are not made within the specified time period. In this latter situation, the PIP also serves as the final written warning.

Also on a follow-up basis, a growing number of organizations are removing raises from the performance appraisal process. It has been found that linking raises with performance appraisals has generated distraction and a misguided focus during the appraisal session, along with decreased cooperation and collaboration and increased dissatisfaction. As a result, many organizations are now separating raises from performance appraisals, a step that has generated increased objectivity in their overall compensation plans. In this framework, discussions about raises are typically held in a separate session with each employee.

You'll find a detailed discussion regarding goal-setting, PIP plans, and managing going forward in Bonus Chapter 3, "Following-Up."

Using Effective Phrases

Your written comments in the performance appraisal process offer an excellent opportunity to present compelling, long-lasting, and motivational feedback and feedforward to your employees. To do so, the phrases you use must be specifically designed to energize your employees to continue and even surpass their excellent performance, while simultaneously helping them to understand and upgrade their questionable performance.

The best way to reach this objective is to identify the key areas of performance and then provide impactful phrases that target the full range of employee behaviors. Chapters 5 through 13 provide more than 3,300 such phrases.

With a state-of-the-art performance appraisal system in place, supported by continuous feedback and backed up by specifically designed phrases to use in this process, you're in an excellent position to build employee engagement, satisfaction, agility, collaboration, and communication while simultaneously enhancing the performance, productivity, growth, and development of your employees, your department, and your company.

In addition, Chapters 14 and 15 respectively, I discuss the top ten words to include in performance appraisals and the top ten behaviors that merit special recognition.

Chapter **2**

What Performance Appraisals Do for You and Your Team

Performance appraisals have the potential to generate numerous measurably positive outcomes for individual employees as well as for their managers, departments, and the company at large. After all, there's no question that employees need feedback to learn, grow, and improve their performance, and those are just a few of the key positive outcomes that can emanate from effective performance appraisals. However, a problem occurs in companies that are still relying on annual performance appraisals with intermittent informal feedback at best. This is a common practice that generates distress, dissatisfaction, resistance, and demotivation for both employees and their managers.

In order to benefit from these myriad positive outcomes, the first step is to take a look at the well-entrenched process of annual appraisals, identify the issues and problems, and present some positive and productive solutions to help these appraisals reach their potential. In other words, annual performance appraisals need to be appraised. That's what this chapter is all about, followed by information regarding the many ways that today's approach to performance appraisals can help you, your employees, and your company.

Appraising Annual Appraisals

If you were to sit down to evaluate the performance of an employee named "Annual Performance Appraisals," it would not be surprising to find that your evaluation ironically includes the comment, "needs improvement." Although annual appraisals can be somewhat improved when accompanied by informal feedback along the way, the lack of formality and regularity accompanying such feedback tends to make those appraisals' impact rather negligible. The most common overall perception is that annual appraisals are isolated time-consuming corporate rituals that reappear at the end of each year and inadvertently foster an aura of organizational negativity that is practically palpable.

When there are organizational issues that generate dissatisfaction across numerous departments and impacting employees at all levels, the typical response of management is to dig deeper into whatever may be causing the problem and then set the wheels in motion to make some changes. It does not take much digging to determine why annual appraisals are causing so much trouble.

Identifying the problems

The problems associated with annual appraisals are widely sensed by employees and their managers, and they are generated by such issues as the following:

>> **Delayed reinforcement:** For learning to occur, it's important for feedback to be provided close to the behaviors in question. This point is totally missed in annual appraisals, with employees conceivably being provided with feedback on their performance long after they engaged in the evaluated behaviors. With this type of delay, the likelihood of an employee internalizing and applying new skills in the

future is significantly diminished. In addition, without timely constructive feedback, your employees' mistakes may well be repeated.

>> **Biased by recent events:** In addition to delaying recognition or constructive feedback on a timely basis, a related problem with annual appraisals is that recent events are more likely to influence the rating that an employee receives. This outcome is particularly problematic when an employee has performed in stellar fashion throughout the evaluation period, only to have a problematic incident right before the performance appraisal session. The manager might not remember much about the employee's terrific work during the year, because much of it has become a blur, but that recent misstep is not going to be forgotten. This is extraordinarily unfair to the employee, and it's likely to create a problematic exchange during the appraisal session, followed by negative feelings experienced by the manager as well as the employee.

>> **Lack of agility:** Agility, namely the flexibility and adaptability associated with adjusting to today's dynamic world of work, is basically missing when annual appraisals are in play. By stretching out feedback over the course of a year, there can be changes, adjustments, upgrades, and adaptations that employees could and would have made in real time if they had been given timely feedback. With such feedback being provided at the end of the year, employees are likely to continue to handle a given project in a mode that is outdated, unnecessary, or counter-productive — or perhaps the entire project has become irrelevant, thereby wasting time, energy, and money while generating frustration and dissatisfaction.

>> **Focused exclusively on the past:** Employees today are looking to work in organizations that are interested in employee growth, professional development, and career advancement. This core value is essentially left unfulfilled and disregarded when formal feedback is provided on an annual basis, because such feedback focuses primarily on the past. For the employees, this sends a message that they are not particularly respected or valued by the company, and this further undermines their loyalty, commitment, and motivation.

>> **One-way communication:** Annual appraisals tend to be premised on one-way communication directed from the manager to the employee. This doesn't offer much in the way of discussion, unless a disagreement occurs over a particular rating or assessment — a relatively common outcome due to issues associated with time delays and accuracy noted above. This one-way approach to communication is not what employees are seeking in their work. Rather, employees are interested in working with a manager who functions more as a coach and engages in open, transparent, and respectful two-way communication with them.

Mapping out the solutions

Although some organizations initially stopped annual appraisals altogether, it was not long before employees expressed dissatisfaction with this approach, especially in an era in which large numbers of employees are showing heightened interest in receiving feedback as well as feedforward. However, going back to outmoded annual appraisals was not the answer.

Fortunately, two central changes in the performance appraisal process have led to far more positive and productive outcomes:

>> More frequent performance appraisals

>> Continuous feedback

Utilizing More Frequent Appraisals

In order to significantly enhance the effectiveness of performance appraisals and generate outcomes that positively impact employee productivity, engagement, and growth, growing numbers of companies are implementing performance appraisals on a more frequent basis — typically every quarter or twice a year at a minimum.

Although reliance on annual appraisals has led to myriad problems, as noted above, no magic number of additional appraisals fits all organizations. Rather, the number of appraisals to be conducted in a given year is best determined by factors specific to each organization. Some businesses that review and report financial results on a quarterly basis have found that conducting performance appraisals in the same timeframe works well. Other companies have increased the number of appraisals based on such factors as their business cycles, nature of their work and projects, seasonality of their business, typical duration of goals, and company size.

REMEMBER

In light of the dynamics and rapidly changing internal and external forces in today's work world, many projects and goals are established for time periods that are significantly shorter than a full year, hence making more frequent appraisals even more useful and productive.

Although the optimum number of reviews can vary by organization, any increase will surpass standalone annual reviews. The demonstrated benefits accrued from more frequent appraisals, especially quarterly appraisals, are particularly compelling:

>> **Increased accuracy, relevance, and real-time information:** Performance-related feedback provided on a timely basis has a far greater likelihood to be accurate and fact-based. The actions, steps, and behaviors carried out by the employee during a shorter appraisal period — such as three months — will be fresh in the minds of the manager and the employee, thereby facilitating a discussion that focuses on demonstrable facts rather than on hazy memories and out-of-date notes. In addition, with accurate feedback, the door is easily opened for the conversation to move from feedback to feedforward.

>> **More forward-focused and growth-oriented:** With a foundation premised on an initial discussion composed of accurate and timely feedback, the conversation can simultaneously focus on the steps for the employee to take in order to upgrade any performance issues, establish updated metrics and goals, and further lay out plans for education and upskilling. In this capacity, the manager functions as a coach rather than a critic, emphasizing strategies that enhance each employee's growth, development, and progress.

>> **Enhanced goal establishment and attainment:** As a result of quarterly appraisal sessions and the real-time feedback associated with them, employees are much more likely to stay on track as they pursue their performance and

professional goals. For these goals, the various metrics along the way can be measured, monitored, and communicated in real time, and any necessary adjustments can be made on the same basis. This means that in addition to tracking goal-oriented progress, managers can further act as coaches by providing employees with timely and specific steps to facilitate goal attainment. With this current information at hand, managers are also able to collaboratively adjust employees' goals and align them with possible changes that were unknown or unknowable when the goals were initially established. The overall impact is the increased likelihood of having employees who will meet or exceed their goals. With increased understanding of performance and objectives, managers are also able to work more effectively with each employee toward establishing new performance and development goals.

>> **Increased agility:** In light of today's rapidly changing corporate landscape, a company's ability to act with agility and effectively shift course, speed, direction, and focus is a central contributor to its success. With its capacity for introducing and implementing new and updated objectives at the employee level in real time, quarterly appraisals serve as an important resource in further enabling companies to truly act with agility.

>> **Enhanced performance:** Employees today want feedback related to their performance, especially feedback provided on a timely and constructive basis. Employees also want to receive coaching and guidance to help them enhance their skills, advance their careers, improve their performance, and attain or even exceed their professional goals. Employees want to feel that they are respected, trusted, and treated as adults. They want to be treated as valuable resources of the company, resources whose needs, well-being, interests, and ideas are genuinely important. When significant amounts of time pass between appraisals, employees can easily believe that their accomplishments are being overlooked, opportunities for recognition are ignored, and their individual importance to the organization is minimal at best. With quarterly appraisals, this type of outcome is eliminated. With regular feedback that constructively reviews performance, includes open two-way communications, and focuses on future development, employees are far more likely to experience increased levels of motivation, job satisfaction, and

engagement — all of which contribute to increases in performance and productivity.

>> **Upgraded identification, resolution, and prevention of problems:** The regular conversations between managers and employees that are the foundation of quarterly appraisals significantly increase the likelihood of identifying potential problems and then jointly establishing strategies to prevent them. At the same time, when unanticipated problems do arise, these sessions also provide employees and managers with the opportunity to collaboratively develop timely resolution strategies. This anticipatory, collaborative, and preventive approach also includes ongoing opportunities for employees to provide input at any point in the problem-solving process, a practice that typically generates more productive solutions while simultaneously further increasing the employees' sense of respect, belonging, and personal value.

TIP

When employees participate in the problem-solving process, they are more likely to be receptive to any changes incurred as a result of the problem being solved.

A NEW ROLE FOR ANNUAL APPRAISALS

A fair question is whether the advent of more frequent performance appraisals, especially quarterly appraisals, spells the end of annual appraisals. The answer is no.

The review session at the end of the fourth evaluation period in the quarterly performance appraisal process — or at the end of the second evaluation period when appraisals are provided biannually — is still an annual appraisal. However, it lacks the stress, angst, frustration, anxiety, wasted time, inaccuracies, and conflict associated with traditional appraisals.

With the implementation of quarterly or biannual appraisals, the annual appraisal includes more than feedback and feedforward appropriate to the specific appraisal period. These annual appraisal

(continued)

(continued)

sessions also provide an opportunity to summarize and recap the full range of employee performance and goal attainment for the entire year.

At the same time, these sessions typically include two-way discussions on such forward-focused topics as clarification of goals and roles, identifying specific resources for performance improvement and upskilling, and spelling out actions that will continue to enhance the employees' well-being, engagement, and probability of success.

Utilizing Continuous Feedback

To fully reap the widespread benefits that come from quarterly performance appraisals, the most important step is to combine these appraisals with what is called *continuous feedback*. This type of feedback, which includes feedforward as well, is the managerial practice of holding regularly scheduled meetings with your direct reports, typically every two weeks and lasting anywhere from 30 minutes to one hour throughout each evaluation period. With the incorporation of continuous feedback, all of the previously noted positive outcomes associated with quarterly appraisals will be greatly amplified and enhanced. Importantly, the real-time component of this type of feedback strengthens the relevance and impact of any messaging that is presented.

These meetings are less structured than appraisal sessions, operating on a more flexible basis that fits into the dynamics of your organization. Continuous feedback is designed to touch base and provoke dialogue with employees, to discuss their performance on past projects, as well as progress and metrics associated with their specific performance and development goals, make adjustments and alignments as needed, clarify expectations, and provide prompts, coaching, guidance, recognition, and support. The overarching approach is collaborative, forward-thinking, and designed to help employees take greater ownership of their goals, meet their goals, enhance their performance and productivity, and continue to experience professional growth and career development.

With real-time and regular feedback and feedforward in place, employees are better able to meet their goals, an outcome directly reflected in improved performance and increased productivity — further building employees' confidence, satisfaction, motivation, and engagement. Continuous feedback expands and reinforces a corporate culture that truly values continuous improvement and continuous employee growth.

At the same time, continuous feedback increases the likelihood of early identification of individual or departmental performance-related issues. The preemptive detection of existing or potential problems also facilitates the prompt and timely actions to deal with them. Continuous feedback also further addresses the interests of many of today's employees in terms of receiving feedback and recognition and sensing that they are valuable members of the team.

Continuous feedback sessions provide opportunities for employees to seek answers to any number of questions they may be reluctant to raise during performance appraisal sessions. With continuous feedback meetings in place, unanswered questions no longer need to fester or be set aside until a distant meeting. In fact, the open and collaborative nature of these meetings makes it easier for employees to approach managers between meetings as well. With the possibility of new questions arising almost every day, continuous feedback generates real-time encouragement and opportunities for them to be asked and answered.

Further, with continuous feedback, managers will be better able to know and understand their employees as individuals. The insights generated through increased collaborative contact help the manager provide tailored opportunities and assignments that are engaging and motivational for the employees, while simultaneously helping managers get to know their employees on a more-than-superficial basis. This increased insight into their employees as individuals further enhances the effectiveness of the communication, collaboration, and coaching between managers and their employees.

Many of today's employees are also quite interested in companies that show concern for their well-being. With increased understanding of employees, managers increase their proficiency at picking up subtle cues indicating any deeper issues employees may be experiencing. For example, although employees may be reluctant to bring up concerns relating to their stress levels, work-life balance, or physical or mental health, managers will be better skilled in identifying these types of issues by observing changes in the employees' behavior, demeanor, enthusiasm, communication patterns, and body language. Such insight is highly valuable and can open the door to additional wellness-oriented coaching.

Continuous feedback is particularly useful and helpful for remote employees. Although some of these employees can feel withdrawn or even excluded from the company communications, developments, and operations, the increased interaction that is provided through continuous feedback can help rebuild the bonds between remote employes and the organization at large.

The bottom line is that the process of carrying out quarterly performance appraisals as well as a year-end appraisal is greatly facilitated as a result of continuous feedback throughout each evaluation period. With continuous feedback, managers can generate and document information that is current, thorough, complete, factual, accurate, and trustworthy regarding employee performance, goal-oriented progress, and goal attainment. There is no need for managers to go back and dig out old performance data and notes or struggle with fuzzy memories. Rather, all of the data for the current quarterly evaluation period is readily at hand as a result of these biweekly meetings.

Importantly, employees enter these evaluation sessions feeling informed, respected, and up-to-date on all performance matters — a mindset that further enhances the likelihood of a positive, open, and engaging feedback and feedforward conversation. As a result, the formal performance appraisal sessions at the end of each quarter throughout the year become more useful, meaningful, effective, and productive for the employees as well as their managers — all without drama, angst, distress, conflict, and dread.

Harnessing the Motivational Power of Appraisals

Motivation is the process that energizes employees and propels them to pursue their goals. Well-designed and well-executed performance appraisals throughout the year, supported by continuous feedback, can have a strong positive motivational impact.

With the feedback and feedforward that are central to this process, appraisals generate a vast array of interconnected motivational benefits:

» **They highlight and clarify questionable performance.** If employees don't have a clear understanding of how they've been performing, they can't be motivated to make any improvements. After all, if they haven't been told that there are issues regarding such matters as their expertise, communication, progress toward goals, or the quality or quantity of their work, and if they therefore don't sense that any improvements are needed, they certainly won't be motivated to work harder in any of these areas. Importantly, for feedback to motivational, it should be provided as closely as possible to the behavior or performance in question. The real-time underpinning of today's appraisals provides this connection.

» **They build a sense of personal value.** Employees today have particularly strong needs when it comes to sensing that they are valued, respected, trusted, and heard. When managers take the time and effort to carefully review, analyze, document, and discuss performance with employees, accompanied by individually tailored coaching and guidance, the underlying message to the employees is that they are indeed important and valuable.

» **They enhance professional growth and career development.** Performance appraisals and continuous feedback also strike a positive chord for employees who are motivated to learn and grow. With specific and timely feedback related to key aspects of their performance that have room for improvement, accompanied by managerial coaching and guidance, employees are increasingly energized to take advantage of the formal and informal learning opportunities, hence increasing their knowledge, expertise, and value to the company.

» **They help employees establish and meet goals.** Establishing and pursuing performance and professional goals has been found to be highly motivational for a broad range of employees. With realistic yet challenging goals in place, employees, accompanied by managerial encouragement and support, are likely to be increasingly energized to meet them.

>> **They increase satisfaction and engagement.** By meeting the employees' needs in such areas as gaining recognition, experiencing achievement, enhancing their knowledge and skills, experiencing growth, sensing self-worth, and meeting objectives, performance appraisals are also contributing to the employees' job satisfaction and engagement, two powerful and impactful outcomes in today's jobs. When employees are satisfied and engaged, some of the more visible outcomes are increased performance, productivity, commitment, and loyalty, along with reduced turnover, absenteeism, and tardiness.

On the flipside, when employees are subjected to a questionable performance appraisal process, the opportunities to fulfill these higher-level needs are substantially reduced. As a result, rather than the positive outcomes noted above, employees are more likely to move in the exact opposite direction — namely, reduced performance, productivity, commitment, and loyalty.

TECHNICAL STUFF

If you think about this in psychological terms, people are motivated by unfilled needs. For example, if you have employees who are highly achievement oriented, they are likely to demonstrate greater levels of energy and drive when working on projects on which success will allow them to fulfill their needs to achieve. At the same time, when these employees are working on projects that offer minimal opportunity to sense achievement and accomplishment, they have a mismatch with their needs, leading to diminished motivation. Importantly, when the employees' needs are not being met on the job, they will still seek to have them fulfilled — if not with this company, then perhaps with another. This can result in their leaving the company or simply spending less time on the job and more time on activities that *do* meet their needs — and those are the very pursuits that can cause them to miss work or be less than productive when they're at work.

Performance appraisals are also important because of the numerous ways in which they contribute to learning, skill enhancement, education, and career development for employees and their managers as well. A key component of learning is timely feedback, and performance appraisals meet this standard by providing clear, specific, and accurate feedback and feedforward that is closely tied to individual behavior and actions.

In this section, you'll see the many ways in which performance appraisals can help you as well as your employees learn, grow, reach goals, and perform at higher levels.

Clarifying performance expectations

As part of doing their job, employees are typically provided with a job description that spells out their key roles, responsibilities, and functions. Although such descriptions definitely help employees understand *what* they are supposed to do, that is not the full picture. In order to perform at peak levels, employees also need to know *how* they are supposed to work. This type of information is not typically found in a job description, but it's nonetheless critical when the time comes for employees to fulfill their responsibilities and perform effectively and productively.

This gap is filled by performance appraisals and continuous feedback, which not only focus on the specific functions, accomplishments, and goal attainment inherent to the employees' jobs, but also focus on key performance-related behaviors that are essential to success. These behaviors include such actions as cooperating, communicating, collaborating, and demonstrating engagement, reliability, and agility. In this way, performance appraisals play a powerful educational role by providing employees with an essential behaviorally-based supplement to their job description. By understanding the contents of their job description as well as the contents of their performance appraisals, employees are armed with a thorough and broad understanding of the job expectations and related performance standards. By looking at their jobs through this wider lens, employees are able to clearly see the *what* and *how* of their job, an outcome that contributes to enhanced performance and productivity.

Building self-awareness

Performance appraisals also provide employees with insight that helps build their self-awareness. As a result of factual, behaviorally based, data-driven feedback, provided on a timely basis, employees are more likely to listen and absorb whatever is being communicated, and to incorporate their new learning in future behaviors. With this self-insight, employees can learn, grow, and perform on the job. After all, if their self-insight is marginal, their work is likely to be marginal as well.

At the same time, performance appraisals can also help build your self-insight as a manager. As part of engaging in continuous feedback with your employees, you're applying and enhancing your own observational, performance analysis, and communication skills. Through your employees' reactions, responses, and behaviors, you'll also gain additional insight into your overall managerial skills and style, and find possible areas for improvement.

This self-insight is further enhanced by the feedback you and your employees receive from other employees. Such feedback is generated through self-appraisals and 360-degree feedback, both of which are discussed in Bonus Chapter 1.

Generating insight for your employees

When you meet with your employees through today's performance appraisals, you're not coming to them out of the blue with a bunch of old and arguably inaccurate data. Rather, your meeting is part of an ongoing process in which you have already been openly communicating with your employees and providing them with updates, corrective strategies, support, coaching, and guidance. As a result, the formal feedback that you provide in a performance appraisal session is not a surprise, but rather is based on previously discussed specific aspects of your employees' performance. By interlacing your feedback and feedforward with specific examples of your employees' work, namely by focusing on performance rather than personality, your employees' receptivity to whatever you may be presenting is perceived as useful, helpful, and worthy of real consideration — and a bona fide source of additional self-insight.

TIP

The most effective way to coach your employees is to focus on them as individuals instead of taking a one-size-fits-all approach. Employees have their own learning style and learn in different ways — some are visual learners, some are auditory learners, and others are kinesthetic learners. As you get to know your employees as individuals, you'll understand their unique approach to learning, and the best step is for you to then adjust your coaching style in kind. For visual learners, it will be helpful to provide them with some extra written documentation so that they can better see the information that you're communicating. For auditory learners, it will be helpful to spend some extra time meeting with them and discussing their performance and development with them. With kinesthetic learners, you'll find that providing them with hands-on opportunities to practice some of the behaviors incorporated in your coaching will help them learn these new skills.

TECHNICAL STUFF

The feedback that your employees receive through performance appraisals has extra credibility for one main reason: You're providing it. In marketing, the concept of *source credibility* plays a central role in determining the impact of whatever message is being sent. Although the content is certainly important, the source determines the level of credibility for that content. For example, information a your doctor gives you regarding the treatment for your sore foot is going to be far more believable than the same information would be if given by a friend. In your role as manager, you have source credibility as a result of your title, role, and expertise, especially when combined with your understanding of your individual employees and their performance.

Generating awareness for yourself

At the same time, as a manager in the performance appraisal process, you have three key opportunities to build your *own* self-awareness:

>> The feedback that you receive from your own manager can be a major help in strengthening your self-awareness, just as your feedback and feedforward do for your employees.

>> If your performance appraisal process includes self-evaluations, you can also gain useful insight by honestly evaluating your own performance.

>> If your company uses a 360-degree feedback program that includes feedback from your direct reports as well as from your manager, the information they provide can further enhance your self-awareness on a wide range of workplace behaviors, including planning, organizing, communicating, delegating, and leading.

Increasing your managerial and coaching effectiveness

When carrying out the various responsibilities that underlie performance appraisals and continuous feedback, you're also further developing your own managerial and coaching skills, especially when it comes to communicating, leading, motivating, data gathering and analysis, planning, organizing, and developing employees. As you continue to participate in the performance appraisal process, one major outcome is that your own skills and effectiveness will continue to grow.

In addition to coaching your employees to help them move more successfully toward their performance and development goals, these sessions also create an opportunity for you to provide and practice some specific skill-related training. Although upskilling can certainly be provided through various courses or programs, you can be a source of upskilling as well. For example, if your employees' written communications are unclear, wordy, cumbersome, or filled with grammatical errors, it can be informative and instructional for you to include actual samples of their writing when providing feedback and feedforward. By doing so, your comments move from the abstract to the realistic, making them far more palatable — especially if you show your employees what can be done to improve documents that they wrote, such as by cleaning up the organization, syntax, and redundancies. As a given evaluation period progresses, you'll be able to measure and adjust your upskilling strategy based on your employees' written communications that follow.

As you continue to provide training that helps your employees build their skills, you're also further developing your own training skills.

Another managerial learning point associated with performance appraisals comes from observing the performance of your employees and subsequently gathering accurate and suitable data to form your feedback and feedforward. Such data can be accumulated directly through your observations and documentation as well as through performance management software. Either way, with such data at hand, managers can provide reliable and impactful feedback, coaching, and guidance. As you engage in the data-gathering and data analysis process, your subsequent interactions with your employees will help you further finetune and enhance your skills in these areas. (See Bonus Chapter 2 for information on performance management software providers.)

In order to further upgrade managerial skills as part of the appraisal process, it's also important for managers to take extra steps to gain a clear picture of their employees' performance. Over the years, one of the more effective ways to gather such additional data has been to engage in a practice called *managing by wandering around*. In today's world, this can be accomplished virtually as well as in person, especially since it complements continuous feedback in many respects. The underlying common premise is for managers to actually or remotely get out of their offices and informally visit with their employees to continuously build managerial understanding of whatever may be going on as well as to identify problematic issues and jointly design and implement corrective strategies

TIP

There is more to observation than meets the eye. If you really want an accurate picture of performance when working with your employees onsite and in person, try to think about observing with *all* your senses. For example, the next time you visit your employees' work area in a hybrid or onsite work environment, turn up your antennae and concentrate on what you're seeing, hearing, touching, and even smelling. This is a powerful way to gather additional data, and it's truly a sensible way to manage. (Additional information on managing with all your senses is also provided in Bonus Chapter 2.)

Transmitting company values

Performance appraisals educate the employees on the company's values, namely the deeply held underlying principles that define what the company is and how it aspires to operate. These values form the foundation of the company's mission, standards, and identity, and they are reflected in terms of expectations regarding employee integrity, inclusion, creativity, leadership, trust, respect, honesty, teamwork, service, and ethics.

Performance appraisals offer an optimal opportunity for managers to spell out the company's values and the kinds of behaviors and actions that align with them. Through the process of managerial feedback and feedforward, employees can gain a clearer picture of these values and consequently adjust their own behaviors to better mesh with them.

A company's values are reflected in the performance appraisal process, especially in terms of the kinds of behaviors that are expected from employees. Importantly, when there is a mismatch or misunderstanding between company values and the employees' understanding of them, the outcomes can include confusion, conflict, distress, and subpar performance.

For example, some employees may operate under the assumption that their company values independence, creative thinking, and assertiveness. At the same time, the company may place a higher value on following proven precedents, having employees who stay in their lanes, and expecting employees to devote full attention to their assigned work. Although arguments can be made either way regarding these values, the key point is that employees need to understand their company's values in order to meet the performance expectations associated with their job. Through the two-way communication that underlies the performance appraisal process, employees gain a clearer and more accurate picture of their company's value system and the kinds of behaviors they need to exemplify to thrive within it.

Strengthening goal alignment

Employees are often provided with the basics of company goals as part of their orientation, and they may also hear about them through town hall meetings or other company communications and publications. However, such outreach does not provide sufficient individualized guidance to effectively inform, shape, and vertically align employee goals.

Goal-setting is a joint undertaking in which managers and their employees work together to establish performance goals and development goals. Importantly, through the process of performance appraisal and continuous feedback, managers can provide ongoing guidance and support to help align the employees' goals with managerial goals, departmental goals, and company goals. This outcome is greatly facilitated as a result of the managers' existing understanding of the overarching goals and the application of that knowledge to the individual goal-setting process.

As part of the performance appraisal process, depending upon the company's objectives, timeframes, and business cycles, the employees' goals can be jointly established during the final performance appraisal session at the end of a yearlong period, or they can be jointly established in separate continuous feedback sessions that are specifically dedicated to goal-setting. (More information on the goal-setting process is discussed in Bonus Chapter 3.)

Jointly developing a career path

Another beneficial outcome that emanates from the performance appraisal process is the way in which it helps employees develop a more focused picture of their career direction and the most effective steps to take to move closer to their career goals. With performance-based feedback and feedforward, employees gain a clearer perspective of what they seek in their work at this point and over the longer term. As a result of today's appraisal process, employees are able to learn more about their work-related skills, abilities, and interests, and this insight helps them generate the most personally suitable and rewarding career path — especially when supported by managerial coaching.

As a result of the performance appraisal process, managers have particularly keen insight into the knowledge, skills, and abilities of their employees — sometimes more than the employees themselves. This knowledge base enables managers to understand each employee as an individual and jointly work-one-on-one to not only identify and address current work-related issues, but also provide realistic and tailored career guidance to help the employee look down the road and identify the most desirable and realistic career pathways.

REMEMBER

When performance appraisals are short on feedforward, employees will still be on a career path, but their navigation systems will be turned off. Under such circumstances, they are likely to either head down the wrong path or simply jump ship.

Identifying development opportunities

As a manager, you may hear about a particularly successful training or upskilling program that was administered in another department or company, and such an endorsement might convince you to utilize the program in your department as well. However, despite the rave reviews, such a program might be a waste in your department. The most important first step in selecting and administering training, upskilling, or educational programs, whether onsite or virtual, is to determine whether such training is actually needed by your employees. Implementing an upskilling program that worked well elsewhere can be a waste of time and money if your employees are already adequately skilled in areas that are targeted by the program.

The performance-related data that you generate through performance appraisals provides a solid basis for determining training and educational needs, whether on an individual or departmental basis. By implementing training and upskilling that focuses on areas in which there are performance gaps, you're far more likely to generate outcomes that are appreciated and applied by your employees — which will be reflected in their performance and productivity.

Take the case in which a significant number of employee evaluations point to problems in teamwork and cooperation. This finding would highlight a need for additional training in these areas, such as a team-building program or exercises. On the other hand, if the performance review data indicates that there are no significant teamwork or cooperation problems, even the best team-building program in the world would be of questionable value at best.

TECHNICAL STUFF

In the world of training and upskilling, effective programs have a high degree of *transference,* meaning that the information, skills, and behaviors learned in these programs can be readily applied to the attendees' jobs. Training that is conducted without consideration of the employees' actual developmental needs is destined to have minimal transference at best, and this means minimal interest, attention, and learning.

When a training program is completed, a key follow-up step is to evaluate its effectiveness. One way to do this is to compare performance appraisal data in the area addressed by the training prior to and after such a program. For example, if the evaluations pointed to consistently low ratings and negative comments related to time management prior to the training in this area, while the ratings and comments became more positive in evaluations following the training, then the training most likely had a measurably positive impact. However, if later evaluations show that the ratings and comments remained poor or even dropped, then the issue needs to be revisited — most likely with a different program and approach.

TIP

When employees are provided with clear and specific examples of performance where they fell short, and they also understand the measurable benefits associated with upskilling or increased knowledge in the area that the training addresses, their interest in taking corrective steps is significantly enhanced. Within such a context, employees enter educational and upskilling programs as motivated learners — an approach that greatly enhances the learning process.

Strengthening the manager/employee working relationship

With the increased contact and two-way communication between managers and employees that form the foundation of the performance appraisal process, one common outcome is that managers get to know their employees as individuals and gain a clearer understanding not only in terms of their performance, skills, and expertise, but also in terms of their personality. For the manager, deeper insight into such characteristics as their employees' likes, dislikes, strengths, and weaknesses, as well as into such personality traits as openness, empathy, agreeableness, conscientiousness, honesty, and emotional intelligence clearly strengthens the efficacy of their working relationships.

With an increased understanding of their individual employees, managers are better able to provide feedback and feedforward, suggestions, assignments, and coaching that truly resonate. Employees today enjoy being treated and respected as individuals and sensing that they are not simply regarded as just another cog in the wheel. The increased individual insight that is generated through today's performance appraisals clearly and effectively addresses and fulfills this need.

At the same time, it's also important to note that this process also enables employees to learn more about their managers and consequently apply the most suitable methods to work productively and successfully with them. Through increased contact with their managers, employees learn a great deal about such qualities as their managers' performance expectations, standards, work style, and priorities. This insight helps employees shape the way in which they approach and carry out job responsibilities.

This combination of increased mutual understanding shared by managers and their employees provides a solid foundation and impetus for a positive, respectful, productive, and successful working relationship.

TIP

By better understanding what makes their employees tick, managers are better able to generate a working relationship that clicks.

Aiding Administration

Performance appraisals generate particularly important administrative information and documentation that play a key role in terms of promotions, transfers, succession planning, and potential claims from employees. Decisions and actions in each of these areas are greatly facilitated and expedited by having solid performance data as a foundation.

Gathering relevant data for promotions

One of the strongest motivators that many employees bring to the job is focused on being promoted and advancing their careers. In this regard, promotions are among the employees' foremost thoughts as they carry out their job responsibilities and continue their growth and development.

As a manager, it's quite normal to have a general impression regarding the promotability of each of your employees. Fortunately, the clear, specific, and real-time data that you have generated and documented regarding each employee's performance elevates your thinking in regard to promotions from general impressions to actual facts. As a result of performance appraisals, the information that is critical in determining promotability and promotions is readily at hand, especially in terms of such key factors as each employee's productivity, expertise, quality of work, interpersonal skills, reliability, engagement, and problem-solving. With this information in place, managers are better empowered to implement promotions that are well-deserved, well-regarded, and successful.

At the same time, when managers' decisions about promotions are based more on feelings than findings, three distinct problems emerge:

>> **Problems for the promoted employee:** Without accurate performance data, one particularly problematic outcome is that the wrong person is promoted. In such a case, the outcome is obvious — namely, the individual is likely to fail. This creates an entirely new range of problems for the manager, especially in terms of spending extra time monitoring, coaching, counseling, disciplining, and possibly terminating this individual. At the same time, this outcome

created another open position due to the loss of the employee who was presumably performing satisfactorily in their original position prior to being promoted.

>> **Problems for the employee who is not promoted:** By promoting the wrong person, managers are also likely to upset at least one other person in the department — namely, the individual whose performance actually merited the promotion. This employee is likely to be upset and believe that promotions in the department are unfair and arbitrary. These types of feelings eat away at an employee's motivation, commitment, and performance, and this means that one of your best employees is now dissatisfied.

>> **Problems for the rest of the team:** Employees typically have a strong sense of which coworkers are actually deserving of promotions. When they see a promotion decision that ignores a truly outstanding coworker, they develop doubts about the role of equity and merit in the department. Such doubts can chip away at their attitudes and performance as well.

REMEMBER

When the wrong person is promoted, dissatisfaction is promoted as well.

Generating key information for job transfers

Job transfers provide employees with an excellent opportunity to advance their careers without necessarily moving to a higher-level position. Although an open lateral position may indeed be at the same level as an employee's current position, transfers allow employees to have expanded opportunities to learn, acquire new skills, work with different people, and even open a wider and more suitable career path. Regardless of the way in which the open position is communicated, whether it's through a job-posting system, internal advertisement, or word of mouth, it's extremely helpful to have accurate performance data in order to make a good decision.

When it comes to making decisions about selecting employees to transfer into your department or recommending employees for transfer to open positions in other departments, performance appraisals can play a major supportive role. In this regard, when considering individual employees for possible transfer into your department, a discussion with the individual's manager combined with a review of the individual's previous performance appraisals can provide excellent data regarding the individual's suitability for the transfer. Just as is the case in hiring a new employee, it's essential to gather accurate job-related information regarding the individual's prior work experience, and this is precisely what is documented in these appraisals. Conversely, this approach can be applied by other managers in determining the next steps when considering any of your employees who are interested in transferring to an open position outside of your department.

With thorough and accurate performance documentation in place, performance appraisals facilitate and expedite the entire transfer process by creating a level and data-based playing field on which all interested individuals are provided with a fair chance to make a lateral move. By reviewing internal performance data that evaluates employees with the same criteria and measures, managers are enabled to match each candidate against the other on comparable work-related skills and behaviors, hence further increasing the fairness, consistency, and reliability of the process.

By relying on fair and accurate performance data in the transfer process, the underlying message is that the company is genuinely interested in retaining employees and providing them with opportunities that enhance their job experiences and widen the focus of their career paths.

Providing data for succession planning

Whether it's a matter of turnover or company growth, it's particularly important to have employees who can step up and fill open or newly established positions. Although in some cases, it's entirely appropriate for companies to look to the outside to find suitable candidates for such positions, promoting from within has several significant pluses — the individuals are known commodities, they understand and mesh with company values and goals, they are already prescreened, and this approach saves time and money. With all of this in mind, the performance appraisal process can be of great assistance when it comes to succession planning.

In the first place, managers are likely to have a clear understanding of open positions, whether by working with individuals who previously held them or by being directly or indirectly involved in the process of creating or redesigning newly opened positions.

This enables the managers to have a clear understanding of the roles and responsibilities that are inherent to these positions, as well as the kinds of skills and abilities that are required to succeed in them.

Complementing their understanding of open positions is the managers' understanding of their employees and their suitability for such positions. By working directly with their employees via appraisals and continuous feedback, managers have accurate and documented insight into the full range of their employees' performance in terms of their expertise, skill levels, motivation, drive, goal attainment, engagement, and professional growth. Managers are in an excellent position to analyze the ways in which their employees currently match the requirements of the open positions, as well as implement steps and coaching strategies that further build employee preparedness to advance in the organization.

Diminishing the likelihood of claims from employees

In today's workplace, it's important for managers to fairly, fully, accurately, and formally document employee performance before taking any kind of administrative action — ranging from promotion to termination. When employees believe that they were not treated fairly in any such matters, the likelihood of their responding with a claim against the company is greatly increased. With this in mind, the accurate, thorough, and well-communicated documentation generated through performance appraisals is extremely helpful not only in preventing employee claims in the first place, but also in dealing with them if they're made.

The documentation associated with performance appraisals can clearly demonstrate that decisions on such matters as work assignments, transfers, training, promotions, raises, and terminations were made equitably and on the basis of performance. The decision-making behind any of these actions can be fully validated and verified by the data that you have gathered and the feedback and feedforward that you have provided.

At the same time, if employees are struggling on the job and are ultimately terminated, their performance appraisals will provide clear documentation showing that such employees were well advised about specific performance issues, received coaching and an opportunity to improve, and were fully informed about the consequences of continued questionable performance.

If employees have received appraisals that contain clear and fair feedback and guidance, but they have failed to show any significant improvement in any noted areas of problematic performance, they should be provided with a written *performance improvement plan (PIP)* that spells out the specific improvements that need to be made, the timeframe in which this must occur, and the consequences if sub-par performance continues. (Performance improvement plans are discussed in more detail in Bonus Chapter 3.)

TIP

If employees are surprised when they are terminated, don't be surprised if they file a claim.

2

Working Your Way through the Process

Chapter **3**

Pre-Appraisal Preparation

With so many appraisal forms, techniques, and strategies at your command, you can easily become sidetracked and overlook the most important element in the entire performance evaluation process: *you!*

Researchers continue to find that although it's obviously important for companies to select and implement performance appraisal systems that match their culture, style, cycles, operations, and standards, it's the individual who conducts the evaluations that is the key factor in determining the effectiveness of the system itself.

Building a Constructive Mindset

Before you start looking at your employees, the first step is to look at yourself. In order to provide the most relevant, compelling, credible, and effective feedback and feedforward, it's essential to have a mindset that is fully supportive of the process. Managers who approach performance appraisals as a ritual, a chore, or an isolated event undercut their own effectiveness before they even start.

To have the right mindset, it is particularly helpful for you to take the following steps:

>> See yourself as a leader and coach.
>> Set positive expectations.
>> Overcome your own fear, reluctance, and resistance.
>> Take steps to further increase your self-awareness.
>> Empathize with your employees.

With this foundation in place, you'll be in a much better position to understand and analyze your employees' performance and ultimately help them achieve greater productivity, growth and development, and satisfaction.

Seeing yourself as a leader and coach

By seeing yourself as a *leader* and a *coach*, you're likely to engage in behaviors that will resonate with your employees and help them build their performance and personal growth. In strengthening your leadership and coaching skills, the first place to look is at your leadership style. After all, if a manager is overcontrolling, autocratic, inflexible, and short-tempered, any coaching imbedded within this type of leadership style is going to be given minimal attention and acceptance by the employees.

As a result, the first step in viewing yourself as a leader is to look at some of the major characteristics and behaviors that are part of effective leadership.

TIP

There is no one best way to lead. Rather, some situations call for leaders to make firm decisions on the spot, typically when the timing is urgent and substantial resources are involved. On the other hand, there can be situations in which the most effective approach is an open, collaborative, and democratic method in which the employees play a key role in presenting their ideas, input, and suggestions, which then shape the forthcoming decisions. Hence, in many respects, the best leadership style is flexible and can be adjusted to meet situational demands.

To better see yourself as a *leader*, look first at the following sampling of leadership behaviors and think of ways in which they are currently part of your leadership style or could be introduced into it. If you truly act as a leader and see yourself as such, your leadership practices, including the feedback and feedforward you provide, will be increasingly impactful:

>> Understanding the employees as individuals

>> Engaging in open two-way communications

>> Treating employees with respect and trust

>> Introducing and applying best practices whenever possible

>> Positively leading and influencing the team to meet goals

Looking now at seeing yourself as a *coach*, the key point to note is that leadership is focused on energizing and motivating others to meet goals, whereas coaching is focused on developing, upskilling, and building others. These are complementary processes which, when working in tandem, further enhance your effectiveness in conducting performance appraisals. Some of the key coach behaviors include the following:

>> Focusing clearly on individual employee growth, training, upskilling, and career development

>> Providing employees with constructive feedback and guidance

>> Collaboratively creating developmental plans with your employees

>> Providing recognition appropriately

>> Helping employees build their strengths and exceed their own expectations

By truly looking at yourself as a manager through these two integrated lenses and making additions, adjustments, inclusions, and tweaks as you see fit regarding your leadership and coaching behaviors, you solidify a framework that reinforces the validity and utility of the feedback and feedforward that you provide through continuous feedback and the performance appraisal sessions. With this outcome, the most likely results include increased employee performance, productivity, commitment, development, and engagement.

TIP

When you envision yourself as a leader and coach and engage in the behaviors noted above, every step of the performance appraisal process becomes easier and more effective. On the other hand, if you don't see yourself as a leader and coach, neither will your employees — and they won't accept or act on the information you give them during their performance appraisals.

Setting positive expectations

Your expectations affect the way in which your employees ultimately perform, and this means that your expectations play a critical role in the performance appraisal process. The reality is that managerial expectations have a clear and measurable impact on employee behavior. It is undoubtedly important to have realistic expectations, but if you truly seek to improve your employees' performance, one important practice is for you to maintain and demonstrate positive expectations regarding their current and potential performance on the job.

If you expect an employee to perform poorly, you're likely to transmit that expectation in many subtle and not-so-subtle ways:

>> **Nonverbal communication.** On the subtle side, your body language can clearly signal your negative expectations, such as through the hint of a frown, a furrowed brow, crossed arms, shaking your head negatively in an almost imperceptible way, or perhaps a quick yet observable roll of your eyes. In fact, regardless of your spoken words, nonverbal elements — such as the tone, volume, inflection, and emphasis — can send a clearer message, often contradicting what you are saying. On the receiving side, employees are more likely to sense that the real meaning of whatever you are communicating comes through nonverbally.

>> **Differential treatment.** On the not-so-subtle side, you may use words and behave in a way that communicates negative expectations. If you have low expectations regarding the performance of any of your employees, you might frequently use the word *no*, give these employees the less significant assignments, ignore them or rush through their comments in meetings, and provide them with minimal thanks, appreciation, and recognition when arguably due.

REMEMBER

Your employees pick up *all* your negative cues — whether subtle or obvious — and internalize them and act accordingly. These cues impact the employees' attitudes, and their attitudes are reflected in their behavior.

However, when you expect your employees to do well, you deal with them in an enthusiastic, upbeat, positive, and supportive style. You tend to smile and nod more, and your speech is likely to be more animated, supportive, and filled with encouraging phrases and the word *yes*. The work you assign and the feedback you provide tell the employees that they're terrific, and they are likely to respond with terrific performance.

TIP

When it comes to employee performance, one way to think about expectations is the following: What you expect is what you get. In many respects, expectations are self-fulfilling prophecies.

REMEMBER

Your expectations have a major impact on your employees' performance and ultimately on the evaluations that you conduct.

As you prepare yourself to appraise your employees, think of your employees as individuals, and then consider the expectations you've established for each of them. It would not be surprising to find that the employees for whom you have low expectations are performing at lower levels, whereas the employees for whom you have higher expectations perform better.

It's also possible that some of your expectations are inaccurate or out of date. A careful and honest review of the expectations that you hold for each of your employees can open the door to more productive coaching and guidance. The quarterly or biannual performance appraisal session is a perfect time to take a look at the expectations you have for your employees and then commit to building more positive expectations for each of them. By doing so, you're more likely to behave in kind and generate the level of performance that you expect. As part of this approach, it's equally important for your employees to sense that you have positive expectations for them, not only from the standpoint of their job performance, but also in terms of their growth and career development.

TIP

With this in mind, be sure to specifically express positive expectations during the performance appraisal sessions.

Overcoming fear, reluctance, and resistance

With the prospect of conducting performance appraisal sessions approaching soon, some managers feel a little queasy and unnerved. If thinking about performance appraisals gives you a discomforting feeling, you're not alone. A key source of managerial distress in this area emanates from the use of annual appraisals accompanied by minimal ongoing feedback and feedforward for the employees.

Fortunately, the implementation of quarterly or biannual appraisals supported by continuous feedback and feedforward greatly reduces much of the underlying distress. Nonetheless, some managers still experience residual angst when it comes to appraisal sessions, typically manifested by such reactions as fear, reluctance, and resistance.

If you're experiencing any of these reactions, the best way to dig yourself *out* of them is to dig *into* them. After all, if you carry these feelings into the performance appraisal process, they'll carry you and the process far from where you want to go.

Eliminating fear

Fear is an emotion provoked by imminent danger — real or imagined. In the case of performance appraisals, fear belongs in the imagined file. There are essentially two common fears that can accompany this process:

>> **Fear of looking foolish:** Managers who harbor this fear are primarily concerned that their ratings, comments, and face-to-face appraisal sessions will put them in situations that highlight their lack of knowledge, lack of accurate information, and even lack of managerial skills.

>> **Fear of confrontation:** Some managers are afraid that these one-on-one sessions with their employees will turn into arguments and disagreements. In order to prevent this type of outcome, some managers simply opt to provide unwarranted positive reviews.

Providing undeserved positive reviews to avoid a confrontation doesn't qualify as a method of *overcoming* fear. Rather, it's a method of *surrendering* to fear.

Fortunately, you can take two major steps to overcome your fears about conducting performance appraisals:

>> **Fully engage in continuous feedback.** By meeting regularly with your employees, you'll be gathering factual, specific,

real-time, and job-related performance data. This not only helps you create and provide a valid evaluation at the end of each period, but it also raises the quality of the feedback and feedforward that you provide. This approach also reduces fears related to the unknowns in the feedback process because you will have already discussed individual performance with your employees and provided coaching and guidance in the areas that warranted improvement. These types of actions basically preempt and eliminate the prospect of confrontation and looking foolish during these sessions.

>> **Fully understand the performance appraisal system.** Regardless of the performance appraisal method and system used in your company, it's critical for you to have clear and full knowledge of how it works. You should understand all the performance criteria and the key actions and behaviors associated with the ratings that you provide. At the same time, it's equally important for your employees to understand the process as well. By having a shared understanding of each component of the process, you and your employees are far more likely to have a positive and productive discussion that focuses on performance as well as growth and career development.

TIP

Just as your expectations about your employees' performance strongly influence how they perform, your expectations about performance appraisal sessions determines how they will go. If you enter these sessions expecting an embattled exchange, that's what you're likely to get. On the other hand, if you approach the process with positive expectations, it's far more likely to go well.

Eliminating reluctance

Managers reluctant to provide performance reviews aren't necessarily *afraid* of conducting appraisals. Rather, they're just hesitant, tentative, and likely to defer the process until a later date — a much later date if possible.

One of the primary sources of this reluctance stems directly from a manager's prior experiences with performance evaluations, especially the reviews they gave to other employees and the kinds of reviews they received from their own managers:

>> **Problems with reviews you gave:** If you've had difficulties providing performance appraisals in the past, you're likely

to feel reluctant to give appraisals now. Perhaps you gave reviews based on information that wasn't fully substantiated, or maybe you gave negative reviews to employees who expected excellent reviews. Either way, the outcomes were probably upsetting, distressing, and frustrating for you and your employees. As a result, it's not surprising that you're reluctant to enter the performance appraisal process again and risk a repeat performance.

>> **Problems with reviews you received:** You can also be reluctant to conduct performance appraisals if you have had dissatisfying experiences with the appraisals that you have received. Perhaps you had a manager who evaluated you unfairly or focused on traits and characteristics that had nothing to do with your performance. Because you don't want to put your employees through this type of ordeal, you're reluctant to appraise them at all.

By definition, *reluctance* is not an absolute refusal to conduct the process. Instead, it's a matter of hesitancy to do so until you reach more of a comfort zone. Fortunately, two key steps can help you enter that zone:

>> **Set goals for yourself.** When you carry out most of your managerial functions, you establish specific objectives, strategies, and deadlines. One way to reduce your hesitancy is to use the same approach for performance appraisals. Namely, try to determine the measurable outcomes that you'd like to achieve from this process, and delineate them as specific goals. Such goals can focus on steps to generate measurable improvements in employee performance, upgrading of employee knowledge and skills, and setting a clear path for employee growth.

TIP

By including clear and specific objectives and action plans as you approach each appraisal, your reluctance will decrease, and your motivation is likely to increase. Goals are indeed motivational, and by including them in the performance appraisal process, you're likely to approach these appraisals in the same way that you approach other responsibilities that are part of your job as a manager.

>> **Maintain a forward focus.** Although these sessions clearly include feedback on past performance, they will be more productive for your employees and more engaging for you

by placing the primary emphasis on your employees' learning, upskilling, development, and growth. By approaching these sessions as a coach rather than as an evaluator, you're likely to feel more engaged in the process and subsequently generate outcomes that strengthen your employees, meet their needs, and add value through improved performance and increased productivity.

Eliminating resistance

When managers resist performance appraisals, they flat-out oppose the process. In many cases, managers who demonstrate resistance tend to believe that the process is an unnecessary intrusion on their time and doesn't generate useful results.

In light of the wide range of benefits that can accrue from performance appraisals, especially quarterly or biannual appraisals accompanied by continuous feedback and feedforward, the real factor behind this resistance is a lack of understanding of how the process actually works. Managerial receptivity is heightened when managers understand that performance appraisals are not a standalone practice that is appended to their job, but rather a key component of managing focused on two-way communication, employee growth and development, and improved individual and departmental performance and productivity.

REMEMBER

With today's continuous feedback and forward-focused performance evaluations, the process is not simply an add-on for managers. Rather, it is another element of effective management that aligns easily with other responsibilities inherent to managerial positions.

If you find that your approach to the performance appraisal process falls under the heading of resistance, here are two key steps that can help you remove this barrier:

>> **Consider the advantages.** Instead of approaching the appraisal process as a time-consuming exercise with minimal usefulness, take a look at the potentially positive outcomes it can generate for you, your employees, and the company at large. By using today's performance appraisal methods — especially quarterly appraisals and continuous feedback — your employees are likely to be more satisfied, energized, and productive, which means that you and your department will be more successful.

>> **Consider some training.** If you have lingering questions, doubts, or concerns about the process, be sure to get some help. More than likely, members of your company's HR team can handle any questions that you might have, as well as provide you with suggestions and strategies to help you carry out the process effectively. In addition, many employers offer training in this area, and if you still find that there are gaps in your understanding of the process, you should ask for this training.

TIP

Asking for training is not a sign of weakness or deficiency — rather, it's a sign of confidence, commitment, and engagement.

Gaining self-awareness

Effective performance appraisals require managers to have considerable insight into their employees, but this task is virtually impossible for managers who lack insight into themselves. When self-awareness is missing, managers can easily miss the main events when appraising their employees and then end up focusing on performance and developmental matters that are of secondary importance, off the mark, or simply meaningless.

Importantly, self-awareness is a soft skill that can be improved. One of the most effective ways to do so is to carefully consider the feedback you've received in the past and continue to receive from the credible sources in your life. This doesn't mean that you have to roll over every time someone says something that doesn't sit well with you, but it does mean that you should truly *listen* to what others are saying, try to make an honest judgment regarding their comments, and look carefully at your specific behaviors in the types of situations where your actions may have seemed appropriate to you but not to others.

TIP

As long as you're willing to listen, learn, and grow, you can gain greater insight into yourself and thereby gain greater insight into those around you, including the employees who report to you.

If the feedback you receive starts to fall into a pattern or common theme, you should definitely give it a second thought, or even a third. In this regard, you can build your self-awareness by paying real attention to feedback from the important people in your life, including the following:

>> **Your manager:** Part of a manager's job is to observe and evaluate employee performance as well as provide tailored coaching and guidance. To carry out these responsibilities effectively, managers need to work with their employees, observe their behaviors, and expose them to new and challenging work. By doing so, managers truly can gain some compelling insight into their employees. In light of managers' regular contact with their employees, their feedback and feedforward can contain a great deal of behavior-based information that can contribute significantly to their employees' self-awareness. As a result, the feedback that you receive from your manager should not be placed on a backburner.

>> **Your coworkers:** In most cases, fellow employees spend a lot of time with members of their team every day. Some of the feedback they provide may come out during informal conversations, and some can also be generated through 360-degree feedback. Either way, your coworkers have considerable information on your personality and performance, and their comments, insight, and suggestions are worth considering carefully.

>> **Your friends:** By definition, true friends are open and honest with each other, which means they can provide particularly revealing feedback that can enhance your self-awareness When you're with your friends, you're free to be authentic yourself — which is not necessarily the case in the workplace. This means that your friends see a much wider range of your behaviors. As a result, when friends give you feedback, it's a good idea to listen.

>> **Your family:** Your family knows you in an entirely different context, and, like it or not, in many cases the members of your family know you quite well. For some people, feedback from family members is wrapped in so much emotional baggage that it's difficult to accept. Nonetheless, if you truly want to build your self-awareness, it's helpful to try to set some of your own baggage aside and listen to what they have to say.

>> **Professionals:** If you've taken any job-related tests during the employment process, it can be quite revealing to go back and look at the results. You don't have to accept everything you find, but there can be some information that can help generate additional self-awareness, especially if it fits into a pattern that aligns with information that you have received from others. In addition, if you've ever met with a career

counselor, member of the clergy, or mental health professional, take a second look at what they may have said to you,
regardless of whether you accepted or rejected their advice
at the time. After all, these are professional observations,
and they do merit some extra consideration.

>> **Yourself:** As noted earlier, you can enhance your self-
awareness through self-evaluations that are part of the
performance appraisal process. By looking carefully and
honestly at your behavior in situations you've handled on the
job — such as dealing with pressure and deadlines, accepting change, interacting with fellow employees, pursuing
goals, listening to others, and accepting constructive
criticism — you can gain considerable insight into your
motivations, interpersonal skills, priorities, persistence,
confidence, judgment, values, and more. Although one
purpose of self-evaluations is to provide your manager with
an understanding of your perceptions of your performance
as well as your career development, they serve the equally
important purpose of helping you gain insight into yourself,
which helps you continue on a path of enhanced performance, learning, development, and advancement.

TIP

By looking honestly at your behavior and listening carefully to
your own messages and the messages from important players in
your life, you'll be better enabled to understand your employees as individuals, accurately interpret and measure their performance, provide meaningful recognition, and help focus their
personal growth and career development.

WALKING THE WALK

One of the primary ways in which your self-awareness directly
impacts the performance appraisal process is the extent to which you
literally and figuratively "walk the walk" in terms of your own behavior.

For example, if you have a casual attitude toward meeting deadlines,
and your employees are aware of your lackadaisical actions and comments in this area, you won't have much credibility and impact if you
focus on meeting deadlines when evaluating your employees. This
applies to every component of the performance evaluations that
you provide.

As a result, it is important for managers to continuously monitor the degree of consistency between their own behaviors and the standards that they use when appraising their employees' performance. This can be accomplished by periodically taking the following steps:

- **Review your self-evaluation**: Look back at your self-evaluation and see how your assessment of your performance and behaviors aligns with the expectations that you hold for your employees. The objective is to honestly determine if you're performing at least at the level that you expect of your own employees. The idea is to go through every component in your self-evaluation, look at your performance on each factor, and then determine if you need to focus additional attention on upgrading your behaviors in any of the noted areas.

- **Review your support for the process**: For your performance appraisals to have real significance, it's important to not only get actively behind them, but also let your employees know that you're doing so. If you make offhand negative comments about the appraisal process, or if your evaluations are casual or run late, your employees will respond in kind, not only verbally but behaviorally.

- **Review your descriptors**: To continue to build your self-awareness, it can also be helpful to ask yourself some key questions along the way — and answer them honestly. Such key questions include "What are my greatest strengths/weaknesses?," "What am I most/least proud of at work?," "What is my greatest success/failure?," and "How would my manager/coworkers/employees/friends describe me?" As you answer these, the self-portrait you paint will help you see yourself more clearly, continue your growth and development, build your performance, send positive messages to your employees, and evaluate their work more accurately.

Empathizing with your employees

Empathy is the quality of sensing the feelings and thoughts of others by putting yourself in their situation and then looking at whatever they may be experiencing. As you may expect, empathy is a particularly valuable and desirable quality for managers, especially when it comes to the performance appraisal process.

During this process, your ability to empathize will help you create and provide written and verbal feedback and feedforward that is highly likely to resonate with your employees. When employees sense that you truly understand them and feel what they may be feeling, their trust in you increases, as does their acceptance of your constructive criticism, coaching, and guidance.

TIP

Managers low in empathy tend to resort to a one-size-fits-all style of performance appraisals, but they soon find that this style doesn't fit at all.

To strengthen and enhance your ability to empathize with others, some of these key steps can help:

>> **Look at your own feelings.** The better you understand your own emotions and feelings, the better you'll be able to experience the emotions and feelings of others. Hence, the first step in building your ability to empathize with others is to step back and look at your behaviors and reactions in situations in which your emotions are actively in play. These situations should run the gamut and include your feelings when experiencing great satisfaction and joy, all the way to your feelings when encountering stress and setbacks. While carefully considering your own behaviors and emotions during these periods, feedback from significant others in your work life and personal life can also help increase your ability to empathize.

>> **Practice empathy-enhancing behaviors.** Various behaviors can also help build empathy, such as focusing more of your energy on listening and observing others. By tuning in more carefully and consciously to the behaviors of others, verbal as well as nonverbal, you can learn a great deal about what they are feeling. By doing so, you'll be better able to look at situations from their perspective. Along with this approach, it's helpful to be curious — try to learn more about the people around you, including your employees, in terms of what makes them tick. This can be accomplished not only by being more observant, but also by asking questions that relate to what you are observing. At the same time, it's also important to take an honest look at any biases, preconceived notions, or assumptions that you hold regarding the people around you. To the extent that any of these predispositions exist, they will prevent you from empathizing with others — and they often lead to an inaccurate rush to judgment.

To continue to enhance and experience empathy, one ancient piece of pithy advice is particularly helpful, especially during performance appraisals. Namely, as you develop and provide feedback and feedforward, try to put yourself in your employees' shoes.

>> **Widen your network.** The more people you know, and the more varied and diverse the situations in which you place yourself, the greater your opportunities will be to enhance your ability to learn about others, understand them, and empathize with them. At the same time, as you experience the ways in which others display empathy, you can learn from their examples and try to emulate their behaviors. Your widened network may take you out of your comfort zone, but it can place you in a learning zone.

TIP

The more you can see, understand, and relate to work from the perspective of your employees, the more compelling and effective your appraisals and coaching will be.

Playing the "What If?" Game

By engaging in continuous feedback throughout a given evaluation period, the likelihood of any surprises during the evaluation sessions at the end of each period is greatly reduced. As part of the ongoing, open, and two-way process of feedback and feedforward, the employees' questions have most likely been asked, addressed, and answered in real time. Nonetheless, a helpful component of the preparation process is for managers to still think about any questions that their employees might raise during the appraisal sessions.

Many of today's highly successful salespeople try to come up with the most difficult questions that a customer can ask and then develop workable answers to them. This is called the "What If?" game, and it applies to this preparatory step in performance appraisal process as well.

To avoid being stunned or stumped by your employees' questions and struggling for answers, try in advance to come up with possible queries that they might raise, along with appropriate and supportive answers. You know your employees best, and you can probably anticipate the kinds of questions they may ask, and who might even be asking them. By thinking about who may be asking what, you can increase the likelihood of keeping your appraisal sessions on track and on target.

However, although such anticipation is important, it's impossible to predict every conceivable question your employees might ask. In spite of ongoing questions and answers during the continuous feedback process, some questions can jump into your employees' mind on the spot, and it can be helpful to try to anticipate what these questions might be. Here's a sampling of a few that can be raised during the appraisal sessions along with supportive responses to each:

Question: What rating did you give to Employee X?

Answer: I really understand and appreciate your interest in other members of the team, but everyone's rating is confidential and private.

Question: I thought my performance was better than that. Why did you rate me so low?

Answer: That's a great question, and that's just what we're going to talk about — especially in terms of the ways to strengthen your performance in any noted areas and also identify upskilling and educational opportunities to help you meet your goals. And I really want to hear your thoughts about all of this.

Question: Who said that about me?

Answer: Actually, your review is based on my overall observations and analysis of data that included your self-evaluation plus feedback from your peers and direct reports, but nothing in it is based on anyone's individual comments.

TIP

If a question comes totally from out of right field and you lack sufficient information to provide a cogent answer, there's no need to scramble for data or proffer a guess — you can always indicate that you'll check out the matter after the session and get back with a response as soon as possible.

In light of the collaborative and forward-focused nature of the performance appraisal process, it not only makes sense to have an agenda in place before the appraisal session, but it also makes sense to incorporate input and suggestions from your employees in putting the agenda together. With this approach, your employees will sense greater involvement in the process, while further eliminating concerns or confusion regarding the topics to be discussed in these sessions. In addition, employees sense increased levels satisfaction and anticipation when they have included topics that they would like to discuss.

Importantly, your agendas should not be ironclad, but rather should have enough flexibility to allow you to engage in in-depth discussions as well as expand into relevant related topics. The overall framework for this agenda can include the following topics:

>> Overview of performance during the period

>> Employee's main achievements and accomplishments

>> Performance areas needing improvement

>> Attainment and progress regarding performance goals and development goals

>> Upskilling, growth, and development during the quarter, and opportunities for continued development

Handling the Logistics

To conduct a collaborative and productive appraisal session with your employees, there are some premeeting logistical steps that can greatly facilitate the process.

Scheduling the day and time

The key step in calendaring these meetings is to make sure that you have provided sufficient advance notice to each of your employees regarding these sessions. Obviously, if time slips by and your availability as well as that of your employees have become quite limited, this can lead to delays while sending an underlying message that these meetings are not particularly important or significant.

As the end of a given evaluation period approaches, the best step is for you to use a continuous feedback session to let your employees know that you'll be holding their individual quarterly or biannual appraisal session with them within the next few weeks, and you wanted to give them an update on the process and make sure that they will be available. This type of advance notice and updating will engage your employees to a far greater extent than if you were to simply look at their calendars and send them an invite. Also, approximately two weeks prior to the end of the evaluation period, you should send the self-evaluation forms to the employees whom you are evaluating along with the 360-degree feedback forms to peers and direct reports who will be participating in this process — this should include a request to receive the completed forms by a specific date within the two-week period.

TIP

One particularly effective way to set the actual dates for these formal appraisal sessions is to let your employees schedule them. This approach implies respect for them and helps set the stage for open and forward-focused discussions.

Clearing the deck

As soon as the days and times are confirmed for theses sessions, it's important for managers to treat them as a high priority and clear the deck of anything that might interfere. If other assignments come your way or other individuals want to meet with you during these blocked-out time periods, you should do all that you can to keep the scheduled appraisal sessions in place. Other than in the case of a real emergency, these sessions should not be cancelled, abbreviated, or rescheduled. When they are moved around because of other appointments, especially at the last minute, this sends a message to the employees that they are not a real priority.

TIP

The concept of clearing the desk also includes preparing your work area for this meeting. If you are meeting onsite with your employees for this session, you should remove or cover all documents and files on your desk prior to the meeting. If these documents are visible during the appraisal sessions, they can easily become a distraction for you as well as your employees — especially if there is the slightest indication that they may contain confidential information. If you are conducting these sessions remotely, it's still important to make sure that your background does not contain any such documents and files, while also making sure that your background is appropriate for the session — a frivolous or cluttered background can also be distracting and interfere with communication.

Blocking extra time

In most cases, these sessions can be scheduled to last one hour. However, just to be safe, managers should not schedule any other appointments that end right before the evaluation sessions start, nor should they schedule any meetings to start right after the appraisal sessions are scheduled to end. The safest approach is to leave yourself at least a 30-minute cushion before and after every session. This also means implementing a hard-stop for any meeting that you have prior to the appraisal session. By blocking 30 minutes before any given session, you'll have some time to get organized and set up before the appraisal session starts.

REMEMBER

Dashing into an evaluation session after the scheduled starting time sends a message of disinterest and carelessness on your part regarding the employees and their performance. In addition, a late arrival increases the employees' distress and anxiety, hence disrupting the session before it begins and undercutting the employees' receptiveness to the feedback and feedforward that you may provide.

Onsite or remote: Selecting the right venue

In setting up appraisal sessions with your employees, it's important to select a venue that is unlikely to interfere with or detract from the feedback and feedforward you'll be providing. If you'll be meeting with your employees onsite, the most suitable place for these sessions is your office, if you have one — or in another enclosed area, assuming that it's private. Holding these sessions in locations where others are within earshot, such as in a cubicle or workstation, clearly undercuts two-way communication.

If you are working in an open environment without offices, you should book a conference room, meeting room, huddle room, or any other private area for these sessions. It's not as if a private workspace automatically increases communication, but it's clear that a wide-open space with others nearby will definitely decrease it.

TIP

If you don't have a private office but your manager has one, ask if you can use it for your evaluations. Many managers will go along with this request, especially those who take the process seriously and expect their employees to do likewise. Your manager may also have some suggestions for other options or meeting areas in the company. Also, with today's hybrid workplaces, another way to conduct a private performance appraisal session is for you and your employees to work remotely on the day of the session and use a videoconferencing platform such as Zoom or Teams to hold a private meeting.

If you'll be conducting performance appraisals for fully remote employees, one approach as noted above is for you to conduct the session through videoconferencing, especially because your employees will be familiar with this method as a result of the continuous feedback you have been providing. In using this approach for appraisal sessions, you will most likely not need to physically clear your desk prior to the conversation, but it will nonetheless be important to remove any possible distractions such as people walking behind you, pets that want your attention, or backgrounds that draw your employee's attention. All the other steps related to blocking out your time also apply when providing feedback and feedforward to remote employees.

Giving reminders

When the times and dates for the appraisal sessions are approaching, be sure to provide your employees with reminders. This does not mean hovering over them or badgering them about their preparedness, but rather just keeping them posted on the approaching date and asking whether they have any questions or need any further information or support along the way. This step can be easily handled through the continuous feedback and feedforward that you provide to them, along with any informal interactions that you may have with them.

Keeping it private

As noted earlier, privacy is one of the important underpinnings of the performance appraisal process, and managers should advise their employees of this fact. Without privacy, employees as well as their managers will be very guarded in these appraisal sessions and basically unable to be totally honest — and without honesty, these sessions are futile at best.

For these sessions to be truly productive and provide employees with useful feedback on past performance plus feedforward that helps them grow, it's essential to have privacy both *during* and *after* the appraisal sessions.

During the session

To have an open and honest exchange premised on two-way communication, these sessions need privacy. This means no visitors, audiences, coworkers, or eavesdroppers present or nearby during these sessions — whether remote or virtual.

After the session

The information discussed in these sessions is private and confidential. As a result, managers should refrain from discussing the contents of these discussions with others unless absolutely necessary, such as when addressing high-priority business matters including promotions, transfers, or staffing adjustments. You should let your employees know that HR will have access to this information, along with a very limited number of senior-level individuals who have a legitimate need for such access.

As part of these sessions, advise employees that they should not discuss their evaluations, ratings, or any other contents of their appraisal sessions with other employees.

Preventing interruptions

By selecting appropriate venues as noted above, you've already reduced the likelihood of interruptions. However, a number of potential interrupters should also be addressed and sidelined before they can interfere with these sessions.

Advising the team

Prior to any evaluation sessions, one preventive step is to let others on your team know you are not to be disturbed — this includes your employees as well as your peers and manager. These individuals need to know that you take this process seriously, and you don't want to be paged or have anyone knocking on your door or peeking into your office to see if you're available.

Eliminating phone call, texts, and email

You should not be taking any calls or reading or sending texts or email during these sessions. Engaging in these behaviors, even if they deal with business matters, immediately tells employees that their individual needs and the appraisal process itself are of secondary importance.

In addition, these sessions have momentum, especially as the conversation continues and employees become more comfortable, open, and engaged. When a manager gets distracted by phone calls, texts, or email, the conversation is brought to a complete standstill. Even if it's a brief interruption, the likelihood of returning to the level of interaction that was previously established is minimal. As a result, one important step for managers is to turn on the "Do Not Disturb" feature on their cellphone during these sessions and to advise their employees to do likewise.

Avoiding your computer

Whether the appraisal session is remote or virtual, managers should also refrain from simultaneously doing any work on their computer while meeting with their employees. Doing this, even just a quick glance at their screen, is another source of interruption, disruption, and dissatisfaction — any of which can completely derail the session. Using your computer during these sessions should be strictly limited to accessing information that is immediately needed and directly relevant to the feedback or feedforward for the employee with whom you are meeting.

TIP

Rather than allowing interruptions of any kind to intervene, the best outcomes in terms of feedback and development are generated when managers approach and conduct these sessions with full attention focused on their employees.

Final Steps to Make the Process Work

As you establish the framework for successful forthcoming performance appraisal sessions, you should take these five additional actions, which are all discussed in more detail in Bonus Chapter 2, "Gathering and Analyzing Performance Data":

>> **Review your notes.** Take a careful look at the notes you put together as part of your continuous feedback, especially in terms of your employees' performance, goal attainment, competencies, and development.

>> **Review employee evaluations.** Take the time to carefully review their self-evaluations and 360-degree feedback if your company uses this method.

>> **Review employee files.** You can gain considerable insight into your employees by reviewing any work-related documentation that may have been added to their files during the current appraisal period, such as complaints, compliments, reprimands, awards, and milestones. It can also be quite useful to review their previous appraisals if they worked for a different manager.

>> **Complete the evaluation forms.** Some of the most effective ways to complete these forms include starting with your best employees, writing first and rating/ranking later, and keeping in mind how your constructive feedback and your comments about areas for improvement, growth, and development will be read.

>> **Consider performance management systems.** Today's performance management solutions have the potential to facilitate, expedite, and enhance the performance appraisal entire process. Bonus Chapter 2 also provides links to a wide range of today's performance management software.

Chapter **4**

Leading a Productive Appraisal Session

At this point in the process, you have already established a solid foundation for conducting successful and productive performance appraisal sessions with your employees by having taken the following steps:

» You've provided continuous feedback, feedforward, and coaching throughout the evaluation period.

» You've gathered, documented, and reviewed accurate and specific performance data for each of your employees.

» You've written performance evaluations that are thorough, fair, and based on actual and measurable behaviors, competencies, and results, while simultaneously having a strong forward-focus on the growth and development of your employees.

As a result of these actions, you will have eliminated a vast array of negative feelings and reactions that are commonly evoked by traditional performance appraisals. Rather than setting the stage for angst, stress, distress, defensiveness, and dissatisfaction, your continuous feedback has opened the door for an open and respectful two-way conversation that reviews progress, performance, and goal attainment across the full range of employee responsibilities during a given appraisal period. Underlying this approach is a clear forward-focus through which you and your employees set the framework to jointly determine and update performance goals and development goals, while also delineating specific pathways for training and upskilling to further enhance employee performance and development.

Preventing the Most Common Mistakes

As you take the final steps in preparing for the appraisal sessions with each of your employees at the end of a given evaluation period, step back and look at some of the more common errors that can occur in the appraisal process and make sure that your appraisals don't include them.

In addition to some of the most common mistakes that occur in the performance appraisal process that were addressed in earlier chapters, such as focusing excessively on the past, being overly influenced by recent events, and talking too much, it's important to be on guard for other potential sources of errors that can distort your feedback and feedforward and ultimately undercut the process. Some of these common mistakes are based on the following:

>> **The halo effect:** This is the tendency to allow employees' exceptional performance in one area positively impact the way that managers appraise their employees in many other areas, regardless of actual performance.

>> **The horns effect:** The horns effect occurs when managers allow their employees' questionable performance in one area to negatively impact the ratings in most other areas, in spite of performance data to the contrary.

>> **The contrast effect:** When managers appraise a truly exceptional employee, the next employee's ratings may be lower than merited, primarily as a result of a conscious or unconscious comparison made by their manager. This same type of outcome occurs in the opposite direction when an employee at any performance level is evaluated directly after that of a poorly performing employee.

>> **Central tendency:** The central tendency describes the behaviors of some managers who regard all employees as

being essentially in the middle range in terms of their performance, regardless of how productively and effectively they performed.

>> **Perceived similarity:** When managers sense that they have a great deal in common with certain employees, they tend to be more lenient, generous, and forgiving when appraising their performance.

Setting the Stage for the Appraisal

A few days before the sit-down sessions at the end of a given period, you can take some additional actions to further help your forthcoming appraisal sessions generate positive and productive interactions and outcomes.

Identifying the key takeaways

As you establish the framework for your performance appraisal sessions with each of your employees, have a clear idea of the most important performance-related points, actions, and suggestions that you would like your employees to understand, remember, and incorporate into their performance going forward. By identifying the desired takeaways prior to each session, you'll be able to ascertain that all of the central topics that need to be addressed and acted upon by your employees are covered in these meetings.

As you look at the forthcoming performance evaluation sessions, some of the key takeaways that you anticipate for your employees can include the following:

>> **Areas of excellent performance:** Your employees should have a clear understanding of the areas in which they demonstrated excellence in their performance, whether in terms of goal attainment and alignment, projects, or personal growth. This not only reinforces and encourages similar behaviors in the future, it also offers a source of additional recognition that contributes to satisfaction, engagement, and productivity.

>> **Areas where performance improvement is needed:** Your employees should also leave these sessions with a clear, full, and accurate understanding of the areas in which their

performance needs some improvement. In order to have further staying power in this area, your feedback should avoid generalities and focus on the specific and documented actions, behaviors, and outcomes that can be upgraded. By using clear and descriptive language, as well as by including your employees' comments and input on the performance that is being discussed, your points will be more likely to resonate and stay with your employees following these sessions.

>> **Steps to improve performance:** In relation to the above point, while discussing areas in which your employees' performance needs improvement, you can increase the likelihood of a more enduring impact by providing your employees with some specific advice, training, upskilling, and guidance during the evaluation sessions. Depending upon the behaviors in question, you may be able demonstrate some of the specific ways in which your employees can upgrade the performance in question. By receiving such on-the-spot guidance and even practicing in front of you, there's an increased likelihood that your support will lead to a useful and productive takeaway.

>> **Upskilling and training opportunities:** Also, in terms of improving employee performance, you can generate a powerful takeaway by presenting your employees with some targeted developmental opportunities for them to pursue following these sessions. Such opportunities can include programs offered by the company, as well as selected and suitable classes, courses, podcasts, and certification programs. Importantly, this type of action on your part further demonstrates your interest in your employees' advancement and career development, two areas that are of particular importance to today's employees — hence making your feedback and feedforward in this area even more compelling and long-lasting.

Depending upon your company's industry, size, operations, marketplace, and major developments, the points above are certainly not the only takeaways to keep in mind when meeting with your employees in the appraisal sessions. Although they may help as you approach these sessions, it will be equally important for you to tailor the specific kinds of takeaways that will be most effective for your employees and the company at large.

TIP

When it comes to developing takeaways for the appraisal sessions that you lead, here's one question to ask yourself regarding each of your employees: What do you want this individual to be thinking, doing, and learning following these sessions?

By identifying the takeaways before the sessions, and then making sure they're addressed during the sessions, you'll greatly increase the likelihood that your employees will leave with a clear understanding of the most important components of your feedback and feedforward.

Maintaining a forward-focused mindset

As you approach the performance appraisal sessions for your employees, remember that you'll be providing feedback along with feedforward. As the word implies, feedback takes a look at past performance and provides the employees with accurate, data-based, specific information on the ways in which their performance exceeded, met, or fell short of the desired and expected outcomes. Although this is useful information for your employees, they will already know about it because of the continuous feedback that you have been providing throughout a given evaluation period. Hence, such performance should certainly be raised during the evaluation sessions, but it should not be the focal point.

Rather, the feedback that is related to your employees' past performance during a given evaluation period should be used as a springboard for a forward-focused discussion that deals with performance improvement, individual training and growth, and career development. In many respects, the areas in which your employees' performance fell short of the mark are actually identifiers of training and developmental needs. You and your employees now have the advantage of knowing the specific areas in which training, upskilling, growth, and development are needed. With this shared information at hand, the stage is set for you to collaborate with your employees to continue to jointly develop, adjust, and implement development goals and the strategies to attain and even exceed them.

TIP

There's no question that employees need to know about the areas in which their performance did not meet the mark, but the central focus of these sessions should not be on what they did wrong in the past, but rather how they can do it right in the future — and continue on an upward path of growth.

At the same time, your comments in these sessions should also include positive feedback as merited by your employees' successes, such as in terms of their goal attainment, project completion, and personal growth. You will have provided your employees with positive feedback in these areas as part of your continuous feedback during the evaluation period, but you should also do so during these sessions. The reason is that as you meet with them at the end of the period, you'll have another opportunity not only to provide them with recognition, appreciation, and thanks, but also to identify new areas in which to build on their successes, identify new areas of growth to pursue, and further jointly define and refine your employees' career path and advancement opportunities.

Reviewing the agenda

As discussed in Chapter 3, one particularly effective way to establish an agenda for these appraisal sessions is to do so with input from your employees. This approach further demystifies the process, while also establishing a framework for an open, honest, and factual two-way conversation. This method also ascertains that all of the issues, developments, and events that impacted employee performance during the evaluation period are included in the discussion.

In addition, having a jointly agreed-upon agenda helps keep the discussion on track and on topic. If the conversation strays from what you had intended, the agenda can help guide the discussion back to the main points that need to be covered.

REMEMBER

The agenda for these sessions should not be cast in stone. If circumstances arise that warrant a change in the agenda — such as new reporting relationships, staffing changes, or altered job responsibilities — you should let your employees know in advance. This step will reduce the element of surprise and maintain your employees' involvement in the process.

TIP

In reviewing the agenda, estimate the amount of time that you're planning on spending on each item. Granted, some areas may take longer than you plan, but having a sense of timing will help you keep each session moving along and focused on higher-priority topics.

Having performance data available

Also prior to the evaluation sessions, make sure you have any performance documentation you may possibly need. You certainly don't need to bring every piece of data that you touched in determining the ratings, but the following points can help in determining which documents to bring and which ones to make available for quick access:

» **Your evaluation form.** Be sure to have your final copy of the individual's performance evaluation form. If you are meeting in person, you should bring a hard copy with you, and you should be ready to send the completed form electronically to your remote employees.

» **Each employee's self-evaluation form.** Have this completed form available because you'll be discussing it during the session and because using the original document as the basis for such a discussion is more effective than relying on your notes or recall.

» **Each employee's 360-degree evaluation forms.** Rather than bringing these forms with you, bring the summary notes that you generated by reviewing these forms. This approach is more private and confidential. As you discuss these reviews with your employees, your notes will help you focus and elaborate on the main points in terms of your employees' strengths and areas for improvement.

» **Information from each employee's files.** You should bring your summaries of any performance-related information that you found through your review of your employees' files, as this can also help you provide more detail and substantiation for your comments if necessary.

» **Each employee's goal attainment.** Your notes on your employees' goal attainment during the period will be helpful in discussing actions your employees took that led to their successes in reaching their goals, as well as the kinds of steps that they can take going forward to meet goals that were unmet. This information will also be helpful in setting the framework and strategies for the coming period and beyond for longer-term goals.

>> **Your notes from continuous feedback.** Although you have generated your assessment and forward-focused strategies for your employees by analyzing all of the performance data that you gathered, your notes can be helpful if specific questions arise regarding the feedback and feedforward that you provided at various specific points during the evaluation period.

Actively listening

As you hold these appraisal sessions with your employees, your effectiveness will be enhanced if you display solid listening skills. By listening carefully to what your employees are saying, not only will you be able to learn more about their actions and their motivations for taking them, you'll also better able to accurately identify areas of potential development. If your employees sense that you have truly heard what they're saying, they will be far more receptive to your suggestions as well as your collaboration in working with them to create specific steps and strategies to help them enhance their learning, growth, and career development.

Regardless of ratings, employees feel better about the evaluation process if they sense that they're truly being heard.

TIP

As part of the open exchange of ideas that is at the heart of appraisal sessions, here are some steps that can help strengthen your listening skills.

>> **Be totally present.** Your employees should sense that they're getting your full focus and attention during your meeting with them. As noted in Chapter 3, this not only includes preventing interruptions and refraining from looking at your phone or computer, but it also includes thumbing through papers, looking around, or just gazing in the distance — possibly deep in thought about something that has nothing to do with the discussion with your employee.

>> **Let your employees talk.** As your employees answer your questions, ask you questions, look over their performance, discuss their growth and achievements, speak about their goals, and eye their future, be sure to let them talk. This means that you should not interrupt them, cut them off, finish their sentences, or use words or phrasing to rush them.

>> **Restate, rephrase, and summarize.** In order to make sure that you fully and accurately understand what your employees may be saying, as well as to let them know that you are truly listening and engaged, you can play back their comments such as by saying, "I want to make sure that I understand," and then put their comments in your own words. In addition, briefly restating and summarizing their comments in a sentence or two demonstrates your interest and involvement, while further enhancing your understanding of whatever your employees may be saying.

>> **Pay attention to what they're *not* saying.** Pay extra attention to your employees' body language, such as their facial expressions, whether they're slouched or sitting forward, whether their arms are crossed, and whether they maintain eye contact. As noted earlier, nonverbal communication sends a wide range of important information, and by focusing carefully on the nonverbal as well as the verbal components and aspects of your employees' communication, you'll be able to obtain a clearer and more complete understanding of whatever your employees may be trying to express.

TIP

While your employees are talking, be sure to focus on what they're saying rather than on what you want to say in response.

>> **Ask open-ended questions.** Rather than asking questions that call for a yes or no response, ask open-ended question, such as those that start with *what*, *why*, or *how*. These types of questions will enable your employees to express and elaborate on their thoughts and ideas regarding the topics that are being addressed, rather than feeling somewhat restricted by questions that call for a yes or no response.

Giving out the appraisals

As you plan the appraisal sessions with your employees, determine when your employees should be given a copy of their evaluation — regardless of whether it's provided in person or via email. Although no hard and fast rule exists about how quickly you should provide your employees a copy of the completed performance appraisal form, the general agreement is that employees should be given a copy at some point as part of this process. The specific timing depends on your company's established practices and processes in this area, but the three prevailing approaches on this matter are as follows:

Before the session

Many managers find that the best time to give the completed performance appraisal forms to their employees is *before* the face-to-face sessions, whether in person or virtual. Some managers give out the forms an hour or two ahead, whereas others give them out a day or two in advance. Providing this document to the employees prior to the sessions helps facilitate the conversation by removing more unknowns, while also showing respect for the employees by including them in this phase of the process.

With this approach, the idea is to give employees a chance to think about their evaluations, review the ratings and comments, formulate productive questions, and come up with their own thoughts regarding the ways to improve their performance and enhance their growth. In addition, by having the employees review their appraisals ahead of the sessions and spend some time thinking about the written feedback, less time will be needed to do so during the meetings. As a result, this will provide additional time for managers and their employees to review performance and the determination of the ratings, as well as more time to look ahead and discuss performance goals and development goals.

When the session starts

Some managers start the evaluation sessions by handing the completed evaluation forms to their employees. On the one hand, this approach reduces any mystery and doubt over the points to be covered in the sessions. The employees have an immediate and upfront idea of the focus and direction of the discussion.

However, when managers provide employees with completed forms at the beginning of the sessions, the employees tend to rush through the forms, typically without absorbing much of the detail. Employees often immediately dwell on ratings that are lower than expected, which can adversely impact their understanding and acceptance of the other information in the forms. As part of this reaction, some of their negativity and skepticism regarding what they have just read can also leak into the discussion that follows during the evaluation session itself. Plus, many employees aren't comfortable sitting and reading their evaluations while their managers are staring at them. As a result, this approach does not typically establish a positive framework for a productive, open, and forward-focused conversation.

TIP

If you give the completed evaluation forms to your employees at the start of their evaluation session, another issue is that they will spend time during the discussion reading it, looking ahead, and even making some notes — instead of listening to you and engaging in a productive two-way conversation.

When the session ends

At the other end of the spectrum, some managers discuss the entire evaluation with their employees during the appraisal sessions, followed by providing them with the completed form at the end of the discussion, again either in person or via email. Although this approach eliminates the speed-reading, negative focusing, and distraction associated with handing out the forms at the outset, it has its own problems. Specifically, when managers conduct the evaluation sessions and discuss the various ratings section-by-section, employees typically hear the first few words of their managers' comments regarding performance in a particular area and then start to wonder how they'll be appraised on the next item.

In some cases, as the sessions wrap up, the forms are provided to the employees, and the discussion is essentially ended at that time. Although the employees can then review the written evaluations on their own following these sessions, a good deal of continuity is lost because of the gap in time between the end of the sessions and the reading of the evaluation form. In addition, if comments or ratings in the form differ from what the employees think they heard during the sessions, a follow-up discussion will be necessary — and this type of disparity is not always easy or comfortable to resolve.

TIP

When you give the completed evaluations to your employees ahead of the discussion sessions — whether by an hour or two or even a day or two — your employees come to these sessions better prepared to have a productive two-way conversation that lends itself more easily and effectively to feedback and feedforward.

Repositioning Raises

In the past, it was quite common to include raises as part of the performance appraisal process and list them as one of the topics for discussion on the agenda for these sessions — especially in year-end annual appraisals. Importantly, along with the introduction of continuous feedback and quarterly or biannual appraisals, there has been a clear and steady movement to separate raises from performance appraisals.

The newer approach is for companies to make raises part of a company's overall compensation planning and policy, with a direct focus on aligning raise practices with corporate goals and strategy, as well as with the company's pay and benefit programs. This approach helps increase consistency, transparency, objectivity, and clarity in the process, while also preventing some of the more common problems that occur when pay and performance appraisals linked together, such as the following:

>> **Overriding the messaging:** When raises are a topic in the appraisal sessions, employees are typically waiting to find out how much of an increase they'll be receiving, or if they'll be receiving an increase at all. Rather than thinking about the feedback and feedforward regarding their successes, areas for improvement, goal attainment, or growth opportunities, they're more likely thinking about the money. When this occurs, employees are likely to engage half-heartedly in these discussions, hence severely undercutting their value and utility.

>> **Creating inequities:** In some cases, the inclusion of raises in the performance appraisal process has been found to contribute to perceptions of inequities and unfairness. In such situations, there's concern regarding the ways in which managers may determine raises for their employees, especially considering the discretionary factors that might not be consistently applied across the board to all employees.

>> **Disrupting development:** Although these sessions should be focused on discussing feedback and feedforward, especially in terms of strategies related to employee growth, upskilling, career development, and advancement, many employees are too distracted by unknown raises to adequately focus on any of this. Rather, they're waiting to hear what kind of a raise they'll be getting, and as soon as they hear about the raise, they're then distracted by their satisfaction or dissatisfaction with the amount. Either way, the primary developmental objective of these sessions can easily be missed when raises are part of the conversation.

Holding the Meeting

At this point in the process, you will have completed all of the preparatory steps in anticipation of the appraisal session that you'll hold with each of your employees at the end of a given evaluation period. Although the agendas you jointly established with each of your employees will help you navigate through these sessions, keep in mind some additional steps to further facilitate and enhance these discussions.

Steps to open the discussion

By the time these sessions arrive, typically at the end of a three-month or six-month evaluation period, you've already established an open, supportive, communicative, and coaching-oriented working relationship with your employees. Nonetheless, because these meetings are more formal than your continuous feedback sessions or your informal contact with the employees, you should open these sessions positively and constructively — especially because your opening comments will have a major impact on the tone, tenor, and atmosphere for the discussion that follows. With this in mind, here are a few steps to keep in mind when opening these sessions:

>> **Greetings.** Rather than immediately getting down to business, you should welcome your employees, ask them how they're doing, and even briefly touch on a light topic that they may have recently mentioned to you — even if it's not totally work-related. This type of welcoming and upbeat opening helps generate a greater sense of comfort and ease for your employees.

>> **Appreciation.** As part of your opening comments, another positive step is to thank your employees for their input on the agenda for this meeting, for taking the time to complete their self-evaluation, and for helping to set up some of the continuous feedback sessions during the evaluation period. This is an excellent time to let your employees know that you truly appreciate and respect their involvement in the appraisal process.

>> **The big picture.** Before diving into the details of the meeting, this is also a good time to provide your employees with an overall picture of the meeting by giving a quick

rundown of the agenda that you jointly established with them. Just in case there was any initial doubt as to the direction and contents of this session, your overview helps them know where the meeting is going, while also increasing their sense of ownership and responsibility for its contents.

Providing feedback and feedforward on performance and goal attainment

At this point in the performance appraisal process, you have established a positive, productive, and open framework for providing your employees with accurate, useful, and relevant feedback and feedforward that they are likely to accept, internalize, and apply productively to their work and development. Such feedback and feedforward focus on the central areas of their performance:

>> **Achievements and successes.** At the beginning of the session, one way to continue the positive momentum generated by your opening remarks is to focus on your employees' particularly notable achievements, accomplishments, and successes during the evaluation period. Bringing up these outcomes at this time demonstrates the relevance that you attach to these positive outcomes, while also providing high-level and significant recognition and reinforcement for your employees' actions, behaviors, and steps that generated these results.

>> **Self-evaluations.** Also, in this early stage of the discussion, talk about your employees' self-evaluations. This further draws them into the conversation, and also opens the door for them to talk further about their successes as well as the areas in which their performance did not match expectations — theirs as well as yours. Their comments in these areas will provide you with an opportunity to gain an even clearer understanding of their insight and perceptions regarding their own performance, developmental needs, and interests, hence shedding additional light on the most effective ways to provide them with feedback and feedforward.

>> **360-degree feedback.** After finishing the discussion regarding your employees' self-evaluations, you'll have an excellent opportunity to share the overarching information

that you gleaned from the 360-degree feedback that was submitted to you from your employees' peers and subordinates (if they have any). You can bring up the major themes from this feedback and solicit your employees' reactions, comments, and thoughts. To the extent that any of this feedback aligns with your employees' responses in their self-evaluations, the discussion can then easily flow into the kinds of steps that the employees can take to enhance their performance in the noted areas. At the same time, if the employees believe that some of the feedback from the 360-degree evaluations is inaccurate or incomplete, it will be helpful to let them fully express their thoughts in such areas, and for you to carefully consider what they're saying. Importantly, your employees' ratings are not determined by 360-degree evaluations. Rather, these types of evaluations are a tool that can serve as a source of recognition for stellar performance, as well as an identifier of possible performance questions as well as training and development needs — all of which should be openly discussed with your employees in these sessions.

>> **Performance results.** Having discussed your employees' appraisals regarding their own performance along with the feedback from their associates, you now have the foundation in place to provide your feedback and initial feedforward regarding your employees' performance. This is the time to discuss and praise your employees for each area in which their specific and measurable performance was satisfactory or better, while providing the same level of specificity in terms of the areas in which performance improvements are needed. One way to frame this feedback is to take out the completed evaluation that you previously provided to your employees and walk through the individual ratings. In doing so, you should pay particular attention to the areas in which your ratings differ from the ratings your employees gave themselves. These differences can provide important insight into the differing perceptions of performance, standards, and results between you and your employees. As you learn more about the rationale behind their self-assessments, and as your employees simultaneously learn more about the rationale behind your ratings, the shared understanding that emanates from such a discussion can generate a clearer alignment of performance expectations going forward.

»» Performance goal attainment. Your employees' goal attainment is directly linked to their overall performance, and the transition to performance goals occurs easily and naturally. These goals focus on specific work-related targets related to output, actions, productivity, and results. They can be longer-term goals that were jointly established before the evaluation period began, or they can be short-term goals that were established as recently as the beginning of the period, with completion dates prior to the end of the period. In terms of the goals that your employees successfully completed during the period, you have another opportunity to provide recognition, credit, and thanks. For those goals which remain uncompleted, you have an opportunity for an open two-way conversation regarding whatever may have caused the shortfall. This can include any number of causal factors such as shifting priorities, altered objectives, work-related barriers and blockages, mismatched skills or expertise, and unclear or unrealistic expectations. This is the time to jointly, openly, and honestly discuss any of the factors that may have impeded goal attainment, followed by identifying possible steps and strategies to increase the likelihood of meeting or exceeding the agreed-upon milestones during the coming period.

»» Development goal attainment. Along with performance goals, your employees also have development goals that are focused on their upskilling, training, growth, and career advancement. Structured similarly to performance goals, these goals are clear, specific, measurable, and time-sensitive, but they're focused on specific actions for employees to take and outcomes to reach in terms of building themselves professionally and moving ahead in their careers. As you review your employees' performance throughout the most recent evaluation period, you'll also have clear data regarding their growth and development. Again, for the development goals or milestones that they met, you should provide appropriate recognition. At the same time, for those goals or milestones that were left incomplete, you should have a two-way discussion regarding any possible blockages that may have interfered with their progress and goal attainment, along with possible steps and strategies to remove or overcome the hurdles and set the framework to jointly determine updated development goals and strategies that support them. At the same time, depending on the factors that impeded their goal attainment, you may be able to provide your employees with some guidance, tips, and training right on the spot to help them hit the ground running after this session.

TIP

In some companies, the process of establishing new performance goals and development goals is carried out as one of the final steps in the performance appraisal sessions. However, many companies prefer to conduct goal-setting in separate meetings. Some of the reasons for this separation include the fact that new ideas, issues, and developments that may have emerged during the appraisal sessions call for thorough review, analysis, and communication by managers and the employees — rather instantly moving into the process of goal-setting. In addition, jointly agreeing upon, establishing, and finalizing goals takes time, and including this step in the appraisal sessions can cause these sessions to become excessively time consuming.

Wrapping up the discussion

Before ending these sessions, you can take a few steps to help generate a more meaningful, impactful, and motivational conclusion for your employees and for you as well:

>> **Q&A.** As part of the two-way conversation that is central to these appraisal sessions, employees have the opportunity at any time to raise any questions that they would like to ask. Nonetheless, as the end of the session approaches, ask the employees if they have any questions about their feedback, feedforward, company goals, new products, equipment, or anything else that is of interest or concern to them. Your responses should be clear, honest, and complete, followed by asking if your response provided the information that they're seeking. If there's a question that you cannot answer on the spot, you should let your employees know that you'll do some checking after the session and will get back to them as soon as possible. After your employees have asked all their questions, be sure to thank them for doing so and remind them that you are open to their questions at any time.

>> **Suggestions.** Although you have already solicited your employees' ideas, input, and suggestions as part of your

continuous feedback as well as during these sessions, it can be helpful to see whether they have any additional suggestions before the appraisal session ends. Their suggestions can be on any topic related to work, such as ventilation issues, charging stations, the breakroom, or a company newsletter. Although most suggestions cannot be instantly implemented during these meetings, you should let your employees know that you'll do more research on each suggestion, adding that you'll keep them informed as you proceed. Again, let them know that you appreciate hearing their new ideas.

» **Feedback to you.** Although your company's 360-degree feedback program may include feedback from members of your team during your own evaluation, the current appraisal sessions with your employees also provide an opportunity for them to provide you with some face-to-face feedback as well. Before the meeting ends, you can ask them if they have any advice, suggestions, or even concerns about their working relationship with you. Many employees are hesitant to provide this type of feedback, but if you have established an open, trusting, and respectful relationship with your employees, they may be inclined to share some useful feedback for you. Be sure to listen carefully and let your employees know that you are doing so. As noted above, be sure to thank them for their honesty and candor.

» **Next meeting.** This is also the time to set up the next meeting which will be focused on your employees' performance goals and development goals. Your employees should use the information that you provided during this session as well as the feedback and feedforward that they have received from you during the appraisal period to draft these goals. At the same time, let them know that they can contact you at any point prior to the goal-setting meeting to discuss any questions that they may have in drafting these goals.

» **Summary.** With all the above feedback, feedforward, and follow-up actions in place, the next step is for you to provide a brief summary and overview of this session, including a recap of your employees' major strengths and areas for improvement. In addition, be sure to cover the specific steps that you and your employees will take going forward, with specific attention focused on the actions to be taken prior to the next scheduled meeting. Be sure to keep the tone of your summary upbeat, confident, supportive, and positive, and let your employees know that you look forward to working with them to jointly establish their performance and development goals at the next meeting. For more detailed information on the process of establishing performance goals and development goals, please see Bonus Chapter 3, "Following Up."

TIP

Upon conclusion or directly following these sessions, the completed performance appraisal form for each of your employees will need to be signed by you and the employee, whether as a hard copy or electronically. In most cases, signing the performance appraisal form does not automatically mean that the employee agrees with its content. Rather, the employee's signature typically signifies that the employee has received the completed appraisal form.

3

Phrases and Expressions That Work

Take advantage of more than 3,300 appraisal phrases that focus on the most important areas of job performance.

Provide impactful and accurate feedback by using specific descriptions ranging from "Exceptional" to "Unsatisfactory."

Select positive phrases that encourage and motivate your employees to keep up the good work.

Select phrases in the less-than-positive categories to help employees clearly understand where improvements are needed.

Use these phrases to open the door to enhanced performance, relevant training, and career development.

Chapter 5

The Best Phrases for Attitude

One of the most common themes in performance appraisals is focused on employee attitude. Unfortunately, much of the feedback that focuses on this topic fails to resonate with employees. The reason is that *attitude* is a term that has many components and meanings, and simply advising employees that they have a great attitude or a poor attitude is not particularly helpful.

Overarching favorable comments about positive attitudes provide no significant information regarding behaviors for an employee to continue, whereas overarching negative comments about questionable attitudes provide no information regarding specific behaviors for the employee to upgrade or eliminate. Plus, vague or general feedback in this area can chip away further at the employees' attitudes.

As a result, the most effective way to provide meaningful feedback regarding attitude is to use descriptive phrases that focus directly on the most compelling behaviors that reflect employee attitudes at work, such as attendance, dedication, commitment, reliability, initiative, energy, handling of pressure and stress, and related topics.

When providing feedback in this area, it's important to remember that as employees improve their performance, their attitude improves as well. In terms of the big picture, attitudes shape behaviors, and behaviors shape attitudes.

Accepting Assignments

Exceptional: Consistently exceeds expectations

>> Reaches out for assignments, especially those that are challenging and demanding

>> Has increased departmental productivity as a result of willingness and eagerness to take on additional work

>> Enjoys the challenges and learning opportunities that accompany new assignments

>> Assumes full responsibility on all assigned work and projects

Excellent: Frequently exceeds expectations

>> Accepts assignments without hesitation

>> Reorganizes and reprioritizes work to fully and effectively carry out all assignments

>> Completes assignments thoroughly and on time or even ahead of schedule

Fully competent: Meets expectations

>> Is always willing to do extra work when asked

>> Approaches all assignments seriously, positively, and energetically

>> Discusses assignments and clarifies expectations and priorities in advance

>> Effectively prioritizes and completes assignments

Marginal: Occasionally fails to meet expectations

>> Begrudgingly accepts assignments

>> Frequently makes excuses to avoid handling assignments

>> Regards assignments as punishments

>> Asks for assignments, and then basically ignores them

Unsatisfactory: Consistently fails to meet expectations

>> Continuously looks for reasons to refuse an assignment

>> Shows signs of exasperation and annoyance when asked to do additional work

>> Instantly looks for other people to do the work rather than take responsibility for it

>> Consistently fails to complete the assigned work

Agility

Exceptional: Consistently exceeds expectations

>> Understands the dynamics of work and adjusts quickly and effectively to internal and external changes

>> Works productively and supportively with the team to facilitate their adjustment to unforeseen developments and demands

>> Pays careful attention to the newest trends and issues and is able to quickly implement strategies and steps to deal successfully with them

>> Able to analyze and understand new challenges and develop a course of action to effectively respond to them

Excellent: Frequently exceeds expectations

>> Makes decisions and adjustments quickly, but not impulsively, while still soliciting and utilizing input from others

>> Demonstrates solid ability to create and utilize innovative strategies for prompt and productive handling of new situations, challenges, and developments

>> Able to maintain focus on the big picture while fully immersed in the details of a new situation that demands flexible and agile thinking and problem solving

>> Approaches setbacks with resilience and strength by focusing on strategies to work around or overcome obstacles

Fully competent: Meets expectations

>> Takes advantage of learning opportunities on and off the job and is able to apply new knowledge and skills in numerous situations

>> Is not wedded to past practices, and takes an open-minded and receptive approach to handling new challenges, situations, and demands

>> Follows companies policies and practices, but is open to updates and revisions in order to increase performance and productivity

>> Takes a proactive approach to the job and keeps an eye out for potential issues, changes, and challenges that need to be addressed

>> Serves as an advocate for necessary changes and builds support for them among the team

Marginal: Occasionally fails to meet expectations

>> Tends to stick to carrying out work by using older and outdated methods rather than applying newer strategies, techniques, and technologies

>> Regards new strategies and expectations as intrusions and interruptions that are of secondary importance

- Overreacts to the change process and often complains about new standards and practices rather than trying to understand and apply them
- Does not devote adequate time and attention to understanding changes on the job and in the industry, often minimizing them rather than adjusting to them
- Occasionally applies new standards and strategies to work, but complains about having to do so

Unsatisfactory: Consistently fails to meet expectations

- Actively refuses to apply new performance standards, measures, and processes, in spite of the immediate need to do so
- Shows ongoing resistance rather than adapting and adjusting to changes and developments that are essential for successful job performance
- Insists that the old approaches are better and actively refuses to learn or bend
- Incorrectly advises others that the new changes and adjustments that are needed in the company are of minimal significance and will soon disappear
- Asserts that employees who demonstrate the ability to adjust to new standards and practices are simply trying to look good
- Has taken no time to seriously consider the need for new processes and programs, while spending excessive amounts of time complaining about them

Attendance

Exceptional: Consistently exceeds expectations

- Consistently utilizes timely advance planning and communication when taking time off under the PTO plan

>> Schedules personal appointments during non-work hours

>> Attends and actively participates in all work-related sessions, including those that are held after hours, during the evening, and on weekends

>> Is a model of exceptional attendance

Excellent: Frequently exceeds expectations

>> Always arrives on time or a few minutes early for work and meetings, whether onsite or remote

>> Has used company sick leave only for personal or family illness

>> Has significantly improved overall attendance in the department

Fully competent: Meets expectations

>> Gets right to work upon arrival in the office, and even earlier when working remotely

>> Follows and enforces company policies regarding breaks

>> Utilizes company PTO plan honestly and appropriately

>> Promptly advises management when unable to work

Marginal: Occasionally fails to meet expectations

>> Regularly makes personal appointments during established work hours

>> Spends the last hour of work preparing to shut down or leave

>> Is frequently late to arrive at work or start working remotely

Unsatisfactory: Consistently fails to meet expectations

>> Consistently abuses the company's PTO plan

>> Ignores the company's break policy

>> Fails to be available for work and doesn't notify anyone

>> Spends excessive amounts of time away from the job

Can-Do Attitude

Exceptional: Consistently exceeds expectations

>> Has a can-do attitude, plus a will-do attitude

>> Actively seeks opportunities to take on the most demanding and difficult tasks

>> Consistently delivers more than expected or requested

>> Focuses on what can be done, rather than on what can't be done

Excellent: Frequently exceeds expectations

>> Has had a positive impact on the attitudes and performance of others through a clearly positive approach to work

>> Demonstrates certainty and confidence when it comes to getting any job done and done right

>> Can be counted on to step forward whenever challenges are encountered

>> Has yet to turn down, equivocate, or avoid any highly challenging project

Fully competent: Meets expectations

>> Is always ready to jump in and get the job done

>> Seeks opportunities to demonstrate skills, drive, and commitment

>> Actively seeks the more challenging tasks

>> Rarely if ever says, "I can't"

Marginal: Occasionally fails to meet expectations

» Talks about having a positive attitude, but falls short in terms of performance

» Only steps forward to work on the least-demanding projects

» Focuses more on what can't be done rather than on what can be done

» Takes on additional responsibilities, but typically tries to push them onto others

Unsatisfactory: Consistently fails to meet expectations

» Initially responds to any request by saying that it can't be done

» Has a "can't-do" attitude

» Is more likely to undo a project than do it

» Says "no" before hearing all the facts regarding any request that is made

Dedication and Commitment

Exceptional: Consistently exceeds expectations

» Becomes fully immersed on all projects in order to make each one a major success

» Foregoes personal opportunities to keep work commitments

» Shows unwavering dedication to the company and its mission

Excellent: Frequently exceeds expectations

» Puts in extra hours without being asked to do so in order to deliver first-rate work

» Works nights and weekends whenever needed

» Demonstrates consistently high levels of dedication and commitment in carrying out job responsibilities

Fully competent: Meets expectations

» Is always willing to accept extra assignments

» Takes pride in demonstrating loyalty and dedication to the company

» Has a strong personal commitment to the company's goals

Marginal: Occasionally fails to meet expectations

» Is dedicated to the company whenever it's convenient

» Gives work intermittent attention, rather than concentrated focus

» Speaks of dedication to the company, but takes no significant steps to show it

Unsatisfactory: Consistently fails to meet expectations

» Airs negative views about the company while praising the competition

» Is critical of the company's vision, values, and goals

» Uses time at work to advance a personal agenda rather than the company's agenda

Emphasizing Safety

Exceptional: Consistently exceeds expectations

» Treats safety as a top priority and encourages others to do likewise

- >> Has consistently taken proactive and productive steps to make employees feel safe at work in every sense of the word
- >> Has designed and implemented programs to maintain the lowest accident rate in the company
- >> Regards personal and group safety as a major concern
- >> Has dramatically reduced accidents in the department
- >> Has received awards for actions and suggestions to improve safety in the workplace
- >> Understands the importance of maintaining psychological safety as well as physical safety across the workplace
- >> Always takes the safest approach in carrying out all responsibilities

Excellent: Frequently exceeds expectations

- >> Continuously building employee awareness of safety issues
- >> Recognizes and rewards employees for safe actions and safety-related suggestions
- >> Has brought in experts to discuss safety with employees
- >> Adheres to high personal standards of safety
- >> Leads classes on workplace safety
- >> Has played an active role in creating and implementing the company's emergency preparedness programs
- >> Is an active member of the company's safety committee
- >> Has not had one accident while employed by the company

Fully competent: Meets expectations

- >> Follows all company policies on safety
- >> Keeps safety in mind in all work activities, assignments, and projects
- >> Serves as a model of safe behavior
- >> Works safely and does not draw other employees into risky or dangerous situations

- » Promptly and thoroughly investigates all accidents
- » Has decreased the number, rate, and severity of accidents in the department
- » Participated in the company's training programs on safety, CPR, and first aid
- » Participated in additional training in emergency preparedness

Marginal: Occasionally fails to meet expectations

- » Focuses a minimal amount of time, energy, and attention on safety
- » Produces vague and general write-ups of employee accidents and safety incidents
- » Instantly blames others when accidents occur
- » Shows little concern for the growing number of accidents in the department
- » Has been involved in X accidents during the evaluation period
- » Provides no significant formal or informal training on safety

Unsatisfactory: Consistently fails to meet expectations

- » Has taken no steps to reduce the number of accidents in the department
- » Pushes production at the expense of safety
- » Engages in risky behaviors on the job
- » Ignores the company's policies on safety
- » Regards the issue of employee safety as a low priority
- » Ridicules employees who insist on working safely
- » Covers up accidents when they occur

Energy

Exceptional: Consistently exceeds expectations

» Demonstrates remarkable energy throughout the day

» Has a boundless energy level

» Brings an unending supply of energy to the job

Excellent: Frequently exceeds expectations

» Is still energized when most others are exhausted

» High personal level of energy serves to energize the entire team

» Maintains a high degree of energy regardless of hours

» Is never at a loss for energy

Fully competent: Meets expectations

» Is always ready to do more work

» Productively channels energy to the job

» Is highly productive all day long

» Actively seeks challenging and demanding projects

Marginal: Occasionally fails to meet expectations

» Consistently focuses on less rigorous and demand-ing projects

» Frequently diverts energy to nonproductive pursuits

» Becomes less productive as the day progresses

» Starts projects with a good deal of energy, but runs out of gas quickly

Unsatisfactory: Consistently fails to meet expectations

>> Falls asleep during the workday

>> Waits for others to do the heavy lifting

>> Never exerts extra effort

>> Devotes more energy to non-work activities than to the job

Engagement

Exceptional: Consistently exceeds expectations

>> Consistently demonstrates a high degree of emotional attachment and connection to the job and the company at large

>> Approaches work with extraordinarily high levels of motivation and enthusiasm which positively impact the performance of the team

>> Demonstrates high levels of passion about the company, its products, its mission, and its objectives

>> Exceeds performance standards and expectations and provides ongoing support to others so that they can do likewise

>> Approaches the job with a deep personal sense of purpose and a mindset that is focused on doing the best possible work

>> Maintains an ongoing focus on continuous improvement

Excellent: Frequently exceeds expectations

>> Channels high levels of drive and energy in order to deliver outstanding results

>> Focuses on continued learning and growth with the goal of making increasingly valuable contributions to the

organization while simultaneously enhancing personal growth and career development

>> Actively supports company products and performance whenever the opportunity arises

>> Takes a highly collaborative approach when working within the department as well as with other departments

>> Fully committed to best practices and continuous improvement in all aspects of work

>> Proactively identifies functions and processes than can be upgraded, followed by taking productive steps to help initiate positive changes

Fully competent: Meets expectations

>> Fully immersed in the job and maintains a high degree of focus, attention, and commitment on all projects

>> Highly motivated to build skills and competencies and do more for the company

>> Goes beyond the established performance expectations and seeks ways to make measurable contributions to the company's success

>> Views work as more than a job and maintains a strong connection to the company at large

>> Seeks ways to highlight and publicize the positive aspects of the company, its products, and the opportunities it provides

Marginal: Occasionally fails to meet expectations

>> Typically ignores opportunities to go the extra mile for the company

>> Does the minimum amount of work on most projects

>> Displays a minimalist attitude in carrying out responsibilities

>> Places intermittent attention on primary workload demands, while spending extended amounts of time and attention on lesser matters, some of which have nothing to do with the job

>> Demonstrates indifference and a lack of interest and enthusiasm toward the job and company at large

Unsatisfactory: Consistently fails to meet expectations

» Misses deadlines and shows minimal concern regarding the problems that this creates for other employees and the department at large

» Openly and publicly criticizes company performance, products, and practices

» Approaches the job with an aloof mindset and demonstrates no serious connection to the work or the company itself

» Has taken no steps to build knowledgebase or engage in upskilling, despite encouragement and support from management

» Output often contains obvious errors that should have been caught and corrected prior to submission

» Comments and reactions in meetings frequently show minimal interest, involvement, attention, and focus

Flexibility

Exceptional: Consistently exceeds expectations

» Has an open mind and carefully considers all new ideas, strategies, and approaches

» Consistently focused on the future and new ways to work more effectively

» Has generated creative strategies and solutions when encountering unanticipated last-minute problems, issues, and challenges

» Effectively adjusts to the dynamics and changing demands of the job and seamlessly reprioritizes to get the work done

» Has an open mind and carefully considers all new ideas, strategies, and approaches

» Encourages and actively listens to new ideas

Excellent: Frequently exceeds expectations

>> Has contributed to an open and communicative climate in the department by demonstrating flexibility

>> Regards employees as valued resources and carefully considers their ideas and input when encountering unforeseen challenges

>> Quickly and professionally adapts to changes and is not automatically wedded to past practices

>> Is genuinely interested in ideas that differ from the established way of doing things

Fully competent: Meets expectations

>> Is receptive to change, but only if it makes sense

>> Is flexible to new ideas, approaches, and techniques without being a pushover

>> Engages in active listening, learning, and observing when dealing with new changes and developments

>> Increases employees' receptiveness to new ideas and practices

Marginal: Occasionally fails to meet expectations

>> Hardly considers new ideas and approaches that differ from previous practices on the job

>> Instantly regards new practices and changes as marginally valuable at best

>> Is overly flexible and easily influenced by others

Unsatisfactory: Consistently fails to meet expectations

>> Is totally resistant to ideas that differ from past practices

>> Insists on doing things the way they have been done in the past

>> Regards employees who offer alternative approaches and ideas as troublemakers

Focus

Exceptional: Consistently exceeds expectations

>> Directs laser-like attention on every project
>> Has an outstanding ability to concentrate
>> Focuses equally well on big-picture items and details
>> Has an excellent perspective and is not distracted by minor issues
>> Keeps the team focused on the work to be done

Excellent: Frequently exceeds expectations

>> Productively channels energy and effort on major projects
>> Has an unbending focus in handling all aspects of the job
>> Never loses sight of the objectives
>> Clearly focuses on the goals to be met, and then tenaciously pursues them

Fully competent: Meets expectations

>> Is a persistent problem-solver who doesn't stop until the solution is found or the matter is resolved
>> Stays focused on projects from start to finish
>> Directs full attention to work-related matters throughout the day

Marginal: Occasionally fails to meet expectations

>> Places excessive attention on issues of secondary importance

>> Drifts from one project to another, without closure on any

>> Is easily distracted by minor points or issues

Unsatisfactory: Consistently fails to meet expectations

>> Fails to fully direct attention and efforts on the work to be done

>> Focuses attention on less significant issues, concerns, and problems

>> Easily distracted by time-consuming non-work matters

>> Takes an excessive number of breaks

Following Company Policies and Procedures

Exceptional: Consistently exceeds expectations

>> Clearly understands and adheres to the company's policies, procedures, standards, and expectations

>> Understands policies and procedures, along with the spirit and intent behind them

>> Offers valuable and viable suggestions to upgrade specific policies or procedures

Excellent: Frequently exceeds expectations

>> Keeps other employees up-to-date regarding changes in policies and procedures that impact their work

>> Explains and clarifies policies and procedures

>> Applies polices fairly, evenly, and consistently

Fully competent: Meets expectations

>> Understands most policies and procedures and is able to quickly find answers when in doubt

>> Takes policies and procedures seriously

>> Follows company policies and sets an expectation for other employees to do likewise

Marginal: Occasionally fails to meet expectations

>> Is always looking for ways to work around company policies

>> Regards policies and procedures as loose suggestions

>> Can apply company policies inequitably

Unsatisfactory: Consistently fails to meet expectations

>> Follows personal preferences rather than company policies and procedures

>> Picks and chooses the policies and procedures to be followed

>> Demands that others follow policies while personally ignoring them

Going the Extra Mile

Exceptional: Consistently exceeds expectations

>> Puts in extra time, energy, and effort to produce the highest-quality work

- » Is always ready to do more for the company, regardless of the time, place, or demands
- » Seeks out the most demanding and challenging projects
- » Won't settle for average performance

Excellent: Frequently exceeds expectations

- » Strives to deliver more than whatever is expected
- » Puts in extra energy, effort, and time to generate excellent results
- » Willingly takes on the most demanding tasks at any time

Fully competent: Meets expectations

- » Works extra hours when extra work is needed
- » Never complains when projects require additional time and effort
- » Is always ready to step up and do more work

Marginal: Occasionally fails to meet expectations

- » Resists doing any extra work for anyone in any situation
- » Begrudgingly goes the extra mile and then complains at every step
- » Typically comes up with excuses rather than taking extra steps to help on a project

Unsatisfactory: Consistently fails to meet expectations

- » Is never available when extra help is needed
- » Frequently responds by saying, "That's not my job"
- » Is unwilling to do anything beyond the bare minimum

Handling Pressure and Stress

Exceptional: Consistently exceeds expectations

>> Maintains composure and focus in high-pressure situations

>> Is a calming influence during stressful periods

>> Has truly remarkable stress management skills and abilities

>> Helps build other employees' stress management skills

>> Demonstrates even higher levels of performance as the pressure increases

>> Is extra-energized in high-pressure situations

>> Helps others remain calm and focused by demonstrating equanimity and exceptional performance in stressful situations

>> Remains unfazed by the pressures of a heavy workload and highly demanding deadlines

Excellent: Frequently exceeds expectations

>> Demonstrates positivity and confidence when under severe pressure

>> Adjusts schedules, priorities, and strategies to effectively handle increased job pressures

>> Tolerates high levels of pressure with no slippage in performance

>> Prevents or reduces the severity of pressure situations through solid planning skills

>> Remains calm, steady, and focused as pressure increases

>> Never falters when under pressure

>> Takes steps to remove unnecessary sources of stress on the job

>> Manages stress, rather than being managed by it

Fully competent: Meets expectations

» Goes into high gear when the pressure is on

» Puts in extra energy and hours when job pressures increase

» Is steadily building stress management skills

» Demonstrates excellent productivity levels under stressful circumstances

» Copes with stress by working even harder

» Maintains wide-open communications in high-pressure periods

» When stress levels increase, uses stress management techniques to remain calm and help others do likewise

Marginal: Occasionally fails to meet expectations

» Tends to lose focus during periods of high pressure

» Experiences high levels of stress in situations that are not particularly stressful

» Creates increased pressure and stress by falling behind on projects

» Becomes nervous and jumpy when under pressure

» Lets productivity slide as pressure increases

» Becomes overly emotional when pressure levels increase

» Loses patience in direct proportion to increases in pressure

Unsatisfactory: Consistently fails to meet expectations

» Displays significant declines in performance with the slightest increase in pressure

» Misses work when the pressure increases

» Constantly complains about the pressures of the job

» Is unable to perform effectively when under pressure

- » Tends to shut down when experiencing even minor amounts of stress
- » Becomes short-tempered when pressure increases
- » Starts to panic at the first sign of pressure
- » Increases stress instead of managing it

Initiative

Exceptional: Consistently exceeds expectations

- » Is a true self-starter
- » Appropriately identifies work that needs to be done and then takes action
- » Is highly proactive in approaching all aspects of the job
- » Steps up and takes action on projects, issues, or concerns whenever and wherever needed

Excellent: Frequently exceeds expectations

- » Shows consistently high levels of initiative, self-reliance, and independence
- » Needs the absolute minimum amount of supervision
- » Seeks assignments instead of waiting for them

Fully competent: Meets expectations

- » Gets right to work when there is work to be done
- » When given an assignment, works autonomously and effectively
- » Helps foster a spirit of initiative among the employees

Marginal: Occasionally fails to meet expectations

» Waits for problems to arise or assignments to be made rather than anticipating and taking action

» Shows initiative primarily on minor tasks and assignments

» Is slow to engage on projects that truly need attention

» Takes initiative, but fails to provide adequate communication regarding the steps that are being taken

Unsatisfactory: Consistently fails to meet expectations

» Needs constant prodding to get the job done

» Does very little work unless given specific directives

» Actively avoids assignments that require initiative and drive

Level of Supervision Required

Exceptional: Consistently exceeds expectations

» Has surpassed goals on numerous projects that included minimal direct supervision

» Works without supervision on many projects and generates consistently outstanding results

» Is highly effective in autonomously managing projects from start to finish

Excellent: Frequently exceeds expectations

» Can be trusted to deliver outstanding results on a wide range of projects with very little direct supervision

» Displays excellent independent judgment, decision making, and problem-solving on projects of all sizes

>> Independently handled numerous projects from inception to highly successful completions

Fully competent: Meets expectations

>> Knows when to ask for additional guidance and direction
>> Is steadily and successfully demonstrating increased levels of independence
>> Actively seeks opportunities to work autonomously

Marginal: Occasionally fails to meet expectations

>> Only devotes full effort when closely monitored
>> Doesn't know when to ask for help
>> Tends to focus on questionable priorities when working independently

Unsatisfactory: Consistently fails to meet expectations

>> Without ongoing supervision, slips to unacceptable performance levels
>> Needs regular reminders to stay on track
>> Becomes nervous and stressed out when working independently

Reliability and Dependability

Exceptional: Consistently exceeds expectations

>> Consistently displays exceptional performance
>> Keeps commitments under all circumstances

>> Regardless of the situation, does everything possible to maintain high-level performance

>> Is undeterred by obstacles, pressures, or additional demands that may arise at any point while working on a project

Excellent: Frequently exceeds expectations

>> Can be counted on to give 110 percent under all circumstances

>> Keeps commitments and works with fellow employees to help them keep theirs

>> Quick to step up and work extra hours if that's what it takes to get the job done correctly

Fully competent: Meets expectations

>> Maintains steady and reliable performance

>> Demonstrates consistently solid performance in all aspects of work

>> Handles projects conscientiously from start to finish

Marginal: Occasionally fails to meet expectations

>> Demands reliability from others, while personally performing inconsistently and erratically

>> Demonstrates inconsistent and unpredictable levels of energy, drive, and performance

>> Talks about deliverables, but does not consistently deliver

Unsatisfactory: Consistently fails to meet expectations

>> Frequently disappoints employees by failing to keep commitments

>> Makes promises and then ignores them
>> Guarantees that deadlines will be met, but consistently misses them

Understanding and Supporting Company Values and Mission

Exceptional: Consistently exceeds expectations

>> Acts in ways that represent the best in company values
>> Takes a wide range of actions that help support and fulfill the company's mission
>> Frequently articulates and reinforces company values for other employees
>> Consistently demonstrates a full and unwavering commitment to the company's mission
>> Establishes and pursues goals that help the company advance toward its mission
>> Believes that the company is pursuing a worthy mission
>> Takes a wide range of actions that encourage other employees to focus more clearly on the company's mission

Excellent: Frequently exceeds expectations

>> Helps employees understand and act in accordance with the company's values and mission
>> Has values that are in direct alignment with the company's values
>> Establishes and follows specific plans and strategies to help the company realize its vision and fulfill its mission
>> Truly believes in and supports the company's mission
>> Takes immediate action to deal with behaviors that contradict company values

- ≫ Recognizes and rewards employees whose behaviors help move the company closer to its mission

Fully competent: Meets expectations

- ≫ Fully understands and accepts the company's values and mission
- ≫ Consistently performs in line with company's vision and values
- ≫ Clearly acts in ways that are reflective of the company's values
- ≫ Keeps company values in mind when carrying out all work responsibilities
- ≫ Has great faith in the company's mission and ability to fulfill it
- ≫ Demonstrates a high degree of respect for the company's values
- ≫ Takes pride in the company's mission

Marginal: Occasionally fails to meet expectations

- ≫ Occasionally engages in behaviors that ignore the values of the company
- ≫ Hasn't taken the time to understand the company's mission
- ≫ Ignores communications as well as remote or onsite meetings that present information on the company's values and mission
- ≫ Doesn't regard the mission of the company as being particularly significant
- ≫ Provides other employees with misinformation regarding the company's mission and values
- ≫ Doesn't believe that issues related to the company's values or mission are particularly important

Unsatisfactory: Consistently fails to meet expectations

» Often acts in ways that are in direct conflict with the company's values

» Has personal values that are significantly different from those of the company

» Actively disagrees with the company's mission

» Speaks negatively about the company's mission

» Has turned some employees against the company's mission

» Regards the company's values and mission as secondary matters

» Acts as if company values only apply to other employees

» Manipulates company values to justify questionable behaviors

Volunteering

Exceptional: Consistently exceeds expectations

» Always the first one to volunteer for committees, task forces, and extra responsibilities

» Not only volunteers, but plays an active role as a volunteer

» Doesn't turn down opportunities to volunteer

Excellent: Frequently exceeds expectations

» Senses a high degree of personal satisfaction by assuming voluntary responsibilities at work

» Has made many valuable contributions to the company through various roles as a volunteer

» Has taken actions that have directly led to increased levels of employee interest in volunteering for various committees

Fully competent: Meets expectations

>> Regards volunteering as part of the job

>> Devotes serious time and energy to voluntary roles

>> Has personally recruited several volunteers

Marginal: Occasionally fails to meet expectations

>> Joins voluntary committees, but then shows very little involvement or support

>> Volunteers to help, but complains about doing so

>> Spends too much time on voluntary functions at the expense of other responsibilities

Unsatisfactory: Consistently fails to meet expectations

>> Hasn't volunteered for anything

>> Signs up to volunteer, but doesn't show up

>> Always has a reason to avoid volunteering

>> Volunteers opinions rather than time

Chapter **6**

The Best Phrases for Collaboration, Communication, and Interpersonal Skills

For your employees to effectively carry out their responsibilities and meet their short-term and long-term performance and development goals, they need to know how well they're communicating, collaborating, and dealing with others.

Ironically, some managers have difficulty communicating assessments in these areas, especially when it comes to written comments. They're often concerned that their written feedback on communication won't be expressed clearly, and they fear that providing such feedback on interpersonal relations and collaboration might strain the working relationships instead of improving them. When written comments are vague, general, and overly wordy or terse, these outcomes are indeed likely to occur.

With the above caveats in mind, this chapter provides clear, succinct, and targeted phrases that focus directly on collaboration, communication, and interpersonal skills, while also focusing on key elements of performance in which these skills play a central role. These performance areas include cooperation, teamwork, listening, negotiating, telephone skills, and more. With focused phrases that cover the full spectrum of performance in each of these categories, this chapter provides recognition and reinforcement for successes while also providing specific information regarding the behaviors and practices that need to be addressed for performance improvement and individual development.

Collaboration

Exceptional: Consistently exceeds expectations

» Consistently and effectively pursues, builds, and applies collaborative processes and strategies

» Generates outstanding levels of innovation and productivity through collaboration

» Approaches work with a collaborative mindset that fosters collaborative thinking and problem-solving across the team

» Is directly responsible for generating several highly valuable solutions to company issues and problems through collaboration

» Effectively contributes to brainstorming sessions with employees to generate creative plans, strategies, and outcomes

» Enhances collaboration by incorporating high levels of respect, trust, and teambuilding when working with others

Excellent: Frequently exceeds expectations

» Successfully utilizes collaboration to prevent problems as well as solve them

» Encourages and supports new ideas and suggestions from others and is highly receptive to their input

- » Has introduced collaboration to projects and programs where none existed in the past, subsequently generating measurably improved performance and outcomes
- » Serves as an excellent role model in demonstrating, utilizing, and engaging in collaborative behaviors
- » Generates widespread feelings of fairness, inclusivity, and belonging

Fully competent: Meets expectations

- » Openly and productively serves as a source of information, expertise, and insight when working with individuals and groups
- » Displays high levels of cooperation, support, and engagement when participating in group projects
- » Listens carefully to others and encourages their participation in collaborative activities
- » Understands the role and importance of collaboration and uses it to generate positive experiences and excellent results

Marginal: Occasionally fails to meet expectations

- » Spends considerable time voicing personal ideas while showing minimal interest in the ideas of others
- » Is more prone to argue than discuss
- » Quickly rejects thoughts and insights expressed by others
- » Withholds relevant data, expertise, and advice, rather than making viable contributions to group discussions
- » Does not pay full attention or listen carefully when working with others

Unsatisfactory: Consistently fails to meet expectations

- » Rigidly adheres to personal views and opinions that undermine collaboration and cooperation

- >> Shows a lack of interest, patience, and respect for others when working in a group
- >> Is totally dismissive when group discussions turn to new strategies or options that differ from past practices
- >> Approaches collaborative projects with negative expectations that undermine the process before it starts

Cooperation

Exceptional: Consistently exceeds expectations

- >> Demonstrates a high level of cooperation that sets an example for the entire company
- >> Builds cooperation within the department
- >> Enhances cooperation across the departments
- >> Creates a climate of cooperation
- >> Is clearly one of the most cooperative employees

Excellent: Frequently exceeds expectations

- >> Is always ready to cooperate
- >> Has a totally cooperative attitude
- >> Genuinely enjoys work that calls for cooperation within and across the departments
- >> Is one of the easiest people to work with

Fully competent: Meets expectations

- >> Can always be counted on to pitch in
- >> Readily cooperates whenever the opportunity arises
- >> Is a solid addition to any group
- >> Has a strong concern for others

Marginal: Occasionally fails to meet expectations

>> Cooperates, but with strings attached
>> Is too self-absorbed to display much cooperation
>> Manipulates rather than cooperates
>> Does not view cooperation as a priority

Unsatisfactory: Consistently fails to meet expectations

>> Is the last person to offer help or support
>> Generates conflict rather than cooperation
>> Cannot be counted upon to cooperate
>> Disrupts even the most cooperative groups

Customer Service

Exceptional: Consistently exceeds expectations

>> Demonstrates exactly what it means to be customer centric
>> Is very responsive to the customers' needs
>> Provides the maximum in customer service
>> Maintains the highest levels of professionalism in all aspects of work
>> Has an upbeat and friendly demeanor
>> Knows the product from A to Z
>> Is the customers' first choice
>> Serves as a great customer service role model
>> Understands the customers as individuals
>> Treats customers as partners
>> Is the go-to person for difficult customers or calls

- » Builds excellent relationships with customers
- » Regards customer service as a top priority
- » Is a regular winner of customer service awards
- » Consistently receives highly positive reviews from the customers
- » Is satisfied only if the customers are satisfied

Excellent: Frequently exceeds expectations

- » Puts customers first
- » Goes the extra mile for the customers
- » Places customer satisfaction at the top of the list of job priorities
- » Is motivated to meet the customers' needs
- » Quickly and effectively solves problems and resolves issues for the customers
- » Is able to satisfy dissatisfied customers
- » Makes each customer feel special
- » Is highly skilled in handling difficult customer service situations

Fully competent: Meets expectations

- » Is always pleasant, patient, and engaging with the customers
- » Listens carefully
- » Gives first-rate service
- » Provides fast and competent service
- » Treats every customer with respect
- » Makes the customers feel important
- » Knows the customers by name
- » Builds customer loyalty
- » Always projects a positive attitude

Marginal: Occasionally fails to meet expectations

>> Underestimates the importance of the customers

>> Doesn't have adequate product knowledge

>> Fails to listen carefully

>> Is more interested in ending the conversation than ending a problem

>> Shows no interest in building positive rapport and relationships with the customers

>> Keeps customers waiting for excessively long periods of time

>> Does not fully understand or respect the important role that customer service plays for the company

Unsatisfactory: Consistently fails to meet expectations

>> Puts the customers second rather than first

>> Interrupts the customers

>> Does not pay attention to what customers are saying or feeling

>> Provides incorrect information

>> Argues with customers

>> Becomes inappropriately emotional

>> Abandons customers

>> Embarrasses and humiliates customers

>> Has a condescending attitude

>> Is rude to the customers

>> Makes inappropriate comments

>> Gets too personal

>> Takes no steps to improve customer service skills

>> Doesn't care about losing customers

Listening

Exceptional: Consistently exceeds expectations

>> Listens actively to what others are saying
>> Restates, repeats, and rephrases
>> Truly cares about the thoughts, ideas, and concerns of others
>> Devotes full attention when speaking with others

Excellent: Frequently exceeds expectations

>> Takes follow-up action on matters that are discussed
>> Does not interrupt
>> Listens to the full story before drawing conclusions
>> Creates a climate that encourages communication
>> Fully engages in two-way communication

Fully competent: Meets expectations

>> Does not make snap judgments
>> Uses dialogues, not monologues
>> Is a patient listener
>> Asks questions whenever there is ambiguity or confusion

Marginal: Occasionally fails to meet expectations

>> Rarely pays attention to what others are saying
>> Rushes others as they try to communicate
>> Insists on being heard, but does not listen
>> Ignores what others are saying

Unsatisfactory: Consistently fails to meet expectations

>> Is preoccupied when others are talking

>> Does more talking than listening

>> Multi-tasks rather than truly listening and focusing when others are talking

>> Repeatedly asks the same questions

Meetings

Exceptional: Consistently exceeds expectations

>> Knows when to meet in person and when to meet virtually

>> Engages in highly effective pre-meeting planning

>> Establishes an agenda and follows it unless there is a real need to cover additional topics

>> Keeps discussions open, productive, and robust

>> Leads meetings that are known for excellent problem solving and decision making

>> Avoids distractions and disruptions

>> Fully understands and applies the latest technologies to conduct highly effective remote meetings and presentations

Excellent: Frequently exceeds expectations

>> Is a valued participant in any meeting

>> Sets up and organizes additional meetings as needed

>> Sends out appropriate pre-meeting information

>> Keeps meetings on track and on target

» Effectively handles interpersonal issues that may arise during meetings

» Ends meetings with specific follow-up actions to be taken by attendees

Fully competent: Meets expectations

» Conducts meetings that start and end on time

» Generates participation from all attendees

» Listens carefully throughout meetings

» Builds communication, collaboration, and cooperation in meetings, whether virtual or onsite

Marginal: Occasionally fails to meet expectations

» Usually arrives late

» Does not take appropriate preparatory steps before meetings

» Constantly asks questions, but ignores the answers

» Holds far too many meetings

» Lets meetings run themselves

» Does not effectively use available technologies to enhance virtual meetings

Unsatisfactory: Consistently fails to meet expectations

» Brings up irrelevant topics

» Attends meetings, but remains uninvolved and unengaged

» Conducts meetings that rarely start or end on time

» Sends off-topic text messages during meetings

» Sleeps during meetings

» Misses many meetings for no reason and without any notice

Negotiating

Exceptional: Consistently exceeds expectations

>> Plans thoroughly before entering negotiations

>> Demonstrates excellent trust-building skills

>> Sets positive expectations

>> Carefully observes and pays attention to whoever may be participating in negotiation sessions

>> Finds creative solutions

>> Actively listens throughout the process

>> Has excellent ability to reconcile differences

>> Focuses on areas of shared interest

>> Has materials ready to make agreement easier for all parties

>> Trades concessions instead of giving anything away

>> Generates win-win outcomes

Excellent: Frequently exceeds expectations

>> Understands the sources of power in negotiations

>> Avoids trickery and deceit

>> Is flexible without being flimsy

>> Takes a collaborative approach

>> Focuses on objective factors, not personal factors

>> Keeps relationships intact, regardless of outcomes

>> Is highly aware of the subtleties of the negotiation process, including speech patterns and body language

>> Tries to create a bigger pie, rather than going for a larger slice of the established pie

Fully competent: Meets expectations

>> Does more listening than talking
>> Carefully considers all alternatives and perspectives
>> Recognizes that there can be more than one acceptable solution
>> Generates a wide range of options and possible solutions
>> Avoids a win-lose mentality and strategy
>> Keeps emotions out of the process
>> Uses constructive and confident language
>> Demonstrates empathy and understanding
>> Has a give-and-take attitude
>> Keeps an open mind

Marginal: Occasionally fails to meet expectations

>> Demands rather than negotiates
>> Doesn't understand the needs of others
>> Focuses too heavily on positions rather than people
>> Approaches every session as win-lose rather than win-win
>> Loses sight of the objectives of the negotiation process
>> Is more combative than collaborative

Unsatisfactory: Consistently fails to meet expectations

>> Views negotiation sessions as "take" rather than "give and take"
>> Uses unethical negotiation tactics
>> Relies more on bluffing than facts
>> Is a pushover during negotiations and gives up far more than necessary
>> Wins negotiations and loses relationships

- » Takes an adversarial position
- » Ignores the suggestions and input from others
- » Displays poor listening skills from start to finish
- » Uses wishy-washy language
- » Displays a lack of planning and organization
- » Is overly emotional
- » Locks into a position and causes others to do likewise
- » Generates more stalemates than settlements
- » Enflames situations instead of defusing them

Persuasiveness

Exceptional: Consistently exceeds expectations

- » Is a master of language and persuasion
- » Always knows the right way to say something
- » Persuades others when no one else comes close
- » Is highly effective in informing and influencing others
- » Increases persuasive impact by adjusting the style of communication
- » Has an excellent ability to build trust
- » Maintains a level of expertise that clearly helps influence and persuade others
- » Uses logic and facts throughout the process
- » Utilizes language and phrasing that make others feel comfortable and receptive to new ideas
- » Uses listening as a powerful persuasive tool
- » Makes others feel that they have truly been heard
- » Uses persuasion but not manipulation
- » Shows others how they win by agreeing
- » Has a great deal of personal charisma

Excellent: Frequently exceeds expectations

>> Is known as a credible person

>> Views others as partners rather than opponents

>> Takes the time to truly understand other people and their needs

>> Positively, ethically, and productively influences others through compelling communication and listening skills

>> Uses the input of others as part of the persuasion process

>> Relies on reason and is totally reasonable when trying to persuade others

>> Is highly skilled in handling objections or concerns

>> Has remarkable diplomatic skills

>> Is trusted, respected, and credible, all of which contribute to increased persuasiveness

Fully competent: Meets expectations

>> Has a solid ability to influence others

>> Persuades without arguing

>> Uses empathy effectively

>> Listens carefully and thinks before responding

>> Knows the facts and uses them to further emphasize and enhance key points

>> Is always well prepared

>> Persuades others effectively, but never with high-pressure or questionable tactics

>> Fully understands the participants and the dynamics of each situation

Marginal: Occasionally fails to meet expectations

>> Is more forceful than tactful

>> Is too impatient and tries to force others into agreement

- » Tries to push answers and ideas on others
- » Ignores the subtleties of persuasion
- » Demands more than persuades
- » Lets personal emotions and feelings interfere

Unsatisfactory: Consistently fails to meet expectations

- » Gets upset when others disagree
- » Gives up when unable to persuade others
- » Resorts to name-calling and bullying when all else fails
- » Is overly interested in taking advantage of others
- » Is hampered by being distrusted
- » Tries to persuade by flexing power
- » Is not regarded as honest, ethical, or credible

Sales Skills

Exceptional: Consistently exceeds expectations

- » Is regarded by all as a sales superstar
- » Prepares thoroughly before any presentation
- » Identifies possibly difficult questions and prepares the best answers
- » Is a master of sales presentations
- » Helps build the sales skills of others on the team
- » Is a true sales professional
- » Provides customers with outstanding levels of service and support
- » Uses a collaborative selling style
- » Treats customers as partners
- » Builds trust rapidly

- Is a major asset at trade shows
- Handles objections skillfully
- Knows when and how to close
- Has an excellent closing ratio
- Finds creative solutions to customers' issues, problems, and concerns
- Is regarded by customers as a great problem-solver
- Consistently surpasses sales quotas
- Is the customers' favorite
- Is a great prospector who often finds sales gold
- Demonstrates the highest levels of professionalism and ethics in all aspects of the sales process

Excellent: Frequently exceeds expectations

- Has an in-depth understanding of customers' needs
- Is regarded as highly credible and trustworthy
- Focuses on meeting customers' needs over personal needs
- Treats customers respectfully
- Is a highly effective listener
- Is honest, fair, open, and transparent
- Is always striving to build sales skills
- Works with other sales reps and has developed several best practices sales techniques
- Is unshaken by rejections
- Knows when to stop talking
- Knows the precise moment to ask for the order
- Is highly skilled in converting prospects to customers
- Asks the most effective closing questions
- Stays current with the latest customer relationship management systems

Fully competent: Meets expectations

>> Establishes and reaches challenging sales goals
>> Easily deals with difficult customers
>> Creates and keeps long-term relationships with customers
>> Generates solid results when cold calling
>> Knows how and when to sell add-ons
>> Meets sales quotas
>> Makes great use of sales questions and sales stories
>> Builds rapport easily and quickly with customers
>> Follows up regularly and professionally
>> Continuously analyzes personal sales performance and makes ongoing improvements
>> Keeps commitments and promises to customers
>> Actively and effectively seeks sales leads
>> Is persistent without being a pest

Marginal: Occasionally fails to meet expectations

>> Is more interested in meeting personal needs than the customers' needs
>> Talks more than listens
>> Arrives at sales calls without necessary materials
>> Assumes that all customers are alike
>> Has a know-it-all attitude and mindset
>> Is poorly prepared for presentations
>> Pushes products that the customer may not need or want
>> Makes promises that can't be kept
>> Voices negative comments about the competition
>> Sees selling as a confrontation, not a collaboration
>> Uses a hard sell that pushes customers away
>> Has an inflated view of personal sales abilities

» Is overwhelmed by even the most basic objections

» Doesn't pay sufficient attention to the high-priority accounts

» Ignores customers after a sale

» Generates minimal repeat business

» Rarely meets sales quotas

Unsatisfactory: Consistently fails to meet expectations

» Doesn't pay attention to customers

» Takes an adversarial position with customers

» Has lost several valuable customers

» Has an unacceptable closing ratio

» Rarely lets the customers get a word in

» Misses appointments with customers

» Shows up late for sales calls

» Misses sales quotas

» Has used the same sales presentation for years

» Isn't fully prepared for sales presentations

» Is overly aggressive with the customers

» Demonstrates low levels of persistence, flexibility, and drive

» Provides minimal follow-up to prospects as well as customers

» Overlooks opportunities to close sales

» Exercises questionable ethics and judgment

Teamwork

Exceptional: Consistently exceeds expectations

» Generates remarkable results through teamwork

» Turns a group into a team

- ▶▶ Applies in-depth knowledge of teambuilding
- ▶▶ Puts "we" before "me"
- ▶▶ Creates teams where there were none
- ▶▶ Strengthens the bonds of teamwork, camaraderie, and cooperation
- ▶▶ Treats all employees as highly valued resources
- ▶▶ Brings energy, enthusiasm, and positivity that are critical to the team's success
- ▶▶ Recognizes and builds the unique abilities of each member of the team
- ▶▶ Helps team members strengthen their competencies, skills, and effectiveness
- ▶▶ Has outstanding conflict management skills
- ▶▶ Communicates effectively with every member of the team

Excellent: Frequently exceeds expectations

- ▶▶ Strengthens teamwork within and between departments
- ▶▶ Creates excellence through teamwork
- ▶▶ Displays insight, empathy, and understanding toward others on the team
- ▶▶ Makes the whole greater than the sum of the parts
- ▶▶ Creates a climate of teamwork
- ▶▶ Makes every member of the team feel important
- ▶▶ Is an excellent team player
- ▶▶ Is an asset to any team
- ▶▶ Is a model member of any team
- ▶▶ Holds the team together through difficult and challenging projects
- ▶▶ Has an infectious positive and cooperative attitude
- ▶▶ Is a true team builder
- ▶▶ Takes any team up a notch

Fully competent: Meets expectations

>> Builds a sense of teamwork
>> Energizes the team
>> Is a key contributor to the team's success
>> Makes the most of the talents of all team members
>> Sets high expectations for everyone on the team
>> Resolves problems and conflicts within the team
>> Works well with all team members
>> Keeps team members well informed and listens to their ideas and suggestions

Marginal: Occasionally fails to meet expectations

>> Is more self-oriented than team-oriented
>> Has personal interests that conflict with team interests
>> Places personal goals above team goals
>> Cooperates only sporadically
>> Unwilling to help others unless others unless they provide something in return
>> Cooperates begrudgingly with team members
>> Agrees to cooperate, but rarely does
>> Devotes minimal time and energy to helping others
>> Takes no significant steps to build teamwork and cooperation

Unsatisfactory: Consistently fails to meet expectations

>> Is a disruptive and distracting influence on team operations
>> Undercuts the cooperative efforts of others
>> Has an uncooperative attitude
>> Constantly pushes a personal agenda

>> Is always ready to say "no"

>> Is insensitive to the needs of others

>> Puts "me" before "we"

>> Ignores requests for help from team members

>> Is more likely to clash than cooperate

>> Needs constant reminding to be more cooperative

Telephone Skills

Exceptional: Consistently exceeds expectations

>> Has remarkable patience

>> Is specifically requested by many callers

>> Is always professional

>> Is customer-centric 24-7

>> Has superb telephone etiquette

>> Makes every caller feel special

>> Follows up with callers until all matters are resolved

>> Receives numerous written and verbal compliments

>> Is frequently sought to handle problem calls

>> Is highly skilled in dealing with outbound as well as inbound calls

>> Finishes calls on a positive note

>> Enjoys taking the most difficult and problematic calls

>> Has a smile that is apparent to all callers

>> Has a file filled with compliments from callers

>> Serves as an excellent role model for best practices telephone techniques

>> Consistently receives the highest ratings in company surveys

Excellent: Frequently exceeds expectations

>> Makes all callers feel welcome
>> Uses an upbeat and engaging tone
>> Has a positive and supportive style
>> Maintains a calm demeanor on all calls
>> Has an uncanny ability to quickly and easily build trust
>> Has a warm and friendly attitude that comes through
>> Is polite throughout every call
>> Covers the most difficult calls with great skill
>> Tirelessly handles tremendous call volume

Fully competent: Meets expectations

>> Develops positive and professional relationships with callers
>> Handles complaints promptly and effectively
>> Is always attentive and courteous
>> Listens carefully to each caller
>> Goes beyond expectations to help every caller
>> Continues to upgrade personal telephone skills
>> Provides every caller with VIP service
>> Trains others in telephone skills

Marginal: Occasionally fails to meet expectations

>> Rushes through calls
>> Talks too quickly and confuses the customers
>> Strands callers on hold
>> Doesn't provide adequate follow-up to callers
>> Has insufficient product knowledge
>> Doesn't always speak clearly, carefully, or accurately
>> Takes too long to answer the phone

- Is quick to say "no," instead of doing some checking and seeking new ways to help customers
- Barely listens to what the callers are saying

Unsatisfactory: Consistently fails to meet expectations

- Is discourteous to callers
- Makes callers feel unwelcome
- Can be rude and impatient with callers
- Argues with callers frequently
- Treats callers disrespectfully
- Makes callers feel like they are an interruption
- Has been named in formal complaints from callers
- Gives any answer, even if it's incorrect
- Enflames problem situations
- Regards calls as a nuisance
- Promises a call-back to customers, but rarely keeps the promise
- Has inadequate product knowledge and has ignored opportunities to learn

Written and Verbal Communication

Exceptional: Consistently exceeds expectations

- Consistently demonstrates excellent written and verbal communication skills
- Is the go-to person when others need help with writing
- Keeps email messages on target and to the point
- Has clear, direct, and concise written communications
- Writes without grammatical errors

- » Creates reports and documentation that are consistently outstanding
- » Is a compelling speaker
- » Says more by saying less
- » Actively listens to others
- » Thinks before writing or speaking
- » Uses captivating and compelling language
- » Gives highly organized presentations
- » Is comfortable and effective in front of others and easily holds their attention
- » Is known as the company wordsmith
- » Is an excellent debater
- » Senses when others are on data overload and when they need more information

Excellent: Frequently exceeds expectations

- » Has very readable writing
- » Hits the perfect level of detail
- » Writes to the point, rather than around it
- » Has raised the writing skills of many employees in the department to a new level
- » Sets the standard for excellent business writing
- » Proofreads carefully
- » Provides written work that is always well organized
- » Selects the appropriate writing style for different readers and situations
- » Holds the interest of others when writing or speaking
- » Is a clear and articulate communicator
- » Has an outstanding vocabulary, but never overdoes it
- » Generates a great deal of interest whenever speaking
- » Communicates easily with everyone
- » Demonstrates sensitivity to subtle cues and nonverbal messages

Fully competent: Meets expectations

>> Is confident and comfortable with projects that require clear writing

>> Prepares thoroughly before making written or oral presentations

>> Communicates easily with employees at all levels

>> Is not inclined to talk for the sake of talking

>> Is an effective listener who is truly interested in what others have to say

>> Uses words effectively and economically

>> Is clear and informative when speaking or writing

>> Avoids excessive use of jargon

Marginal: Occasionally fails to meet expectations

>> Uses a writing style that can be difficult to understand

>> Written work demonstrates a lack of planning and organization

>> Hasn't shown interest in improving writing skills

>> Procrastinates on projects that involve writing

>> Sends email messages that are unclear and unfocused

>> Writes too much on every project

>> Provides written documents that lack adequate detail and specificity

>> Doesn't listen carefully to others, and communication suffers as a result

>> Speaks without first organizing thoughts and objectives

>> Provides excessive and unnecessary details

>> Uses overly general language and insufficient detail

>> Needs to listen more and talk less

Unsatisfactory: Consistently fails to meet expectations

>> Writes with numerous grammatical errors and typos
>> Places insufficient focus on organizing a message and its objectives before sending it out
>> Takes a long time to get to the point
>> Is often the loudest voice in the room
>> Writings often lack clarity and focus
>> Interrupts and cuts others off when they are communicating
>> Ignores punctuation and basic grammar
>> Tends to ramble and delay getting to the point
>> Often mumbles and expresses thoughts that are difficult for others to understand
>> Uses inappropriate terms and expressions
>> Is unaware of nonverbal messages
>> Produces work that always needs significant editing
>> Often uses incorrect or inappropriate language
>> Rushes when writing, and it shows

Chapter 7

The Best Phrases for Creative Thinking

One of the hallmarks of successful employees is their ability to think creatively and generate innovative solutions to problems they encounter on the job. Companies that support this type of thinking are not only better able to cope with today's myriad challenges, but they are also better enabled to predict and prepare for challenges going forward.

Identifying, reviewing, enhancing, and reinforcing your employees' applications of creativity to their work are precursors to improved performance and employee development. Your continuous feedback provides ongoing opportunities for you to strengthen innovative thinking among your employees, and you have additional opportunities for such support through informal feedback as well as through quarterly or biannual appraisals.

The formal appraisals you hold with your employees do more than provide them with specific and accurate feedback regarding their creativity on the job. They also provide them with guidance, suggestions, and support to help build these skills, such as generating new suggestions, being receptive to new ideas, thinking outside the box, encouraging and supporting innovation from others, and more.

The phrases in this chapter are designed to provide feedback and feedforward to help employees gain insight into the level of creativity that they display on the job, the kinds of behaviors that foster creativity, and the areas in which steps can be taken to enhance their creative input and output.

Applying Innovative Thinking to Company Policies and Procedures

Exceptional: Consistently exceeds expectations

>> Has created several new policies that have had a measurably positive impact on employee performance

>> Is always looking for ways to improve departmental operations

>> Has taken several highly productive steps to streamline numerous procedures

>> Stays aware of best-practices approaches for a wide range of policies and procedures, and consistently makes productive suggestions for improvement

>> Has implemented new cost-saving procedures

>> Reviewed current policies and removed language that was either out of date or out of compliance with current regulations

>> Has designed and implemented new policies in several important emerging areas

>> Generates ideas to improve policies and procedures that are consistently appropriate, well researched, and a clear improvement over current practices

Excellent: Frequently exceeds expectations

>> Listens to employees for recommendations regarding potential enhancements to existing policies and procedures

- » Has reduced the company's exposure to claims by implementing changes in policies
- » Is always looking for ways to upgrade operations that directly impact the bottom line
- » Carefully studies the flow of work before presenting ideas for improved procedures
- » Finds conflicting and overlapping policies and procedures and recommends specific steps to realign them
- » Includes an appropriate level of detail when presenting ideas for changes in policies and procedures
- » Is systems-minded and consistently presents state-of-the-art methods to upgrade company practices, procedures, and operations
- » Has outstanding systems expertise and is frequently sought for advice regarding writing or revising policies and procedures

Fully competent: Meets expectations

- » Takes a creative look at company policies and procedures and recommends improvements where needed
- » Always provides clear and well-written documentation to support recommended changes in company policies or procedures
- » Continues to study and take classes to build operational expertise
- » Keeps an open mind when presenting ideas to upgrade policies and procedures
- » Provides a broad range of viable options when making suggestions to improve policies and procedures
- » Is directly responsible for new policies that have led to improvements in employee morale, performance, and satisfaction

Marginal: Occasionally fails to meet expectations

- » Recommends new procedures without fully understanding current procedures

- Suggests policy or procedural changes without adequate analysis or understanding of their potential impact
- Formulates changes in policies and procedures that tend to be too general
- Makes recommendations for new policies and procedures prior to adequate analysis and documentation
- Gives presentations on new policies and procedures that are filled with too much extraneous detail
- Disregards concerns about potential shortcomings or problems associated with suggested changes in policy
- Ignores questions that are asked regarding suggested improvements to policies and procedures
- Rarely considers costs when recommending changes in policies or procedures
- Suggests changes in policies and procedures that tend to focus only on the short term
- Refuses to consider input from others regarding proposed changes to policies and procedures
- Tends to complain about policies and procedures rather than recommend specific improvements
- Believes that policies and procedures being used in other companies will automatically work here

Unsatisfactory: Consistently fails to meet expectations

- Maintains a narrow and self-serving approach to policy change
- Recommends changes in policies or procedures that are far too costly to implement
- Becomes defensive when asked to provide more detail on the rationale behind recommended changes in procedures
- Insists on having recommendations implemented, regardless of their value
- Discourages employees from offering their ideas regarding changes in policies and procedures

>> Continues to recommend implementation of policies that are out of date or have failed in the past

>> Takes it personally when suggested changes in policies and procedures are not implemented

>> Hasn't offered one usable suggestion to improve policies and procedures

>> Encourages others to ignore newly implemented policies and procedures

>> Shows no interest in improving company policies and procedures

Brainstorming

Exceptional: Consistently exceeds expectations

>> Uses brainstorming sessions to generate a large number of creative ideas, many of which have been implemented

>> Encourages employees to present as many ideas as possible

>> Actively encourages and supports outside-the-box thinking

>> Takes appropriate follow-up action on all ideas generated in brainstorming sessions

Excellent: Frequently exceeds expectations

>> Lets employees know that no idea is a bad idea in brainstorming sessions

>> Conducts brainstorming sessions that are both playful and productive

>> Sets positive expectations ahead of brainstorming sessions, which help lead to consistently positive outcomes

Fully competent: Meets expectations

>> Picks interdepartmental topics and includes employees from other departments

>> Leads discussions that are free of criticism and reprisals

>> Has motivated other managers to implement brainstorming sessions

Marginal: Occasionally fails to meet expectations

>> Provides no follow-up after brainstorming sessions

>> Does most of the talking during brainstorming

>> Cuts discussions short during brainstorming sessions

Unsatisfactory: Consistently fails to meet expectations

>> Refuses to hold brainstorming sessions

>> Criticizes employees for their suggestions

>> Takes reprisals against employees if their ideas don't conform with current practices

Embracing Change

Exceptional: Consistently exceeds expectations

>> Creates a dynamic environment in which productive change is sought, implemented, and embraced

>> Acts as a change agent and regards this role as a key component of personal effectiveness

>> Utilizes a high degree of two-way communication when implementing change

>> Includes employees in the change process

- » Keeps employees involved at every step of the change process
- » Solicits and incorporates employee input when changes are being considered
- » Identifies areas in which changes are needed, and then generates employee suggestions and support
- » Uses excellent business insight and judgment in suggesting changes
- » Plays a central role in introducing changes to keep the company at the forefront of new strategies, technologies, and programs

Excellent: Frequently exceeds expectations

- » Builds employees' receptiveness to change as well as their abilities to adjust and adapt
- » Avoids change for the sake of change
- » Excels at analyzing proposed changes and implementing those that are most likely to be effective
- » Regards change as a key force behind learning, growth, and development
- » Helps employees see how they'll benefit from changes that are being implemented
- » Maintains employee participation throughout the change process and treats employees with trust and respect at every step
- » Introduces changes that contribute to measurable improvements in employee performance
- » Has created an atmosphere that is highly supportive of change

Fully competent: Meets expectations

- » Adjusts to most changes quickly and easily
- » Works directly with employees to help them adjust to change
- » Is a highly effective change agent

- » Maintains a positive and receptive attitude toward proposed changes

- » Reacts to change initially by learning more about it

- » Approaches change with a positive, upbeat, and supportive mindset

- » Maintains positive expectations toward changes that are being implemented

- » Uses ongoing formal and informal two-way communication with employees to reduce resistance to change

- » Enjoys playing an active role in the change process

- » Carefully considers the potential impact when proposing changes

- » Focuses on the gains associated with changes that are being implemented

Marginal: Occasionally fails to meet expectations

- » Becomes nervous and anxious at the first sign of change

- » Accepts change in a half-hearted manner that is then emulated by other employees

- » Avoids discussions to determine changes, but then complains about the changes that are made

- » Pushes for changes that are likely to create confusion and dissention

- » Only embraces self-serving changes

- » Doesn't provide adequate analysis, reasoning, or documentation when suggesting changes

- » Pushes for changes without adequately considering their potential outcomes

- » Frequently introduces changes that are neither necessary nor productive

- » Has caused widespread productivity problems among the employees by introducing one change after another, many of which are questionable at best

- » Places more attention on making changes than making progress

Unsatisfactory: Consistently fails to meet expectations

» Campaigns against proposed changes without fully understanding them

» Regards most changes as personal threats

» Introduces major changes without prior discussion or approval

» Voices support for new changes, but then ignores them

» Offers ideas for changes outside the department, but never within the department

» Is unwilling to listen to the employees' suggestions for changes

» Excludes employees from discussions regarding departmental change

» Makes decisions about proposed changes without hearing facts or input from others

» Generates a climate of resistance to change

» Initially reacts to change by rejecting it or fighting it

» Becomes upset with employees who support proposed changes

» Continuously brings up changes that have failed in the past

» Approaches proposed changes with negative expectations

» Takes actions to undermine newly introduced changes

Encouraging and Supporting Innovation from Others

Exceptional: Consistently exceeds expectations

» Consistently encourages and supports innovative thinking

» Provides significant tangible and intangible rewards to employees who try to create new ideas, solutions, or suggestions

- Helps encourage innovative thinking by practicing it
- Holds frequent discussions on innovative problem-solving techniques to enhance employee awareness and effectiveness in this area
- Works directly with employees to help build their skills in generating new ideas
- Shares creative thinking expertise with others
- Provides employees with coaching and guidance when their efforts at innovative thinking fall short

Excellent: Frequently exceeds expectations

- Provides employees with significant recognition for their efforts and successes at innovation
- Works with employees to analyze and improve their innovative ideas
- Maintains an open mind regarding employee attempts at innovation
- Initially reacts to employees' innovative ideas by listening rather than judging
- Provides employees with constructive and supportive feedback and follow-up on the innovative ideas that they present

Fully competent: Meets expectations

- Creates a climate that is open and supportive of new ideas and suggestions
- Provides employees with ongoing encouragement to continue to generate and develop innovative ideas
- Supports educational programs to build employee skills in this area
- Holds frequent brainstorming sessions with employees
- Regularly meets with employees to discuss their new ideas

Marginal: Occasionally fails to meet expectations

>> Lets employees present new ideas, but only on relatively unimportant matters

>> Rarely has time to discuss new ideas

>> Expects minimal innovation from employees, which is exactly what they deliver

>> Expresses interest in meeting with employees to brainstorm, but never does so

>> Asks for innovative ideas from employees, but rarely considers any of them

Unsatisfactory: Consistently fails to meet expectations

>> Convinces employees that they aren't creative

>> Ignores employees' innovative comments, ideas, or suggestions

>> Provides strictly negative feedback on the employees' innovative ideas

>> Is quick to criticize employees if their efforts at innovative problem-solving strategies fall short

>> Regards innovative thinking and problem solving as detracting from the work that needs to be done

>> Frequently advises employees that they aren't paid to be creative

>> Ridicules employees' attempts at innovation

>> Doesn't fully understand employees' new ideas, but reacts negatively nonetheless

Generating New Ideas

Exceptional: Consistently exceeds expectations

>> Is a constant source of outstanding new ideas

>> Takes good ideas and turns them into outstanding ideas

>> Finds new and better ways to get things done within the department and interdepartmentally as well

>> Continuously generates ideas that improve performance and productivity

>> Applies numerous creative approaches to problems that appear to be unsolvable

>> Looks at old problems in new ways and solves many of them

>> Is highly regarded as a major source of new ideas and creative thinking

>> Demonstrates remarkable creativity on any assignment

Excellent: Frequently exceeds expectations

>> Generates ideas that are innovative and practical

>> Comes up with ideas that consistently show insight and foresight

>> Keeps chipping away at problems until discovering new pathways to solve them

>> Is a source of creative ideas for employees in many different areas

>> Consistently finds ways to work smarter

>> Doesn't merely generate new ideas, but generates new ideas that are practical, functional, and productive

>> Revisits old ideas in new ways and gets excellent results

Fully competent: Meets expectations

>> Is consistently on the lookout for new and better ways to handle job responsibilities

>> Enjoys working on projects that call for new ideas

>> Has used innovative thinking to solve several complicated problems

>> Always striving to come up with new ideas

>> Regards creative thinking as an important part of the job

>> Seeks challenging problems that call for innovative solutions

>> Strives to apply innovative thinking to every project

Marginal: Occasionally fails to meet expectations

>> Comes up with new ideas that have little applicability to work

>> Is more interested in the quantity than the quality of new ideas

>> Generates new ideas but does nothing with them

>> Focuses on generating new ideas to solve insignificant problems

>> Takes old ideas, slightly rewraps them, and then insists that they're entirely new

>> Becomes overly upset when questioned about new ideas

Unsatisfactory: Consistently fails to meet expectations

>> Hasn't taken any steps to generate new ideas

>> Is uninterested in seeking new ways to handle responsibilities or solve problems

>> Isn't inclined to devote extra effort to come up with new ideas

>> Insists on implementing new ideas without adequate analysis or planning

>> Has implemented new ideas that led to serious performance and productivity problems

>> Doesn't regard innovative thinking as part of the job

- » Insists on pushing old ideas
- » Takes credit for new ideas that come from others

Problem Solving

Exceptional: Consistently exceeds expectations

- » Uses an arsenal of creative strategies to productively solve a wide range of problems
- » Consistently generates outstanding solutions to the most demanding problems
- » Focuses on solving problems, not symptoms
- » Applies highly effective analytical skills to every stage of the problem-solving process
- » Establishes workable, prioritized, and highly effective problem-solving plans for each problem, rather than jumping in and trying to generate instant solutions
- » Uses a varied problem-solving style to meet the nature and demands of a given problem
- » Approaches every problem with confidence and the expectation that an innovative and productive solution will be generated
- » Actively seeks out problems that require the most creative thinking

Excellent: Frequently exceeds expectations

- » Is a highly effective problem solver from start to finish
- » Comes up with creative strategies when other employees are stuck
- » Is frequently sought for a second look at problems that have stumped other employees
- » Takes a fresh look at problems and identifies new inroads to solve them

>> Effectively uses state-of-the-art technology to help in the problem-solving process

>> Finds solutions that have eluded many others

Fully competent: Meets expectations

>> Defines and understands problems before attempting to solve them

>> Is a tenacious problem solver

>> Has a broad range of problem-solving skills that are applied effectively to all problems and problem situations

>> Demonstrates confidence in personal creative skills and seeks to develop the same in others

>> Creatively works around, over, under, or through obstacles in the problem-solving process

>> Solves problems before they become crises

Marginal: Occasionally fails to meet expectations

>> Gets stumped on the more challenging problems and quickly moves to others that are easier to solve

>> Generates average solutions to problems that could yield far more positive results if approached more creatively

>> Is uninterested in new problem-solving strategies

>> Focuses excessively on superficial issues, while often overlooking the deeper cause of a given problem

>> Identifies problems, but takes inadequate steps to resolve them

>> Rushes through problems that require more thorough analysis

Unsatisfactory: Consistently fails to meet expectations

>> Uses a problem-solving strategy that often creates more problems than solutions

>> Overlooks or underestimates problems until they've become major issues

- » Analyzes minor issues and lets larger problems fester and grow
- » Decides on the solution to a problem before doing any work on it
- » Comes up with solutions that are incorrect, insufficient, and invalid

Receptiveness to New Ideas

Exceptional: Consistently exceeds expectations

- » Consistently demonstrates a high degree of interest in ideas and suggestions from others
- » Has a totally open mind when it comes to hearing new ideas
- » Encourages innovative thinking from others
- » Regards new ideas as an essential component of personal growth
- » Is not only receptive to new ideas, but also works with employees to further shape and refine them
- » Emphasizes that individual and company success emanates from new ideas
- » Truly believes that excellent ideas can come from anyone at any level of the organization

Excellent: Frequently exceeds expectations

- » Always makes time to listen to the employees' new ideas
- » Is seen by employees as being genuinely interested in their innovative thinking
- » Follows up with employees after discussing their creative ideas with them
- » Takes appropriate action on employees' ideas
- » Actively solicits new ideas from employees

>> Always provides thanks, credit, and recognition for new ideas, regardless of whether the ideas can be used

Fully competent: Meets expectations

>> Is open to ideas and suggestions that differ from the established ways of doing things

>> Rewards employees for suggestions that are implemented

>> Implements employee ideas and suggestions whenever possible

>> Displays encouragement, positivity, and high expectations regarding innovative thinking from others

>> Never misses an opportunity to ask for new ideas and suggestions from others

>> Has created an atmosphere in which all employees are totally comfortable presenting their new ideas

Marginal: Occasionally fails to meet expectations

>> Shows minimal interest when employees want to discuss their ideas

>> Goes through the motions of listening to employees' new ideas, but doesn't really pay attention

>> Rarely takes steps to do anything with the employees' new ideas

>> Believes that employees lack the expertise and insight to come up with useful suggestions on significant matters

>> Is satisfied with current operations and doesn't see the need for new approaches

Unsatisfactory: Consistently fails to meet expectations

>> Is uninterested in hearing ideas from employees

>> Advises employees to do their work and stop trying to come up with new ideas

- » Tells employees that all their ideas have been tried, and they don't work
- » Regards employees' ideas as interruptions
- » Is aloof and abrupt when employees try to present their ideas
- » Doesn't listen when employees present new ideas
- » Repeatedly cancels meetings with employees to discuss their ideas
- » Criticizes employees whose ideas differ from current practices
- » Lives by the philosophy that employees should "stop thinking and start doing"

Seeking Improvements

Exceptional: Consistently exceeds expectations

- » Maintains a continuous improvement mindset in all aspects of work
- » Consistently seeks ways to generate measurable improvements not only in terms of performance, growth, development, and goal attainment, but also in terms of communications, planning, organization, systems, and technologies
- » Has presented several new ideas to measurably reduce costs
- » Comes up with excellent strategies to build revenues
- » Is responsible for operational improvements that are having a positive impact on the bottom line
- » Regularly scans the marketplace, new technologies, social media, and professional networks for new strategies, initiatives, programs, and business development opportunities
- » Uses knowledge of business processes to help streamline operations

Excellent: Frequently exceeds expectations

>> Regularly applies proven steps, strategies, and programs that make the department and company more effective

>> Is highly knowledgeable in terms of company operations and works with key employees to discuss and implement improvements

>> Meets formally and informally with employees to openly discuss ways to design and implement improvements at the company

>> Is able to find creative applications for ideas that others may have overlooked

>> Reads and attends courses, webinars, and podcasts that focus on successful business operations, followed by sharing the information and working with others to implement new strategies

Fully competent: Meets expectations

>> Interprets job functions broadly and looks beyond assigned responsibilities for ways to generate improvements in the department and company at large

>> Is always on the lookout for ways to build the company's brand and success

>> Provides employees with support and recognition for their efforts to make improvements to the company

>> Is never satisfied with the status quo

Marginal: Occasionally fails to meet expectations

>> Occasionally comes up with new ideas for improvement, but does nothing with them

>> Rarely devotes serious attention to seeking and creating improvements

>> Shows minimal interest in hearing about planned improvements for the company

- Continuously focuses on the need for improvements in areas that are of minimal importance to the success of the company
- Attends strategy sessions, but doesn't participate in the discussions
- Encourages employees to make suggestions for improvements, and then ignores them
- Doesn't focus on improvements beyond the department

Unsatisfactory: Consistently fails to meet expectations

- Has an "it's not my job" attitude when it comes to generating improvements for the company
- Hardly focuses assigned responsibilities, let alone looking for improvements
- Suggests strategies that contradict the company's values and ethics
- Gathers improvement ideas from employees and then takes credit for them
- Discourages employees from seeking ways to improve the department or company
- Changes the subject when employees start talking about improvement strategies
- Shows complete disinterest in making any significant improvements to the department or company

Thinking Outside the Box

Exceptional: Consistently exceeds expectations

- Approaches problems with an open mind and without preconceived notions
- Questions assumptions regarding the significance of each piece of data and reassesses the value of each

- >> Looks at issues, questions, and dilemmas from several angles and generates entirely new ways to resolve them
- >> Is unrestrained by traditional problem-solving approaches, strategies, or expectations
- >> Generates productive outcomes by including unlikely people or resources in the problem-solving process
- >> Clearly communicates the rationale behind new approaches and strategies, easily bringing others onboard
- >> Keeps an ongoing log of creative ideas in order to continuously enhance them
- >> Thinks outside the box by changing venues, remote or onsite, in order to literally look at a problem in a different light

Excellent: Frequently exceeds expectations

- >> Productively integrates people, processes, and systems that seemingly don't go together
- >> Takes concepts that are cast in stone and then shatters, reshapes, or redefines them to generate more productive ideas and solutions
- >> Excludes seemingly essential components to open the door to a wider range of creative solutions
- >> Is open to totally different ideas, assumptions, and strategies
- >> Isn't afraid to make mistakes
- >> Doesn't give up in the face of doubtful comments by others who challenge an unorthodox approach

Fully competent: Meets expectations

- >> Avoids dated or antiquated problem-solving strategies
- >> Enjoys working on projects that require creative thinking and solutions
- >> Has attended training sessions that focus on creative thinking and problem solving
- >> Uses excellent observational skills to find overlooked pieces of data that can open up new ways to solve problems

>> Has an unconventional problem-solving style that yields better-than-conventional results

>> Is always looking for new and productive ways to use everyday items

Marginal: Occasionally fails to meet expectations

>> Overly satisfied with the status quo

>> Is afraid of making a wrong decision

>> Regards unconventional thinking as too risky

>> Has negative feelings and expectations when engaged in thinking that is slightly different from a traditional approach

>> At the first sign of a problem, immediately reverts from creative thinking to overly structured thinking

>> Talks about thinking outside the box, but actions indicate otherwise

Unsatisfactory: Consistently fails to meet expectations

>> Is far more comfortable thinking inside the box

>> Rarely challenges assumptions

>> Is unwilling to change thinking style, regardless of recent questionable decisions

>> Refuses to attend programs that focus on creative thinking

>> Only takes on projects that can be handled with very conventional thinking

>> Avoids projects that call for creative thinking

>> Regards the concept of thinking outside the box as a fad

Chapter **8**

The Best Phrases for Ethics

E thics in the workplace have a major impact on employee satisfaction, performance, and commitment, all of which directly impact individual and organizational productivity and success. As a result, as you engage in continuous feedback and appraisal sessions with your employees, the topic of ethics plays an important role.

When unethical behaviors arise in organizations, they should obviously be addressed as soon as they occur. Through your continuous feedback, you're in an excellent position to identify ethical issues and take real-time action to deal with them. As part of the process, addressing these types of issues during the quarterly or biannual appraisal sessions that you conduct with your employees is also important. By doing so, you not only demonstrate the company's ongoing commitment to ethical behavior and actions, but you're also able to further positively reinforce ethical behaviors by your employees as well as identify and redirect behaviors that are ethically questionable.

As part of the process, using wording that is clear and direct is important. Such wording should be designed to reinforce ethical behaviors while further alerting employees to behaviors that are not in sync with the company's ethical standards and code of conduct. This feedback helps generate an opportunity for employees to receive coaching and guidance to realign their behaviors in accordance with the company's established ethical standards.

Within this context of feedback and feedforward, the phrases that are provided in this chapter look at the key components of ethical behaviors on the job such as diversity, inclusion, sustainability, honesty, and integrity.

Diversity and Inclusion

Exceptional: Consistently exceeds expectations

>> Truly committed to diversity and inclusion

>> Demonstrates strong advocacy for the equitable treatment of all employees

>> Has reinforced a culture that enhances the employees' feelings of belonging and safety

>> Highly focused on maintaining an equitable and inclusive culture

>> Makes all employees feel safe and welcome

>> Shows great respect for individual differences

>> Approaches programs, policies, and decisions with an inclusive mindset

>> Very effective in working with diverse teams to generate creative ideas, suggestions, and results

>> Introduced and implemented successful initiatives and programs to enhance diversity

>> Solicits and incorporates employee suggestions to build diversity

>> Creates and implements programs that support diversity and inclusivity

>> Conducts diversity training programs and workshops

>> Recognizes, develops, and supports the unique talents of each employee

Excellent: Frequently exceeds expectations

» Highly effective in leading, developing, and supporting diverse teams

» Builds on the diversity of fellow employees to generate creative problem-solving strategies and results

» Actively supports company initiatives, policies, and programs on diversity and inclusivity

» Seeks and utilizes ideas, thoughts, and contributions from others regardless of background

» Identifies and breaks down barriers that separate employees

» Genuinely interested in the diverse backgrounds of fellow employees

» Demonstrates high levels of sensitivity to employees of all backgrounds

» Continuously monitors and actively strives to build the levels of diversity and inclusiveness

» Played a key role in widening the company's recruitment reach and generated increased levels of diversity across the applicant pool

Fully competent: Meets expectations

» A strong supporter of diversity and inclusiveness in the workplace

» Regards diversity and inclusivity as competitive advantages

» Treats all employees with respect and trust

» Continues to attend training sessions on diversity and equity

» Understands how to prevent and deal with discrimination

» Supports company actions and practices to increase diversity and inclusion

» Has a great deal of interest in the ideas, input, and suggestions from all employees

» Demonstrates strong advocacy of equity and diversity training programs

Marginal: Occasionally fails to meet expectations

>> Tends to exclude rather than include

>> Allows stereotypes and bias to influence dealings with others

>> Has a diverse team, but plays favorites

>> Takes minimal steps to draw upon the individual talents of employees

>> Demonstrates decreasing levels of willingness to abide by the company's diversity policies

>> Is slow to adjust to employees with diverse backgrounds

>> Is increasingly resistant to the company's efforts and programs that focus on diversity and inclusiveness

>> Shows passive resistance to all efforts to increase diversity

Unsatisfactory: Consistently fails to meet expectations

>> Is unsupportive of programs to increase diversity and inclusion

>> Has sidestepped every opportunity for diversity training

>> Takes actions that undermine the company's diversity and inclusivity efforts and practices

>> Avoids taking any steps that support diversity and inclusion

>> Makes derogatory and divisive comments that directly contradict company policies and practices regarding diversity and inclusion

>> Has consistently rejected opportunities to participate in diverse teams and task forces

>> Is uncommunicative and uninterested when working with a diverse group of employees

Fairness

Exceptional: Consistently exceeds expectations

>> Places major emphasis on fair treatment of all employees
>> Has a solid reputation as a fair and unbiased team player
>> Has helped others truly understand fairness and how to implement it
>> Has made significant changes in policies and programs to eliminate unfair elements
>> Has a strong sense of fairness that is apparent in all decisions
>> Keeps fairness at the core of the decision-making process
>> Takes immediate action to remedy inequitable situations

Excellent: Frequently exceeds expectations

>> Treats all employees in a fair and just manner
>> Regards fairness as one of the most important criteria in decision making
>> Leads a department that is widely regarded as a bastion of fairness
>> Listens carefully to employees' concerns about fairness and takes appropriate corrective actions
>> Clearly communicates standards and expectations regarding equitable treatment of all employees
>> Has a great deal of expertise on established guidelines regarding equitable practices in the workplace

Fully competent: Meets expectations

>> Ascertains that all employees are treated fairly
>> Takes prompt action to counsel employees who engage in unfair behaviors

- » Has obtained training that specifically focused on fairness in the workplace
- » Provides employees with ongoing coaching to increase their understanding of the role and importance of fairness at work
- » Keeps employees fully aware of company standards, expectations, and values regarding fair treatment of fellow employees
- » Has widened the reach and effectiveness of many programs that support fairness in the workplace

Marginal: Occasionally fails to meet expectations

- » Has been advised about engaging in unfair behaviors, but continues to repeat and condone them
- » Implements activities and programs without adequate consideration of their fairness
- » Provides inadequate attention to inequities in the workplace
- » Treats workplace inequities as minor matters that do not require prompt or major attention
- » Focuses more on the symptoms of unfair treatment rather than the causes
- » Makes pronouncements about fairness on the job, but does not take action when issues arise

Unsatisfactory: Consistently fails to meet expectations

- » Plays favorites in spite of the problems that are caused by doing so
- » Rationalizes that unfair treatment makes employees stronger
- » Treats employees unfairly, and this has led to formal complaints
- » Is unresponsive to employees' concerns regarding unfair treatment

>> Reprimands employees who voice concern about inequities at work

>> Makes decisions without considering how fair or unfair they may be

>> Is unconcerned about the impact that unfair actions have on others

Giving Back to the Community

Exceptional: Consistently exceeds expectations

>> Truly values the opportunity to help those in need

>> Is actively involved in volunteer programs supported by the company

>> Plays a leadership role in various community organizations

>> Helps raise substantial contributions for nonprofit organizations aligned with the company

>> Has taken actions that increased voluntarism among many other employees

>> Serves as a model of the company's values, focusing on helping and serving the community

>> Has been singled out for awards for voluntarism from community organizations

>> Has led various drives to help disaster victims

Excellent: Frequently exceeds expectations

>> Always makes time to help community organizations in conjunction with company initiatives

>> Consistently supports causes, events, and organizations that help those in need

>> Is truly committed to helping those who are less fortunate

- >> Has generated increased company-wide support for important causes and charitable organizations
- >> Has a genuine sense of compassion toward the less fortunate
- >> Has built goodwill for the company through civic-minded actions

Fully competent: Meets expectations

- >> Has strong personal values focused on voluntarism
- >> Takes actions to increase employee awareness of the value of community service
- >> Encourages employee involvement in community activities, but never pressures anyone
- >> Is able to effectively balance community service with the demands of the job
- >> Is highly regarded for work that supports the neighboring community
- >> Serves as an excellent role model for other employees when it comes to voluntarism
- >> Actively supports company policies regarding community service

Marginal: Occasionally fails to meet expectations

- >> Is slow to support company-wide efforts to help those in need
- >> Makes comments that discourage employees from participating in volunteer activities in the community
- >> Ignores company policy regarding community service
- >> Keeps pushing the company to do more for a personally favored charity and less for other charities
- >> Uses many company resources and materials for charity work, and does so without permission

>> Solicits contributions on behalf of a personally favored charity or organization during work hours rather than during breaks

Unsatisfactory: Consistently fails to meet expectations

>> Is quick to disparage the volunteer activities of others

>> Provides no scheduling flexibility for employees who engage in community service

>> Resists company policies regarding community service

>> Is overly involved in community activities and lets job responsibilities falter

>> Provides favorable treatment for employees who participate in personally favored volunteer activities

>> Misses too much work as a result of volunteer activities

>> Pressures employees to give time or money for personally favored charities

Health and Wellness

Exceptional: Consistently exceeds expectations

>> Takes an ongoing and genuine interest in helping employees attain and maintain good health

>> Fully understands the benefits of wellness and has introduced programs and initiatives to help employees improve their wellbeing

>> Provides employees with opportunities and support to maintain a healthy work-life balance

>> Has developed and implemented policies and programs that directly contribute to employee health and wellness

>> Leads by example in encouraging and enhancing employee wellness

- » Has taken effective measures to remove potential health hazards from the workplace
- » Actively supports educational and physical fitness programs that are designed to enhance employee health
- » Consistently and actively supports company wellness programs

Fully competent: Meets expectations

- » Demonstrates sensitivity to the health and wellness of other employees and supports programs and initiatives that help them boost their wellbeing
- » Understands the damaging impact of high levels of job stress and considers it carefully in assigning or delegating work to others
- » Provides excellent support, understanding, guidance, and accommodation for employees who are dealing with personal health issues
- » Encourages employees to use company sick time or PTO to deal with personal or family health issues
- » Clearly understands and lets other know about the ways in which employee health and wellness directly help the employees as well as the company at large
- » Has helped create an open and transparent culture in which employees feel comfortable in expressing their ideas, concerns, and suggestions regarding ways to improve safety, health, and welfare on the job

Marginal: Occasionally fails to meet expectations

- » Can show impatience and a lack of understanding when employees are sick and unable to work
- » Rushes sick employees to return to work
- » Shows little concern for the levels of stress that employees may be experiencing

- » Reports to work when ill, often spreading the illness to other employees
- » Displays annoyance when employees need time off for themselves or members of their family

Unsatisfactory: Consistently fails to meet expectations

- » Makes insensitive and inappropriate comments about personal and private medical conditions of other employees
- » Places overly demanding and stress-inducing expectations on employees, followed by publicly voicing critical comments about their performance
- » Falsely accuses sick employees of malingering and taking time off when they are healthy
- » Totally ignores employee comments and suggestions regarding health hazards and dangers in the workplace

Honesty

Exceptional: Consistently exceeds expectations

- » Is 100 percent trustworthy
- » Is widely respected for honesty
- » Is regarded as totally credible by all
- » Completes projects that are based on honest data gathering and analysis
- » Is above-board, straightforward, and candid
- » Displays intellectual honesty in all aspects of work
- » Is the go-to person for honest answers and opinions
- » Signs off on projects only when the work is totally accurate and reliable

Excellent: Frequently exceeds expectations

>> Digs in and finds the right answers to difficult questions, instead of trying to bluff

>> Has established a high degree of personal trust

>> Can always be counted on to keep promises and commitments

>> Is fully trusted, believed, and respected

>> Regards honesty as a top priority in dealings with others

>> Has fostered a climate of honesty within the department

Fully competent: Meets expectations

>> Doesn't stray from the truth

>> Has clearly contributed to a culture of honesty, openness, and transparency in the department

>> Gives credit where credit is due

>> Is willing to make personal sacrifices in order to keep commitments

>> Successfully establishes and maintains honest and open two-way communication with others

>> Provides honest feedback in order to help others learn, grow, and develop

>> Uses honest facts, figures, and data to support decisions, actions, and conclusions

Marginal: Occasionally fails to meet expectations

>> Believes that having a "fudge factor" in every project is not a problem

>> Tends holds back highly pertinent data

>> Rarely gives the full story

>> Is inclined to bend the truth

- » Occasionally provides misleading updates on projects
- » Demonstrates a tendency to embellish accomplishments
- » Can make promises while knowing that they cannot be kept
- » Says anything to get an advantage

Unsatisfactory: Consistently fails to meet expectations

- » Makes comments that always must be taken with a grain of salt
- » Gives different people different stories regarding the same situation
- » Caused the XYZ project to fail because of a lack of forthright behavior
- » Shows a basic lack of honesty that has led to numerous complaints
- » Produces projects and reports that always need extra scrutiny and fact-checking because of questionable analyses and misleading conclusions
- » Takes credit for work done by others
- » Generates questionable results by manipulating the data
- » Is held in questionable regard by others because of issues regarding honesty, credibility, and trust
- » Ignores facts and makes untrue statements, assertions, and pronouncements
- » Makes up facts to support dubious positions

Integrity

Exceptional: Consistently exceeds expectations

- » Maintains the highest standards of personal integrity
- » Displays exemplary behavior in every aspect of work

>> Is highly regarded for integrity both within and outside the company

>> Is a true embodiment of the company's values regarding integrity

>> Sets the high-water mark for integrity

>> Identifies the most worthy and ethical steps and then takes them

>> When given a choice, always opts for the fair, honest, and trustworthy route

>> Finds and implements the best way to handle any ethically challenging situation

Excellent: Frequently exceeds expectations

>> Sets high personal standards of integrity which are then emulated by others

>> Will not consider less-than-honorable plans, strategies, or behaviors

>> Consistently engages in meritorious behavior

>> Can be counted upon to act honorably in all situations

>> Builds a climate of integrity in the department

>> Demonstrates the highest levels of integrity in all dealings with employees, customers, and vendors

Fully competent: Meets expectations

>> Adheres to principles of integrity in all workplace behaviors

>> Consistently acts with integrity and is not tempted or interested in actions that deviate from this approach

>> Appropriately counsels employees who engage in disingenuous behaviors

>> Has a strong sense of right and wrong and applies it in all aspects of the job

>> Maintains high standards of integrity across the department

- » Makes decisions that consistently reflect a strong commitment to acting with integrity
- » Quickly dismisses less-than-exemplary options to solve problems

Marginal: Occasionally fails to meet expectations

- » Places expedience over integrity
- » Sets integrity aside when pursuing goals
- » Rationalizes less-than-meritorious behaviors
- » Does not regard integrity as a high priority
- » Fails to consistently act with integrity, but always expects it from others
- » Rarely demonstrates acceptable levels of integrity
- » Has had several recent lapses in integrity

Unsatisfactory: Consistently fails to meet expectations

- » Violates company standards and expectations regarding employee integrity
- » Has put the company at risk with disingenuous actions
- » Engages in underhanded behaviors
- » Has taken actions that have led to complaints from other employees about integrity
- » Has generated complaints from customers because of actions that demonstrated questionable integrity
- » Has been the cause of concern from vendors because of a lack of integrity
- » Has cost the company customers and money because of disingenuous behaviors
- » Has engaged in questionable behaviors that have led to corporate embarrassment

Judgment

Exceptional: Consistently exceeds expectations

» Is highly regarded for judgmental ability

» Keeps company values, standards, and ethics in mind in any situation requiring astute judgment

» Is comfortable with transparency at any stage of the judgmental process

» Applies excellent judgmental skills by carefully listening and observing, maintaining high levels of expertise, and an ability to focus on the big picture as well as the details

» Is sought in myriad situations that call for honest, insightful, and well-reasoned judgment

Excellent: Frequently exceeds expectations

» Gathers full, complete, and reliable data when making decisions

» Includes significant others in significant decisions

» Refrains from making instant judgments by using deliberation, inquiries, and patience in order to gain a full understanding of whatever the situation may entail

» Can be counted on to make judgment calls that are sound, solid, and well-reasoned

Fully competent: Meets expectations

» Has a commitment to high ethical standards that underlie judgments

» Immediately counsels employees who display questionable judgment

» Has conducted formal sessions with employees to further educate them on business ethics

>> Uses solid judgment in all business spheres to avoid unnecessary risk or danger

Marginal: Occasionally fails to meet expectations

>> Occasionally displays questionable judgment that has led to problematic behaviors and outcomes

>> Personal judgments can be hampered by a refusal to fully consider input and insight from others

>> Is overly judgmental when others are trying to express their views and opinions

>> Judgment shows a disconnect between personal ethics and the company's ethical standards

Unsatisfactory: Consistently fails to meet expectations

>> Demonstrates questionable judgment by engaging in behaviors that disregard company ethics and values

>> Displays lapses in judgment by breaching confidences, distorting facts, blaming others, and approaching new issues with a closed mind

>> Brags about personal actions on the job that clearly contradict the company's ethical standards

>> Has damaged the company's image, goodwill, and reputation through questionable judgment and subsequent behaviors

Maintaining Professionalism

Exceptional: Consistently exceeds expectations

>> Demonstrates consistently high levels of professionalism not only by virtue of personal expertise, but also by treating all employees with respect, trust, fairness, and consideration

- » Has a strong commitment to maintaining, demonstrating, and reinforcing high levels of professionalism
- » Is continuously building professional skills and a wider knowledgebase
- » Stays at the cutting edge of knowledge in the field
- » Is highly effective in applying professional skills and expertise to the job
- » Adheres to a deeply held code of ethics regarding professional behavior
- » Approaches work with a strong sense of accountability and responsibility
- » Gives professional advice, analyses, and recommendations that are well-founded, insightful, and trustworthy

Excellent: Frequently exceeds expectations

- » Places a great deal of emphasis on providing valuable professional suggestions and advice to others
- » Is known for sound decision making
- » Attends numerous programs and classes to continue to augment professional expertise
- » Gravitates into formal and informal leadership roles as a result of in-depth expertise
- » Takes time to coach, guide, and educate others in the field
- » Generates a wide range of new and creative ideas that contribute to the department and the company at large

Fully competent: Meets expectations

- » Continuously networks with professional peers and stays actively involved in professional associations
- » Demonstrates a high degree of pride in all aspects of the job
- » Actively seeks opportunities to continue to participate in company educational programs
- » Is able to effectively apply myriad professional skills to the job

>> Continues to expand professional expertise

>> Is truly passionate about maintaining and applying professional behaviors at work

Marginal: Occasionally fails to meet expectations

>> Has ignored training and educational opportunities and has let professional expertise slide

>> Makes negative comments about personally burning out

>> Has stopped reading professional journals and magazines

>> Has lost enthusiasm and passion for the field

>> Is becoming increasingly involved in peripheral interests instead of focusing on further developing and utilizing professional skills

>> Takes no time to help employees learn and grow

>> Is uninterested in discussing new trends and developments in the field

>> Has lost contact with most professional peers

Unsatisfactory: Consistently fails to meet expectations

>> Ignores the professional code of ethics and regards such guidelines as an unnecessary burden

>> Has engaged in inappropriate behaviors that have demonstrated questionable ethics and professionalism

>> Has caused serious productivity problems because of out-of-date knowledge

>> Uses outmoded problem-solving techniques and strategies

>> Demonstrates minimal professionalism in carrying out job responsibilities

>> Has let professional designations, certifications, and licensing expire

Sustainability

Exceptional: Consistently exceeds expectations

» Is truly committed to sustainability and doing what's best for the environment

» Is the prime force behind the company's award-winning sustainability program

» Has saved the company thousands of dollars by creating and implementing sustainability initiatives

» Has built companywide awareness about sustainability

» Has inspired employees to take a wide range of sustainable steps

» Has devised systems and measurements to track, monitor, and upgrade the company's sustainability programs and practices

» Maintains an expert level of knowledge of sustainable practices

Excellent: Frequently exceeds expectations

» Encourages and supports employee suggestions regarding sustainability

» Has fostered a department-wide climate of sustainability

» Played a key role in saving the company x gallons of water per year

» Is the driving force behind an x percent reduction in the use of paper

» Is directly responsible for an x percent increase in the amount of recycled trash

» Is responsible for an x percent reduction in the use of electricity

>> Led the company's effort to buy environmentally friendly products

>> Established and leads the sustainability committee

Fully competent: Meets expectations

>> Provides employees with appropriate recognition for actions that help sustainability

>> Is steadily building knowledge of sustainability and application of sustainability practices

>> Supports the company's sustainable policies and programs

>> Monitors employee performance to be sure that sustainability guidelines are being followed and standards are being met

>> Works with vendors and customers to help them with sustainability efforts

>> Focuses efforts on recycling, reducing waste, buying recycled goods, and reusing products where possible

>> Is a member of the sustainability committee

>> Circulates important articles on sustainability and the actions that employees can take to help in this area

>> Is a source of outstanding ideas for sustainability

Marginal: Occasionally fails to meet expectations

>> Pays limited attention to sustainability and does not demonstrate a serious commitment to it

>> Asks employees for suggestions on sustainability, but then does nothing with them

>> Has made no effort to understand the company's sustainability programs, policies, initiatives, and objectives

>> Ignores requests to attend company meetings that deal with sustainability

>> Takes minimal sustainability steps and believes that no further steps are needed

Unsatisfactory: Consistently fails to meet expectations

>> Is unconcerned with issues of sustainability

>> Makes no effort to reuse or recycle

>> Ignores company polices and guidelines on sustainability

>> Refuses to take even the most basic sustainability steps

>> Regards sustainability as a fad

>> Continues to engage in behaviors that contradict the company's sustainability programs, practices, policies, and objectives

>> Shows a lack of concern for the amount of paper, electricity, and water that is wasted in the company every day

Chapter 9

The Best Phrases for Job Knowledge and Expertise

Your employees' knowledge, expertise, skills, and abilities are critical to success on the job, and they merit specific attention in the performance appraisal process. However, there's more to these factors than meets the eye.

When appraising your employees in these areas, you may be tempted to focus on the depth of their knowledge base, the skills they have developed, and the range of their expertise. There's no doubt that these are important factors to include in the appraisal process, but they're not the entire story. Rather, two related factors should be considered simultaneously.

The first is your employees' ability to *apply* their knowledge, skills, and abilities to the job. Although your employees' wide-ranging and in-depth competencies are certainly admirable, they're not really of much help to the employee or the company if they're not applied to the job.

The second factor is your employees' ability to *share* their competencies with their fellow employees. By sharing their expertise with others, such as through informal help and support, mentoring, or conducting training sessions, your employees' special competencies are then adding measurable value to the company — such as by enhancing employee skills and growth, meeting employees' needs, and contributing to individual and organizational productivity.

Hence, the phrases in this chapter focus not only on your employees' knowledge, skills, and abilities, but also on the ways in which your employees apply and share these competencies on the job.

Acting as a Positive Role Model

Exceptional: Consistently exceeds expectations

>> Consistently models the most effective and productive behaviors

>> Is a highly respected and industrious individual whose behaviors are emulated by others

>> Is highly conscious of the impact that workplace behaviors have on the actions of other employees

>> Consistently aligns behaviors with the company's standards, ethics, values, and objectives

>> Recognizes that one of the most powerful training tools is modeling excellent actions and behaviors for others to learn

>> Has built a high level of respect and trust with employees which has contributed to their desire to learn from the behaviors they're seeing

>> Has developed employees to the point that they, too, exhibit model behaviors

Excellent: Frequently exceeds expectations

>> Takes specific steps to model the behaviors that are expected from employees

>> Has a positive impact on employee performance by demonstrating enthusiasm, an upbeat attitude, and high levels of energy

>> Engages in behaviors that have helped improve the productivity of all employees

>> Never asks employees to adhere to standards which are beyond those that are demonstrated and modeled

>> Sets an example that has contributed to an atmosphere of learning, growth, and outstanding performance within the department

>> Maintains and demonstrates excellence in all aspects of work

Fully competent: Meets expectations

>> Sets a clear example of behaviors for employees to follow

>> Is always aware of the impact that personal behaviors and actions are having on the performance of others

>> Provides appropriate reinforcement and recognition when employees emulate positive behaviors

>> Is comfortable and successful as a role model

>> Shows employees what to do and how to do it, while also providing the rationale behind the desired actions

>> Is genuinely committed to demonstrating model behavior

Marginal: Occasionally fails to meet expectations

>> Doesn't always recognize the impact that personal behaviors can have on the learning and performance of others

>> Inconsistently follows company policies, sending a mixed message to employees

- » Has engaged in some questionable behaviors that are now being displayed by other employees
- » Tries to serve as a positive role model, but frequently falls short of the mark

Unsatisfactory: Consistently fails to meet expectations

- » Demonstrates questionable behaviors that negatively influence the actions of the employees
- » Ignores the standards that others are expected to meet
- » Serves as a poor role model, and then becomes upset when employees engage in questionable behaviors
- » Cuts corners while expecting perfection from employees
- » Is uncomfortable with the concept of serving as a role model
- » Advises employees to look to other individuals as role models
- » Lives by the adage "Do as I say, not as I do"

Applying Expertise to the Job

Exceptional: Consistently exceeds expectations

- » Approaches and resolves a wide range of challenges skillfully, thoroughly, and effectively
- » Has applied expertise to address and resolve problematic developments in several areas and has generated solutions that led to substantial cost savings
- » Has used technical, operational, and organizational expertise to generate numerous improvements in company processes, procedures, and operations
- » Applied expertise to the XYZ project and contributed directly to the project's success

>> Transformed the XYZ project from a failure to a success by effectively analyzing the full situation and then applying state-of-the-art knowledge to resolve it

>> Makes highly technical or specialized information interesting and understandable

>> Enhances the effectiveness of group meetings by sharing expertise on issues or questions that arise

Excellent: Frequently exceeds expectations

>> Presents complicated information a highly understandable and usable format

>> Uses wide-ranging expertise to upgrade problem-solving

>> Creatively applies expertise and innovative insight to upgrade and streamline operations and systems

>> Enhances the expertise of many fellow employees by providing formal training as well as informal coaching and guidance

>> Is able to take theoretical information and make practical use of it on the job

>> Has helped find solutions to several long-term problems by applying expertise

>> Provides technical information in user-friendly language

Fully competent: Meets expectations

>> Shows a high degree of intellectual effectiveness

>> Easily absorbs and applies new information

>> Communicates effectively with technical and nontechnical employees

>> Uses expertise to raise the quality and quantity of work

>> Shows tenacity in solving technical as well as nontechnical problems

>> Always seeks ways to apply expertise in ways that generate improvements in the department as well as in the company at large

>> Focuses on causes rather than symptoms

Marginal: Occasionally fails to meet expectations

>> Relies on outdated knowledge

>> Is impatient with employees when presenting new information to them

>> Is more interested in quick answers than the right answers

>> Provides a great deal of extraneous detail when asked a question

>> Uses technical jargon to such an extent that communication is unclear and confusing

>> Provides information that is not consistently regarded as credible

>> Starts providing an answer before hearing the entire question

>> Provides too many answers that are either fluff or bluff

Unsatisfactory: Consistently fails to meet expectations

>> Presents out-of-date solutions to employees, and then becomes defensive if the employees raise questions

>> Provides inaccurate technical information

>> Responds to technical questions with an arrogant, degrading, and demeaning style

>> Ignores requests from others for help, assistance, or guidance

>> Is more interested voicing technical jargon than getting the job done

>> Lacks expertise in areas in which it is most needed on the job

>> Provides solutions that have created larger problems

Conducting Research

Exceptional: Consistently exceeds expectations

>> Has cutting-edge online research skills

>> Generates excellent data from the most reliable sources and resources

>> Has state-of-the-art skills in designing, administering, and interpreting surveys

>> Produces high-quality and reliable research-based work

>> Uses a broad range of appropriate statistical measurements and tests

>> Has an outstanding ability to differentiate relevant data from less significant data

>> Knows how and when to effectively, ethically, and productively use AI

>> Produces research reports that are well reasoned, well written, and well received

Excellent: Frequently exceeds expectations

>> Uses research methods that are thorough and well-organized

>> Strengthens the research skills of other employees

>> Develops a solid research plan while remaining open to further data-gathering and analysis if the findings warrant such actions

>> Differentiates between trustworthy and untrustworthy sources

>> Digs through and analyzes a vast array of data before reaching any conclusions

>> Has a solid understanding of statistical analyses and is able to see through questionable statistical methodologies

>> Takes full advantage of the most appropriate technologies when conducting research

>> Continuously conducts relevant research in the field, independent of assignments to do so

Fully competent: Meets expectations

>> Has wide-ranging expertise in the field and uses it for a jump-start on research projects

>> Doesn't waste time with questionable sources or resources

>> Uses a variety of search engines to check and crosscheck sources and gather additional current information

>> Is comfortable and effective in handling research-oriented projects

>> Begins research projects with an open mind

>> Completes research projects on time

>> Continues to build personal research skills

Marginal: Occasionally fails to meet expectations

>> Conducts research randomly and jumps from one resource to another

>> Spends too much time with questionable sources of data and too little time with valuable sources of data

>> Can get sidetracked during the research process

>> Rushes through research projects

>> Is more focused on gathering data than analyzing it

>> Uses outmoded data analysis techniques and technologies

>> Asks for advice when conducting research, but rarely follows it

>> Relies on summaries and overviews, rather than facts and figures

Unsatisfactory: Consistently fails to meet expectations

>> Actively avoids projects that require research

>> Expects AI to do all of the work, leading to inaccurate and skewed results and reports

>> Reacts to research requests by trying to delegate the work to someone else

>> Is easily influenced by small amounts of data

>> Tends to rely on questionable resources

>> Is more influenced by the appearance of websites than by their content

>> Is unfamiliar and uncomfortable with most search engines

>> Relies on outdated materials and sources

>> Produces research reports that lack clarity and credibility

Demonstrating Computer Literacy

Exceptional: Consistently exceeds expectations

>> Has expert-level knowledge regarding a wide range of computer programs, databases, and languages

>> Has finely tuned technical troubleshooting skills

>> Helps fellow employees use software programs that are required on the job

>> Has in-depth knowledge of several operating systems

>> Sets the standard for outstanding web and internet skills and usage

>> Is able to create upgrades, patches, and functionality improvements

>> Fully understands and communicates issues related to computer security

Excellent: Frequently exceeds expectations

>> Is continuously upgrading computer software knowledge and digital skills

>> Quickly learns and applies new computer programs

>> Creates tailor-made training strategies to help employees learn new computer systems

>> Has an excellent understanding of computer operations

>> Helps keep company operating systems at state-of-the-art levels

>> Is always on the lookout for new cost-effective computer systems and applications

Fully competent: Meets expectations

>> Is receptive and responsive in utilizing new computer programs and software upgrades

>> Helps fellow employees with computer-related questions and problems

>> Follows company policies regarding computer usage

>> Maintains a solid understanding of new computer applications

>> Is familiar with a broad range of computer hardware and software

>> Has made several successful presentations to provide support and encouragement to employees in further developing their computer skills

>> Stays current on computer technologies, developments, and advances relevant to work

>> Is highly effective with spreadsheets and databases

>> Demonstrates a high degree of proficiency with social media

Marginal: Occasionally fails to meet expectations

>> Is slow to adjust to new or upgraded computer programs

>> Is unmotivated to increase computer knowledge

>> Doesn't take advantage of many features available on company computers

>> Lacks adequate digital skills and shows no interest or initiative in doing anything about this

>> Frequently interrupts others with basic computer questions

>> Relies on manual processes that can be easily handled on company computer systems

>> Wastes time on social media during work hours on matters that are unrelated to the job

Unsatisfactory: Consistently fails to meet expectations

>> Downloads programs in violation of company policy

>> Actively resists computer upgrades

>> Pays no attention when new computer programs are introduced

>> Forwards inappropriate e-mail messages

>> Totally disregards matters of computer security

>> Doesn't respond to e-mail that requires a response

>> Repeatedly contacts the IT Department for technical support on matters that have been addressed multiple times

>> Recently downloaded a computer virus

Mentoring Others

Exceptional: Consistently exceeds expectations

>> Always makes time to mentor other employees

>> Genuinely enjoys helping others learn

» Takes great pride in seeing employees build their skills, productivity, and personal effectiveness

» Has generated major improvements in employee performance through mentoring

» Is comfortable and effective working side-by-side with employees to help them learn

» Targets mentoring efforts on areas in which critical skills need upgrading

» Provides mentoring on a scheduled basis, as well as spontaneously when needed

Excellent: Frequently exceeds expectations

» Organizes time to allow mentoring

» Engages in two-way communication that serves as a powerful mentoring tool

» Shows employees what to do and how to do it, and then provides opportunities for hands-on practice

» Serves as a mentor without being asked to do so

» Mentors new employees and brings them up to speed quickly

» Regards mentoring as an ongoing process rather than an intermittent task

» Consistently receives praise and appreciation from mentored employees

Fully competent: Meets expectations

» Readily volunteers to mentor others

» Is undergoing training to continuously improve mentoring skills

» Is able to complete assigned work while still providing first-rate mentoring to others

» Provides mentoring that adheres to all company standards and guidelines

- Develops employees to the point that they can help in the mentoring process
- Includes a high degree of support and positive feedback when mentoring others
- Approaches mentoring with positive expectations every step of the way
- Has an excellent base of knowledge and shares it effectively in the mentoring process

Marginal: Occasionally fails to meet expectations

- Can rely on outdated knowledge and practices when mentoring others
- Provides brief answers to questions that require more thorough responses
- Mentors employees at inconvenient or inopportune times
- Doesn't consistently follow up in the mentoring process
- Ends mentoring sessions abruptly, even when employees have additional questions
- Is uninterested in mentoring, and this is apparent to all who are being mentored
- Rushes through mentoring from start to finish

Unsatisfactory: Consistently fails to meet expectations

- Provides information on shortcuts and workarounds that violate standards and compromise quality
- Focuses on employee mistakes, and then provides inadequate corrective information
- Makes far more negative comments than positive ones during the mentoring process
- Places unrealistic expectations on employees, and then reprimands employees who fall short
- Focuses more on discipline than on development

>> Has no patience with employees who are struggling

>> Tends to be more of a tormentor than a mentor

Sharing Knowledge

Exceptional: Consistently exceeds expectations

>> Genuinely enjoys sharing expertise to help build employee productivity, performance, and confidence

>> Is approached by many employees with questions and always makes time to answer them

>> Manages to complete assigned work with distinction while always making time to share knowledge

Excellent: Frequently exceeds expectations

>> Is generous in sharing time and ideas

>> Holds informal discussion sessions with interested employees on numerous workplace questions

>> Lives by the philosophy that "anything worth knowing is worth sharing"

Fully competent: Meets expectations

>> Seeks opportunities to share insight and information with other employees

>> Has raised employee performance and satisfaction by sharing knowledge

>> Runs training sessions that are regarded as valuable perks

Marginal: Occasionally fails to meet expectations

>> Doesn't have much up-to-date knowledge to share

>> Regards questions from others as an intrusion

>> Spends a minimal amount of time sharing knowledge

Unsatisfactory: Consistently fails to meet expectations

>> Refuses to make time to share insight and information

>> Makes employees feel unwelcome when asking questions

>> Uses an arrogant and condescending tone when responding to inquiries

Supporting Technology

Exceptional: Consistently exceeds expectations

>> Is directly responsible for introducing new digital systems that have increased productivity and output while reducing costs

>> Provides hands-on support to others to build their understanding of company applications and digital systems

>> Consistently on the lookout for ways in which new technology can enhance existing systems, processes, and programs

>> Serves as a leader in informing and guiding employees in new technological advances for the company

>> Has solved myriad operational problems by utilizing the latest technological applications

>> Is the go-to person for technical questions

>> Keeps technical skills on the cutting edge

Excellent: Frequently exceeds expectations

>> Fully embraces and utilizes new technology across a wide range of company projects and programs

>> Applies a vast technological knowledge base to the job

>> Clearly analyzes and identifies areas in which new technologies can generate measurable improvements in the company, followed by making appropriate recommendations and spearheading the changes that are approved

>> Communicates effectively with non-technical employees to help build their understanding and utilization of new technologies on the job

>> Is on top of new developments in field

>> Takes ongoing steps to maintain state-of-the-art technical knowledge

Fully competent: Meets expectations

>> Open and receptive to utilizing new technologies to enhance personal performance and productivity

>> Listens carefully to technology-related questions instead of jumping in with an answer

>> Frequently participates in technical upskilling programs

>> Always takes advantage of technology-oriented learning opportunities, whether on or off the job

>> Keeps all licenses and certifications current

Marginal: Occasionally fails to meet expectations

>> Has let technical expertise fall behind

>> Gives superficial answers to detailed questions

>> Has no interest in continuing technical education

>> Builds technical expertise in areas that have little to do with the needs of the company

- ›› Has in-depth knowledge in too narrow of an area
- ›› Has impressive credentials, but spends too much time talking about them
- ›› Relies on information that has since been updated
- ›› Shows declining interest in personal areas of expertise
- ›› Focuses more on yesterday's knowledge than tomorrow's challenges

Unsatisfactory: Consistently fails to meet expectations

- ›› Bases decisions on knowledge that is out of date
- ›› Turns away from opportunities to build expertise
- ›› Lets licenses and certifications lapse
- ›› Is unfamiliar with the latest developments in the field
- ›› Gets caught up in the technical details and fails to see the larger issues
- ›› Becomes argumentative when questioned on technical matters
- ›› Hasn't taken a class or attended a technical seminar, webcast, or podcast in years

Utilizing Analytical Skills

Exceptional: Consistently exceeds expectations

- ›› Effectively incorporates a problem-solving style that is both analytical and creative
- ›› Conducts credible, thorough, and reliable analyses
- ›› Has come up with new problem-solving strategies and solutions by thinking analytically
- ›› Quickly sees through specious arguments

- Has successfully applied analytical skills to solve several long-term problems
- Effectively uses analytical skills to solve technical as well as nontechnical problems
- Has raised the standards of analytical thinking and problem-solving among peers
- Makes high-quality decisions that measurably contribute to the bottom line

Excellent: Frequently exceeds expectations

- Bases conclusions on thorough analyses of all relevant data
- Supports conclusions with solid reasoning
- Identifies and focuses on relevant details
- Is a highly analytical problem solver
- Breaks problems into their individual parts and solves them piece by piece
- Is a clear and logical thinker
- Regards listening as a key component of analytical thinking and problem-solving
- Has business sense and analytical skills that are a powerful combination

Fully competent: Meets expectations

- Uses a logical and orderly problem-solving approach
- Relies on specifics, not generalizations
- Has a deliberative problem-solving style, but never loses sight of the deadlines
- Discerns relevant data from irrelevant data
- Is able to separate hype from facts
- Helps fellow employees build their analytical skills
- Asks the right questions at the right time

- **>>** Is receptive to a wide range of new ideas, suggestions, and strategies
- **>>** Is a tenacious investigator

Marginal: Occasionally fails to meet expectations

- **>>** Bases decisions more on opinions than analyses
- **>>** Uses analytical skills, but relies on limited data
- **>>** Is more interested in a quick solution than a thorough analysis
- **>>** Becomes defensive when asked about the reasoning behind decisions
- **>>** Relies on less-than-credible sources
- **>>** Has a disorganized strategy that has led to lost documentation and marginalized outcomes
- **>>** Is overly involved in the analysis process and loses sight of the objectives

Unsatisfactory: Consistently fails to meet expectations

- **>>** Manipulates facts to reach self-serving conclusions
- **>>** Produces results that lack credibility
- **>>** Draws conclusions based on inadequate analysis
- **>>** Uses antiquated data to support conclusions
- **>>** Lets personal bias influence analyses
- **>>** Often rushes through projects that call for more in-depth thinking and analysis
- **>>** Overlooks critical data and developments
- **>>** Focuses on one idea and refuses to consider others
- **>>** Criticizes rather than analyzes

Chapter **10**
The Best Phrases for Leadership

Effective leadership is premised on influencing, motivating, guiding, and coaching employees to pursue and meet common goals. As a result, individuals in leadership positions play a central contributory role in impacting and ultimately determining company success.

This means that accurately appraising the leadership skills of anyone who plays a leadership role is critical. If you look at all your employees, you'll see that many of them have leadership responsibilities, regardless of their titles. These varying degrees of leadership responsibilities cover a broad range of positions that span from senior management to employees who have no formal leadership titles but carry out occasional leadership functions, such as chairing a committee or running an event.

At the same time, leadership isn't a one-dimensional activity that's either present or not. Rather, it's a combination of many functions that include motivating the team, coaching and training, providing feedback, screening and hiring, managing conflict, making decisions, and more — all of which need to be considered during the performance appraisal process.

In light of the critical role that leadership plays in any organization, choosing the right words to include in performance appraisals is quite important — not only in terms of performance, growth, and development of your employees, but also in terms of performance, growth, and development of your company.

Building a Team

Exceptional: Consistently exceeds expectations

>> Has outstanding team-building skills

>> Builds a team-oriented attitude among all employees

>> Has taken a marginally functional department and converted it into a highly productive team

>> Uses specific exercises and activities to strengthen the team

>> Manages a department that is well known for its high level of teamwork

>> Has an extraordinary ability to turn a group into a team

>> Pulls employees together into a cooperative, supportive, collaborative, and highly successful team

>> Creates a team-oriented environment, climate, and culture

Excellent: Frequently exceeds expectations

>> Possesses a strong goal orientation, which contributes to the solidarity and focus of the employees

>> Develops a winning attitude among the employees

>> Structures projects and assignments to further strengthen teamwork

>> Makes all employees feel that they're valued members of the team

>> Implements state-of-the-art teambuilding programs that further enhance teamwork and cooperation

>> Uses a teamwork approach to further develop and utilize the unique talents of each employee

Fully competent: Meets expectations

>> Recognizes and rewards team-oriented behaviors and actions
>> Consistently emphasizes the importance of teamwork in the department and company at large
>> Is highly effective in bonding employees together
>> Is a solid team player
>> Builds highly productive teams
>> Generates positive measurable performance and productivity as a result of teamwork
>> Sets consistently high expectations regarding teamwork among the employees

Marginal: Occasionally fails to meet expectations

>> Has minimal concern for teamwork which is sensed by the employees and evident in their behavior
>> Makes comments that place employees in conflict with each other
>> Doesn't differentiate between healthy competition and conflict
>> Undercuts teambuilding by providing preferential treatment to certain employees
>> Rarely takes action to deal with conflicts or disagreements among the employees
>> Makes overlapping assignments that undercut cooperation
>> Takes no action to deal with disruptive team members
>> Needs to focus less on team activities and more on team productivity

Unsatisfactory: Consistently fails to meet expectations

>> Engaged in behaviors that turned a successful team into several splintered factions

>> Provides no recognition or rewards for teamwork

>> Takes credit for team successes, and blames the team if projects fall short

>> Never works with the team as a whole

>> Communicates with the team primarily through reprimands

>> Makes no effort to be part of the team

>> Focuses on personal needs, rather than on the needs of the team

>> Interrupts team meetings with comments and behaviors that are far off topic

Coaching

Exceptional: Consistently exceeds expectations

>> Works with employees on an individual and group basis to build skills, performance, and goal attainment

>> Provides ongoing coaching, guidance, and training

>> Recognizes outstanding performance

>> Is more inclined to coach than to discipline

>> Treats employee performance issues as opportunities for coaching and development

>> Is widely regarded as a source of excellent advice

>> Includes formal coaching as part of the development plans for the employees

>> Uses a variety of highly productive coaching techniques

Excellent: Frequently exceeds expectations

» Tailors coaching techniques to best fit the individual employees

» Uses coaching methods that build motivation and enthusiasm

» Has a coaching style that bonds employees together

» Knows when and how to coach in public as well as in private

» Provides excellent follow-up to monitor coaching results

» Accurately tracks and measures the effectiveness of coaching

» Utilizes a coaching style that involves and energizes the employees

Fully competent: Meets expectations

» Truly enjoys coaching and building the employees' skills

» Regards coaching as a central component of the job

» Has helped employees meet their performance objectives as well as their development objectives through coaching

» Helps employees learn to coach themselves in many areas

» Uses innovative coaching strategies to generate measurable improvements in employee performance

» Is regarded by employees as a first-rate coach

» Creates a winning atmosphere through effective coaching

» Is genuinely committed to working with employees to build their skills, enhance their performance, and further their career development

» Provides employees with the tools and guidance they need to succeed

Marginal: Occasionally fails to meet expectations

>> Is more inclined to discipline than coach

>> Frequently reprimands and rarely recognizes employees

>> Has a sink-or-swim mentality in practically every situation

>> Provides employees with far more information than they can absorb

>> Acts more like a critic than a coach

>> Regards coaching as a one-way process and rarely listens to employees

>> Provides minimal follow-up after coaching

>> Quickly becomes impatient when trying to coach

>> Uses a one-size-fits-all style of coaching

Unsatisfactory: Consistently fails to meet expectations

>> Ignores the coaching side of the job

>> Ridicules employees who do not instantly understand and follow coaching advice

>> Equates coaching with lecturing

>> Focuses coaching on areas that are of secondary interest and importance

>> Implements coaching based on inadequate performance data

>> Lets favoritism influence coaching practices and techniques

>> Turns coaching into nagging

>> Coaches employees as if they are children

Delegating

Exceptional: Consistently exceeds expectations

» Effectively manages time by including delegation when appropriate

» Uses delegation as a method to enhance employee skills and build their performance and confidence

» Provides employees with the tools, resources, and support to successfully complete the delegated projects

» Understands the importance of maintaining responsibility when delegating authority

» Has successfully increased productivity through effective delegation

» Builds a stronger team through delegation

» Delegates in a way that sends a message of trust and respect to the employees

» Provides highly effective follow-up on all delegated work

Excellent: Frequently exceeds expectations

» Carefully reviews projects and personnel prior to delegating

» Successfully delegates work to individuals and teams and generates excellent results

» Monitors employee performance without stifling it

» Has excellent insight into the kinds of projects that should and should not be delegated

» Understands how much independence and autonomy can be granted to each employee

» Is able to put faltering delegated projects back on track

» Includes delegation as part of the employee development process

» Provides employees with a clear understanding of the standards, expectations, and goals on delegated projects

Fully competent: Meets expectations

>> Delegates and follows up as needed

>> Has had considerable success by effectively delegating projects

>> Knows when and how to delegate

>> Delegates and then provides highly effective coaching, guidance, and feedback

>> Grants employees authority and autonomy to get the delegated work done

>> Accurately monitors and measures the status of delegated projects

>> Understands employees' strengths and weaknesses, and keeps them in mind when delegating

Marginal: Occasionally fails to meet expectations

>> Needs to review delegated projects more frequently, instead of waiting until such projects are completed

>> Delegates, but then intervenes and tries to take control

>> Totally revises and reworks delegated projects after they have been completed

>> Provides inadequate information regarding standards and expectations on delegated work

>> Delegates work, but provides employees with minimal freedom to carry it out

>> Delegates projects, but can't really let go of them

>> Only delegates the most trivial work

Unsatisfactory: Consistently fails to meet expectations

>> Delegates high-priority or sensitive work that should not be delegated

>> Delegates too much work and overwhelms the employees

- » Fails to provide adequate follow-up on delegated work
- » Delegates work and essentially never looks at it again
- » Refuses to delegate anything
- » Is afraid to delegate
- » Keeps changing expectations and objectives after projects have been delegated
- » Insists on controlling delegated projects

Developing Employees' Skills

Exceptional: Consistently exceeds expectations

- » Varies training methods to meet the employees' learning styles
- » Is highly successful in developing the employees' expertise and skills
- » Provides training that is readily applicable to work that needs to be done on the job
- » Has measurably improved performance and productivity by training the employees
- » Has had a positive impact on the bottom line through upskilling efforts and programs
- » Actively supports a true learning environment
- » Creates and implements outstanding on-the-job and off-the-job employee development programs
- » Provides training and guidance to prepare employees for promotions

Excellent: Frequently exceeds expectations

- » Provides timely feedback to reinforce learning
- » Gives employees numerous opportunities to practice newly acquired skills

- » Consistently and effectively engages in training-oriented behaviors and roles
- » Is approached by many employees who want to learn about best practices
- » Ensures that employees in the department are always well trained
- » Regards employee development as a key part of the job
- » Follows up regularly after training others
- » Identifies and addresses areas in which employees need further training and development

Fully competent: Meets expectations

- » Gladly helps and guides fellow employees
- » Takes no shortcuts when training
- » Builds employee skills by utilizing two-way communication rather than one-way communication
- » Is always looking for ways to continue to strengthen the employees' skills and abilities
- » Is open and communicative when teaching
- » Never turns down an opportunity to train
- » Takes great pride in employee growth and development
- » Conducts highly successful training programs

Marginal: Occasionally fails to meet expectations

- » Does little more than lecture the employees
- » Plays favorites in selecting employees for training
- » Has employees who emerge from the department with no additional skills
- » Provides no follow-up after training
- » Waits for employees to fail before taking any steps to train them
- » Builds employee skills in areas that have little to do with successful performance on the job
- » Expects employees to train themselves

Unsatisfactory: Consistently fails to meet expectations

>> Shows no interest in building the employees' knowledge, skills, or abilities

>> Never has time to train employees

>> Takes training-related complaints personally and then retaliates against employees who voiced them

>> Typically provides training that is out-of-date

>> Is unresponsive to employee questions

>> Has taken no recent steps to upgrade personal skills and competencies

>> Fails to build employees' skills, but reprimands employees for questionable performance in areas that require such skills

Inspiring Enthusiasm and Commitment

Exceptional: Consistently exceeds expectations

>> Has a genuinely positive attitude that spreads across the department

>> Energizes others by maintaining and expressing an upbeat outlook

>> Serves as a model for fellow employees by demonstrating high energy and positive expectations

>> Consistently makes extraordinary efforts to achieve extraordinary results

>> Makes major sacrifices to help the company

>> Frequently expresses appreciation for the opportunities provided by the company

>> Consistently surpasses expectations and standards, leading to similar behaviors from other employees

>> Creates a culture of enthusiasm, loyalty, and productivity

Excellent: Frequently exceeds expectations

» Maintains an upbeat and positive attitude, and draws the same out of others

» Is bursting with contagious enthusiasm

» Helps turn around negative situations and attitudes through genuine positivity and optimism

» Is truly excited about work

» Never misses an opportunity to build goodwill for the company, both internally and externally

» Is willing to go the extra mile and sets a positive example for others to do likewise

Fully competent: Meets expectations

» Is able to make any project more interesting, fulfilling, and rewarding

» Serves as an excellent role model by demonstrating high levels of enthusiasm, energy, and drive

» Puts in long and productive hours, inspiring many employees to do so as well

» Seizes every opportunity to make positive comments about the company

» Generates suggestions and new ideas rather than complaints

» Is always looking for ways to improve performance, productivity, and the company itself

Marginal: Occasionally fails to meet expectations

» Inflames problematic situations

» Encourages fellow employees to rock the boat

» Regards the company as the opposition

» Does the minimum amount of work

- » Frequently talks about how much better things are at other companies
- » Is always looking for a reason to miss work
- » Frequently says "no," and encourages others to do the same

Unsatisfactory: Consistently fails to meet expectations

- » Places job responsibilities a distant second behind other interests and pursuits
- » Speaks negatively about the company
- » Is indifferent to developments in the company
- » Ridicules employees who show energy and enthusiasm
- » Looks for problems rather than solutions
- » Is a constant source of complaints
- » Puts a negative spin on company policies, programs, and developments
- » Is always looking for ways to do less for the company
- » Fabricates malicious stories about coworkers or the company at large
- » Shows the most excitement when the workday is drawing to a close

Making Decisions

Exceptional: Consistently exceeds expectations

- » Uses participative decision-making when appropriate
- » Bases decisions on facts
- » Gathers facts in advance and utilizes them
- » Is sensitive to time constraints when making decisions
- » Approaches decision-making with an open mind
- » Is well regarded as a first-rate decision maker

>> Clearly understands the costs and benefits associated with decisions

>> Is receptive to innovative ideas and suggestions

>> Conducts effective research prior to making major decisions

Excellent: Frequently exceeds expectations

>> Truly values the input of other employees

>> Makes difficult decisions that measurably improve operations

>> Deliberates on decisions, but never overlooks the timing

>> Involves employees in many decisions that affect them and their work

>> Acts decisively, but not impulsively

>> Makes unilateral decisions when needed

>> Shares the credit when decisions generate excellent outcomes

>> Accepts responsibility if decisions don't yield desired outcomes

Fully competent: Meets expectations

>> Separates significant data from insignificant data

>> Makes timely decisions

>> Is trusted by employees when it comes to making decisions

>> Takes decision-making responsibilities seriously

>> Is able to clearly explain the rationale behind decisions

>> Relies on facts rather than emotions

>> Keeps the goals, vision, and mission of the company in mind when engaged in decision-making

>> Reaches decisions that are fair, ethical, and trusted

Marginal: Occasionally fails to meet expectations

>> Turns every decision into a group decision

>> Takes excessive amounts of time to make a decision

>> Is overly influenced by insignificant details

>> Lets corporate politics play too great a role in the decision-making process

>> Tends to waver back and forth

>> Ignores most input from others

>> Makes snap decisions

>> Relies on questionable sources and resources

>> Is overly influenced by emotions

>> Is easily swayed by others

>> Procrastinates on important decisions

Unsatisfactory: Consistently fails to meet expectations

>> Has difficulty making decisions

>> Has made a string of questionable decisions

>> Ignores or misinterprets the facts when making decisions

>> Acts impulsively on major decisions

>> Spends considerable amounts of time laboring over minor decisions

>> Asks for input from others, and then ignores it

>> Shows no flexibility or agility in the decision-making process

>> Lets bias and stereotypes influence decision-making

>> Enters decision-making with a closed mind

>> Ignores new and different ideas

>> Abandons decisions at the first sign of a challenge

Managing Conflict

Exceptional: Consistently exceeds expectations

>> Creatively resolves conflicts large and small

>> Has transformed conflicts into sources of innovative ideas

>> Understands conflicts and manages them effectively

>> Uses team-building strategies to help resolve conflicts

>> Manages conflicts, instead of being managed by them

>> Recognizes the inevitability of conflicts and applies highly effective strategies to manage them

>> Is truly gifted in getting to the heart of a conflict and resolving it

>> Is known for being fair, level-headed, and honest when dealing with conflicts

Excellent: Frequently exceeds expectations

>> Defuses conflict situations before they erupt

>> Prevents conflicts from escalating

>> Builds conflict management skills among the employees

>> Varies conflict management strategies to best fit the situation

>> Has solid mediation and arbitration skills

>> Successfully mediates interpersonal conflicts

>> Identifies potential conflict situations and takes proactive steps to deal with them

>> Is frequently sought to resolve conflicts

Fully competent: Meets expectations

>> Remains calm and focused in conflict situations

>> Is sensitive to conflict situations and acts promptly to deal with them

>> Separates causes from symptoms in resolving conflicts

- Listens carefully to all disputants
- Takes a fair and level-headed approach
- Isn't afraid to get involved when conflicts arise
- Continuously works to improve conflict management skills
- Has pursued and obtained training in conflict management
- Possesses a wide range of conflict management skills and applies them effectively

Marginal: Occasionally fails to meet expectations

- Tends to create conflicts rather than resolve them
- Takes sides in conflict situations and can let favoritism interfere
- Decides on the resolution of a conflict situation without hearing and reviewing all the facts
- Tries to dominate and control conflicts
- Is uncommunicative in conflict situations
- Fails to actively address conflicts that arise
- Creates win-lose situations rather than win-win situations when addressing conflicts
- Lets conflicts fester for too long

Unsatisfactory: Consistently fails to meet expectations

- Is a source of conflict within and between departments
- Puts employees into conflicts with each other
- Implements policies and practices that cause conflicts
- Believes that conflicts will resolve themselves if left alone
- Fails to listen carefully to all sides
- Tends to argue rather than listen
- Develops projects and assignments that create conflicts
- Has a management style that generates conflicts
- Creates conflicts in situations where none existed previously

Motivating Employees

Exceptional: Consistently exceeds expectations

>> Successfully implements a broad range of motivational programs

>> Treats employees as individuals and focuses on their unique motivations

>> Establishes programs in which employees meet their needs while pursuing departmental goals

>> Provides employees with opportunities to fulfill their needs for achievement and accomplishment

>> Serves as an excellent role model for motivation and drive

>> Relies on different motivators for different employees

>> Is a truly motivational speaker

>> Has outstanding observational skills which contribute to the utilization of strong motivational methods

Excellent: Frequently exceeds expectations

>> Implements creative recognition programs

>> Energizes seemingly unmotivated employees

>> Eliminates key sources of employee dissatisfaction

>> Successfully motivates employees by enriching their jobs

>> Understands the uses and limitations of money as a motivator

>> Builds motivation by building the employees' skills

>> Has a great deal of insight and understanding when it comes to employee motivation

>> Effectively utilizes recognition, achievement opportunities, and employee development programs in motivating employees

>> Has raised employee motivation to new heights

Fully competent: Meets expectations

>> Links meaningful rewards to desired behaviors

>> Increases employee motivation by demonstrating significant levels of support, coaching, collaboration, and enthusiasm

>> Is becoming an increasingly effective motivator

>> Offers a variety of programs to tap into employees' individual motivations

>> Has creative ideas regarding new ways to motivate employees

>> Uses positive feedback as a powerful motivator

>> Creates an energizing and uplifting work atmosphere

>> Builds the employees' self-motivation

Marginal: Occasionally fails to meet expectations

>> Treats employees as if they all have the same motivations

>> Asks for employee ideas and suggestions on motivational programs, and then ignores them

>> Establishes motivational programs that have little to do with the employees' needs

>> Uses outdated motivational practices

>> Provides employees with random rewards

>> Uses overly competitive motivational programs that undermine unity and teamwork

>> Has only a minimal understanding of what truly motivates employees

Unsatisfactory: Consistently fails to meet expectations

>> Uses fear as a motivator

>> Creates an aura of intimidation that dissatisfies employees

>> Has caused highly motivated employees to shut down

- Has a lack of self-motivation which interferes with the motivation of other employees
- Undermines employee motivation with arbitrary treatment
- Ignores opportunities to provide employees with thanks, credit, and recognition
- Has no interest in learning about motivation or being a better motivator
- Has a motivational style based primarily on threats and bullying

Proactive Behaviors

Exceptional: Consistently exceeds expectations

- Anticipates problems and takes steps to prevent them
- Is always thinking two steps ahead
- Made the XYZ project successful through proactive thinking and action

Excellent: Frequently exceeds expectations

- Prepares for the unexpected
- Has an eye for potential barriers and blockages
- Creates strategies today that prevent problems tomorrow
- Builds a proactive mindset among the employees

Fully competent: Meets expectations

- Establishes contingency plans
- Has a proactive mindset
- Acts on situations before they turn into problems
- Works with employees to prevent future issues, problems, or crises

Marginal: Occasionally fails to meet expectations

>> Only plans for expected outcomes

>> Takes a wait-and-see approach when potential problems arise

>> Is frequently caught off-guard by unexpected outcomes

>> Acts more like a spectator than a participant

Unsatisfactory: Consistently fails to meet expectations

>> Is reactive instead of proactive

>> Waits until tomorrow to plan for tomorrow

>> Moves from one preventable crisis to another

>> Contributed to the failure of the XYZ project because of a lack of proactive steps

Providing Feedback

Exceptional: Consistently exceeds expectations

>> Provides feedback as close as possible to the behavior in question

>> Uses feedback and feedforward as powerful tools to enhance employee performance and development

>> Effectively incorporates two-way communication as part of the feedback and feedforward process

>> Makes excellent use of positive feedback

>> Includes specific examples as part of the feedback process

>> Provides appropriate recognition when merited

>> Provides positive feedback in public, and constructive feedback in private

» Makes employees feel coached rather than disciplined

» Always concludes constructive feedback with an action plan and positive expectations

Excellent: Frequently exceeds expectations

» Provides timely feedback and feedforward

» Teaches others how to provide effective feedback

» Provides performance-based constructive feedback that is accurate, timely, and well-received by employees

» Takes extra steps to be sure that employees understand the feedback they receive

» Provides constructive feedback that helps employees learn, grow, and improve their performance

» Consistently gives feedback that is fair and factual

» Displays a great deal of empathy when designing and delivering feedback

Fully competent: Meets expectations

» Provides appropriate feedback based on employee performance

» Is sensitive to employees and their situations when providing feedback

» Gives feedback that is clear and specific

» Picks the right venues for providing feedback

» Includes corrective actions and guidance when providing constructive feedback

» Is becoming increasingly effective in providing feedback

» Listens to employees and encourages their input when providing them with feedback

» Goes to great lengths to provide constructive feedback

Marginal: Occasionally fails to meet expectations

>> Waits too long to provide feedback

>> Rarely provides thanks, credit, or recognition

>> Misses many opportunities to provide valuable feedback

>> Gives feedback that is too general to be useful

>> Tends to be more destructive than constructive when providing feedback

>> Is reluctant to provide any feedback when employee performance is slipping

>> Tends to label employees during feedback sessions

>> Is long on negative feedback and short on positive feedback

Unsatisfactory: Consistently fails to meet expectations

>> Gives feedback that is based more on impressions than facts

>> Reprimands employees in public

>> Ignores employees' comments or explanations

>> Never recognizes the employees' successes

>> Is quick to provide negative feedback

>> Is overly harsh with certain employees

>> Gives feedback that has a degrading and insulting tone

>> Avoids situations in which employees need constructive feedback

Recognizing Excellent Performance

Exceptional: Consistently exceeds expectations

>> Always seizes opportunities to provide employees with thanks and credit for strong performance

>> Truly understands the importance of recognition and provides it when due, but without going overboard and making it perfunctory

>> Has provided employees in leadership roles with training and guidance regarding the best ways to provide recognition to others

>> Consistently applies state-of-the-art recognition practices and simultaneously serves as an excellent role model in this area

Excellent: Frequently exceeds expectations

>> Looks for new and innovative ways to provide formal and informal thanks and credit to employees

>> Takes advantage of opportunities to provide public recognition to the employees

>> Is highly sensitive to the importance of job satisfaction and understands the way in which it is enhanced by providing employees with recognition when due

>> Has considerable awareness of the needs and feelings of the individual employees and provides forms of recognition that resonate particularly well with each of them

Fully competent: Meets expectations

>> Understands and monitors the work that is being carried out by the employees and provides appropriate and timely recognition

>> Maintains a genuinely positive attitude that contributes to the authenticity of recognition that is provided

>> Provides support and guidance to employees that increase the likelihood of successful performance, which is then followed by recognition

>> Takes active steps to remove barriers that could interfere with employee performance, hence increasing the likelihood of employee success and recognition

Marginal: Occasionally fails to meet expectations

» Displays no consistent practices in providing recognition, often leaving employees confused as to the job standards and expected results

» Frequently overlooks opportunities to provide recognition to employees who have performed extremely well

» Perceived as being more interested in focusing on employees' mistakes and shortcomings than on their successes and accomplishments

» Tends to delay providing well-deserved recognition until weeks after behaviors that merit prompt and appropriate feedback

Unsatisfactory: Consistently fails to meet expectations

» Does not provide any significant thanks, recognition, or appreciation to employees, regardless of their excellent performance

» Believes that effective employees do not need recognition, and those who do are overly dependent or insecure

» Only provides recognition to certain favorite employees, whereas all others are excluded

» Frequently seeks self-recognition and appreciation

» Ignores advice and suggestions from others regarding the importance of employee recognition

Screening and Hiring

Exceptional: Consistently exceeds expectations

» Identifies, screens, and selects outstanding employees from all backgrounds

- Always adheres to all pre-employment rulings, guidelines, and laws
- Attracts outstanding job candidates with highly diverse backgrounds
- Bases decisions on thorough and complete job-related information
- Only asks job-related pre-employment questions
- Treats all job applicants fairly, equitably, and professionally
- Listens and observes carefully during the interview process
- Spends more time listening than talking during job interviews
- Bases job requirements on skills and abilities that are demonstrably necessary to perform the job

Excellent: Frequently exceeds expectations

- Makes every applicant feel welcome
- Treats all applicants fairly
- Knows when to talk and when to listen
- Bases decisions on each applicant's work history along with their job-related training and skills
- Is fully committed to maintaining diversity
- Has excellent knowledge of equal employment opportunity guidelines and follows them judiciously in the hiring and screening process
- Uses a structured interview format
- Takes time to prepare before every interview
- Never loses outstanding applicants

Fully competent: Meets expectations

- Treats all applicants fairly and equitably
- Takes notes during the interview process

- » Gathers thorough and complete job-related information
- » Clearly explains job responsibilities to each applicant
- » Effectively answers all questions about the job and the company
- » Avoids interruptions during job interviews
- » Follows company processes on background checks and employment eligibility before making a job offer

Marginal: Occasionally fails to meet expectations

- » Asks "pet questions" that are unrelated to the job
- » Conducts totally unstructured interviews that generate questionable information while simultaneously upsetting job candidates
- » Makes snap decisions in hiring
- » Bases hiring decisions more on feelings than facts
- » Ignores appointments and keeps applicants waiting
- » Rushes applicants through job interviews
- » Fails to fully prepare before job interviews
- » Settles for superficial answers, instead of probing deeper
- » Takes no notes during job interviews

Unsatisfactory: Consistently fails to meet expectations

- » Asks personal questions that are unrelated to the job
- » Lets personal bias and stereotypes influence the screening process
- » Has no understanding or concern about equal employment opportunity rulings or guidelines that impact the hiring process
- » Has exhibited behaviors in the hiring process that have led to complaints against the company

- >> Tries to upset applicants to see how they react
- >> Makes offers of employment prior to completing all of the steps in the screening process
- >> Loses excellent candidates
- >> Argues with applicants
- >> Makes promises to job candidates that cannot be kept

Chapter **11**

The Best Phrases for Planning, Administration, and Organization

As employees carry out their job responsibilities and simultaneously pursue jointly established goals that focus on performance and development, they may possess and apply many highly effective skills that can directly lead to successful outcomes. However, their performance may still fall short because of questionable supportive skills and actions in terms of their abilities to plan, organize, and administer their work. Interestingly, skills in these areas are often applied specifically to managerial performance, but the reality is that employees at virtually all job levels engage in many of these kinds of actions in order to keep their work on track, on target, and on time.

Effective planning and organizing skills underlie and contribute to successful performance by helping employees in terms of such job components as scheduling their work, dealing with change, controlling costs, establishing goals, and meeting deadlines. Feedback in these types of areas provides employees with recognition and reinforcement where due, while also further identifying areas in which development is needed.

In light of the impact that planning, organizing, and administrative skills can have on employee performance and growth, it is particularly helpful for employees not only to receive coaching and guidance from their managers on these topics throughout the evaluation period, but also for such feedback and feedforward to be further supported, clarified, and documented through written comments that are included in the performance appraisals. The phrases that follow are specifically designed to target and appraise the employees' skills, behaviors, and actions in these areas.

Adjusting to Change

Exceptional: Consistently exceeds expectations

>> Not only adjusts to change, but is a key source of positive and productive changes

>> Is a positive change agent

>> Is a quick study when it comes to adapting to change

>> Works with fellow employees to help them understand changes and adjust to them

>> Regards the change process as a source of creativity and innovation

>> Holds brainstorming sessions for the sole purpose of generating needed changes

>> Treats change as a major contributor to employee growth and development

>> Regards adaptation to change as a survival skill

>> Doesn't view any of the traditional systems, policies, or procedures as being sacred

>> Creates a climate that encourages and supports change

Excellent: Frequently exceeds expectations

>> Helps other employees adapt to changes

>> Reduces resistance to change by openly communicating about it

>> Has a high degree of intellectual curiosity and applies it to understanding and managing change

>> Has made changes that have led to creative solutions to departmental problems

>> Adjusts to changes by studying and understanding them

>> Utilizes positive changes as springboards for further changes

>> Is an active advocate for change

Fully competent: Meets expectations

>> Recognizes the rapid pace of change in the workplace and readily adapts to it

>> Is receptive to new ideas

>> Continues to build personal knowledge, skills, and competencies to be ready for change

>> Digs in and understands changes and the reasons for them

>> Serves as a role model for others by effectively adjusting to change

>> Has an open mind when it comes to new ways of doing things

Marginal: Occasionally fails to meet expectations

>> Immediately tries to find fault with any changes that are introduced

>> Looks for ways to avoid change

>> Makes disparaging remarks about changes

>> Shows resistance to change whenever the opportunity arises

>> Tries to influence others to resist change

>> Keeps talking about how things worked in the past

Unsatisfactory: Consistently fails to meet expectations

>> Refuses to give change a chance

>> Makes disparaging remarks about individuals who suggest or implement changes

>> Will not give up the old ways of doing things

>> Sabotages new programs, processes, or procedures

>> Makes false claims about specific changes

>> Taunts coworkers who accept changes

>> Becomes visibly upset when changes are discussed

>> Is highly vocal in expressing disdain for changes

>> Refuses to use new methods, strategies, systems, or technologies

Applying Managerial Skills

Exceptional: Consistently exceeds expectations

>> Effectively manages workload responsibilities and demands

>> Builds the managerial skills of others

>> Develops high-performing teams

>> Selects and hires outstanding individuals

>> Has A-level coaching and employee development skills

>> Values ideas, input, and suggestions from others

>> Treats all employees with respect and trust

>> Is up-to-date on the latest management practices

>> Is the resident expert on management.

- » Helps employees build their organizational and managerial skills
- » Maintains ongoing two-way communication with the team
- » Remains calm and steady under pressure
- » Has totally organized a formerly chaotic department
- » Communicates effectively with others whether working onsite or remotely
- » Applies the highest standards of honesty, integrity, and ethics
- » Makes all employees feel welcome and safe

Excellent: Frequently exceeds expectations

- » Stays current on new developments in the field of management
- » Is highly focused on developing the employees
- » Treats employees as valued resources
- » Helps maintain very low turnover in the department
- » Creates highly effective motivational and incentive programs
- » Understands employees as individuals and treats them with empathy and sensitivity
- » Encourages and supports employee learning and growth
- » Keeps the employees well informed
- » Consistently incorporates fairness and equitable treatment in dealing with others

Fully competent: Meets expectations

- » Listens to all employees
- » Is responsive to employees' inquiries, concerns, and suggestions
- » Adheres to company standards and policies
- » Reads management books and magazines

>> Regularly attends management development seminars, podcasts, and programs

>> Is more proactive than reactive

>> Effectively manages multiple high-priority projects simultaneously

Marginal: Occasionally fails to meet expectations

>> Is rarely accessible whether working onsite or remotely

>> Relies on antiquated managerial programs and strategies

>> Micromanages in every situation

>> Hoards responsibilities that should be delegated

>> Ignores employees' interests, accomplishments, and questions

>> Keeps employees uninformed and out of the loop

>> Demands respect instead of earning it

>> Provides minimal thanks, credit, and recognition

Unsatisfactory: Consistently fails to meet expectations

>> Plays favorites in assigning and evaluating work

>> Provides employees with no room for growth or support for career development

>> Tells employees exactly how to work, even if they have better ways to proceed

>> Takes no steps to train or develop employees

>> Is usually inaccessible, even when needed for important discussions or meetings

>> Blames employees for failures

>> Takes credit for the successes of others

>> Treats employees as expendable

>> Yells at employees and demonstrates minimal patience

>> Engages in behaviors that contribute to turnover

>> Has a high rate of accidents

>> Has a high rate of absenteeism

>> Acts in ways that show minimal concern for employee health and welfare

>> Is overly controlling

>> Bullies employees

Bottom-Line Orientation

Exceptional: Consistently exceeds expectations

>> Generates excellent ideas for increasing revenue as well as cutting costs

>> Has made suggestions that have clearly had a positive impact on the bottom line

>> Makes direct contributions to the company's profits

>> Is fully dedicated to the company's success

>> Builds a strong bottom-line orientation among the employees

>> Creates and implements strategies to enhance the bottom line

>> Has taken a wide range of steps to cut wasteful expenditures

>> Takes specific actions to improve earnings before interest, taxes, depreciation, and amortization

>> Establishes goals that are directly linked to the bottom line

Excellent: Frequently exceeds expectations

>> Helps others focus more clearly on the bottom line

>> Is profit-minded

>> Understands and implements solid financial planning

>> Engages in numerous ongoing steps to improve profits

>> Is very comfortable reading and analyzing financial data

» Has a solid understanding of balance sheets and income statements

» Has directly contributed to reshaping the department into a profit center

» Has implemented changes in production, design, systems, and strategies that have helped the bottom line

» Implements incentives and motivational programs that help increase employee productivity

Fully competent: Meets expectations

» Never loses sight of the bottom line

» Works with employees to streamline operations and save money

» Discusses bottom-line issues with employees

» Approaches the job with a best-practices mindset

» Works with employees to develop and implement best practices

» Helps employees understand the link between their performance and the company's financial success

» Is always on the lookout for steps, strategies, and programs to improve profits

» Helps employees understand the ways in which they can contribute to the bottom line

» Stays current with financial news that impacts the company and the industry at large

Marginal: Occasionally fails to meet expectations

» Takes few steps that actually contribute to the company's profits

» Talks about contributing to the bottom line, but the numbers don't show it

» Does little to build employees' financial knowledge and skills

>> Shows little interest in the company's financial condition

>> Does nothing with financial data when presented with it

Unsatisfactory: Consistently fails to meet expectations

>> Makes unnecessary costly purchases

>> Engages in behaviors that hurt the bottom line

>> Regards the bottom line as someone else's concern

>> Implements new programs without considering their impact on the bottom line

>> Is not interested in the bottom line

Controlling Costs

Exceptional: Consistently exceeds expectations

>> Is highly cost conscious in every decision

>> Is excellent at projecting costs

>> Creates highly effective systems and processes to monitor and control costs

>> Is financially astute

>> Has developed a high degree of cost consciousness among the employees

>> Keeps the company's financial goals clearly in mind

>> Generates significant savings by implementing sustainability programs

>> Encourages and rewards successful cost-saving suggestions from the employees

>> Creates and implements highly productive cost-saving practices, policies, and programs

Excellent: Frequently exceeds expectations

>> Develops financial management skills in others

>> Places a high priority on cost-benefit analysis in thinking, problem-solving, and decision-making

>> Maintains excellent financial control

>> Is budget-minded

>> Negotiates fees effectively and professionally

>> Has an excellent ability to focus on the big financial picture as well as the details

>> Digs deeply into the numbers and finds additional ways to control costs

>> Is fiscally conservative, but not cheap

>> Accurately analyzes costs

>> Avoids wasting money, materials, or resources

Fully competent: Meets expectations

>> Monitors department expenses daily

>> Has a proven ability to control departmental costs

>> Carefully monitors and controls costs, and encourages other employees to do the same

>> Effectively manages the financial side of the job

>> Operates within the budget

>> Clearly communicates cost-related issues to the employees

Marginal: Occasionally fails to meet expectations

>> Rarely considers cost when making decisions

>> Lets costs slip out of control

>> Approves invoices without reading them carefully

>> Rarely pays attention to costs

>> Is too liberal with company money

- » Is too quick to cut expenses
- » Cuts expenses without adequate consideration of the consequences
- » Is overly aggressive when cutting costs

Unsatisfactory: Consistently fails to meet expectations

- » Lets costs run totally out of control
- » Makes purchases without approval
- » Overlooks the budget
- » Is unable to develop a workable budget
- » Ignores the expense reimbursement policy
- » Ignores per-diem travel allowance guidelines
- » Approves any expense
- » Regards the company credit card as a gift card
- » Puts a budgetary stranglehold on the department
- » Starts cutting costs and doesn't know when to stop
- » Cuts expenses to the point that customers suffer

Establishing Goals

Exceptional: Consistently exceeds expectations

- » Establishes challenging yet achievable development and performance goals
- » Builds fellow employees' goal-setting skills
- » Works collaboratively with employees to set realistic and motivational goals
- » Establishes a goal-oriented mindset among the employees
- » Jointly creates goals that bring out the best performance in others

>> Works with employees to tailor development goals to their individual needs and career aspirations

>> Has raised the standards for goal setting throughout the department

>> Jointly establishes goals that are aligned with company goals

>> Is an expert in setting goals

>> Implements user-friendly methods to help employees design and meet their goals

>> Generates enthusiasm around the goal-setting process

>> Clearly showcases the positive measurable outcomes that result from goal attainment

Excellent: Frequently exceeds expectations

>> Approaches goal-setting with positive expectations

>> Establishes and utilizes checkpoints and deadlines for every goal

>> Has excellent skills in developing goals that are clear, specific, measurable, time sensitive, and supported by solid action plans

>> Effectively applies collaboration in the goal-setting process, generating increased levels of commitment, performance, and achievement

>> Uses a goal-setting strategy that serves as a model for others

>> Includes well-crafted action plans and strategies in goal setting

Fully competent: Meets expectations

>> Jointly establishes challenging, realistic, and relevant performance and development goals

>> Sets specific and measurable goals that include timelines and deadlines

>> Works effectively with employees to set goals

>> Attaches meaningful priorities to every goal

- » Regards goal setting as a major priority
- » Relies on factual data rather than general impressions in shaping and defining goals
- » Helps employees write, refine, and update their goals

Marginal: Occasionally fails to meet expectations

- » Establishes vague goals
- » Creates easily attainable goals
- » Sets reasonable goals, but fails to actively and aggressively pursue them
- » Primarily establishes low-priority goals
- » Sets goals at the last minute
- » Sets goals for employees without their input
- » Devotes very little time and effort to establishing goals
- » Regards goal setting as a process for others to carry out
- » Focuses on personal goals that have little to do with the company's goals

Unsatisfactory: Consistently fails to meet expectations

- » Creates goals without thinking them through
- » Forces goals onto employees without their input or participation
- » Comes up with the same goals every year
- » Sets goals without any provision for follow-up discussions and review
- » Sets goals that lack action plans
- » Fails to establish clear and measurable goals
- » Provides employees with no guidance or support in goal setting
- » Treats goal setting as a cut-and-paste activity
- » Establishes impossible goals

Meeting Deadlines

Exceptional: Consistently exceeds expectations

>> Plans and organizes work to beat deadlines, rather than meet them
>> Never misses a deadline
>> Completes work ahead of deadlines
>> Is energized by tight deadlines
>> Remains unshaken by demanding deadlines
>> Keeps employees highly focused on the deadlines
>> Approaches demanding deadlines with a calm and steady resolve
>> Would miss just about anything before missing a deadline

Excellent: Frequently exceeds expectations

>> Regards deadlines as a top priority
>> Does whatever has to be done to meet deadlines
>> Plans work to avoid last-minute crunches
>> Meets deadlines without sacrificing quality
>> Never loses sight of the deadlines
>> Establishes realistic deadlines and then meets them
>> Plans and organizes work to consistently meet deadlines
>> Treats deadlines as goal lines

Fully competent: Meets expectations

>> Prioritizes work to meet high-priority deadlines
>> Meets every major deadline
>> Carefully monitors employee progress to be sure that deadlines are met

>> Is deadline oriented

>> Communicates openly about deadlines

>> Establishes contingency plans if unexpected obstacles get in the way

>> Maintains an ongoing focus on deadlines, undeterred by unanticipated interruptions

>> Takes deadlines very seriously

>> Is highly committed to meeting deadlines

Marginal: Occasionally fails to meet expectations

>> Meets many deadlines, but with questionable quality of work

>> Meets lower-priority deadlines, while missing major deadlines

>> Waits until the last minute and then notices deadlines

>> Makes promises about deadlines but doesn't keep them

>> Turns most deadline situations into crises

>> Gets sidetracked and misses deadlines

>> Misses deadlines because of inadequate planning

>> Occasionally panics under the pressure of deadlines

>> Is far too lax and casual when it comes to meeting deadlines

Unsatisfactory: Consistently fails to meet expectations

>> Has missed every major deadline

>> Misses totally reachable deadlines

>> Gets close to many deadlines, but meets few

>> Makes excuses rather than deadlines

>> Regards deadlines as suggestions

>> Loses sight of the deadlines

>> Misses deadlines and blames others

>> Causes delays, instead of planning for them

>> Runs late and tells no one

>> Sets impossible deadlines

>> Sets extremely lax deadlines

>> Shows minimal concern when deadlines are missed

>> Has no sense of urgency

Organizing

Exceptional: Consistently exceeds expectations

>> Applies outstanding organizational skills to all projects

>> Maintains a high level of organization within the department

>> Reorganized a totally chaotic department

>> Organizes for the short term and the long term

Excellent: Frequently exceeds expectations

>> Is highly regarded within the department and across departments for having excellent organizational skills

>> Organizes projects to prevent overlaps or gaps in responsibilities

>> Logically organizes the work and the work area

>> Is always able to access needed items or information

Fully competent: Meets expectations

>> Helps fellow employees get organized and stay organized

>> Sets aside time regularly to organize work

>> Utilizes an excellent system for organizing work

>> Approaches projects with a high degree of logic, order, and coordination

Marginal: Occasionally fails to meet expectations

>> Is more concerned with being organized than getting the job done

>> Has an organizing system that is overly personalized, to the point of being incomprehensible

>> Has a work area that lacks order and organization

>> Is unable to access backup data and information associated with completed projects

Unsatisfactory: Consistently fails to meet expectations

>> Projects show a lack of organization from start to finish

>> Can spend hours looking for items that should take seconds to find

>> Is unconcerned about the negative impact that the lack of organization is having on others

Planning

Exceptional: Consistently exceeds expectations

>> Is highly skilled at planning and generating employee buy-in on plans

>> Demonstrates outstanding planning skills on all projects

>> Helps others design and implement plans

>> Is well regarded for planning skills

>> Applies a systems-minded approach as part of the planning process

>> Establishes plans, policies, and practices that improve performance and productivity

>> Creates contingent strategies that can be implemented when situations require plans to be altered or refined

>> Establishes realistic plans

>> Is typically well ahead of plan when it comes to progress and performance

>> Establishes plans for success and then effectively implements them

>> Is equally skilled at long-term and short-term planning

>> Includes other employees as part of the planning process

Excellent: Frequently exceeds expectations

>> Establishes usable, realistic, and highly effective plans

>> Creates plans that are down-to-earth and workable

>> Sets a standard for planning that many others strive to follow

>> Effectively communicates plans to all who need to know

>> Makes plans, but is never overwhelmed by them

>> Makes excellent use of technology to establish and communicate plans

Fully competent: Meets expectations

>> Stays on plan and helps others to do the same

>> Monitors plans and progress at each step and phase of a given project

>> Creates plans that are thorough without being cumbersome

>> Develops plans and strategies, but never loses sight of the goals

>> Lets others know when plans need to be changed or adjusted

>> Supports plans with all the necessary documentation

>> Leaves very little to chance

Marginal: Occasionally fails to meet expectations

>> Creates plans that are so detailed that they stifle other employees

>> Tends to make plans at the last minute, often leading to inadequate planning and projects falling behind

>> Establishes unrealistic plans

>> Plans for the expected outcome, without adequate consideration for the unexpected

>> Makes derogatory comments about the planning process

>> Waits for problems, instead of anticipating them

>> Waits until the last minute to determine the necessary resources, which by then are often unavailable

>> Shows minimal interest in planning

Unsatisfactory: Consistently fails to meet expectations

>> Leaves everything to chance

>> Does not see the need for extensive planning on complex projects

>> Refuses to use project management software

>> Establishes unworkable plans

>> Creates plans that are skimpy and unusable

>> Regards planning as a waste of time

>> Takes a wait-and-see approach on every project

>> Has been responsible for a number of projects that fell short because of a lack of planning

>> Relies on plans that are out of date

>> Believes that there's no need to plan

>> Ignores the established plans

>> Commits to formulate plans, but then does nothing

Setting and Adhering to Schedules

Exceptional: Consistently exceeds expectations

>> Uses state-of-the-art scheduling systems and technology

>> Maintains the appropriate level of detail when scheduling

>> Has a clear understanding of the projects and the players, which leads to highly effective scheduling

>> Consistently runs ahead of schedule

>> Collaborates with team to establish and adhere to schedules

>> Creates schedules that include back-up plans to deal with the unexpected

>> Solicits employee input when establishing schedules

>> Regularly communicates scheduling updates, adjustments, and realignments

>> Carefully balances the needs of the employees with the needs of the company

>> Is meticulous in establishing schedules

Excellent: Frequently exceeds expectations

>> Regularly follows up to be sure that work is being performed on schedule

>> Sets schedules that lead to timely delivery of high-quality work

>> Establishes schedules that are clear, logical, and reasonable

>> Builds employee motivation and commitment to stay on schedule

>> Helps employees get back on schedule if they're running behind

>> Creates outstanding scheduling based on outstanding planning

>> Operates on schedule or ahead of schedule

Fully competent: Meets expectations

>> Consistently upgrades scheduling skills

>> Creates realistic schedules

>> Keeps the team on schedule through highly effective communication, collaboration, and follow-up

>> Develops the scheduling skills of other employees

>> Provides regular status updates and support

>> Demonstrates flexibility, agility, and guidance when unplanned events interfere with progress

Marginal: Occasionally fails to meet expectations

>> Waits for others to do the scheduling

>> Sets unworkable schedules

>> Schedules at the last minute

>> Sets schedules, but fails to track progress along the way

>> Frequently changes the schedule, often without communicating with others

>> Uses antiquated scheduling practices

>> Confines scheduling to scraps of paper

>> Has taken no steps to upgrade scheduling skills

>> Regards schedules as loose guidelines

>> Has difficulties staying on schedule

>> Utilizes overly rigid scheduling practices

Unsatisfactory: Consistently fails to meet expectations

>> Is inflexible with scheduling

>> Sets schedules at the last minute, if at all

>> Establishes schedules, and then disregards them

>> Shows no interest in scheduling software

- » Is regularly behind schedule and demonstrates minimal concern when this occurs
- » Has shown no inclination or desire to complete a project ahead of schedule
- » Generates issues and problems with other employees and departments by paying inadequate attention to schedules
- » Creates schedules that are too vague to be useful
- » Sets schedules that appear to be random

Chapter **12**

The Best Phrases for Quality and Quantity of Work

Two additional core components that are central to successful performance are the quality and quantity of each employee's work. At the same time, success in these two areas is highly influenced by performance in several related areas, all of which warrant inclusion in this part of the performance appraisal process.

This means it's important to focus written comments not only on the actual quality and quantity of work produced by each employee, but also on the related behaviors and actions that contribute directly to the measurable outcomes in these areas, especially in terms of proficiencies associated with such factors as accuracy of work, goal attainment, setting priorities, and time management.

This is accomplished by using phrases that encourage employees to keep up the solid work in any of the areas in which they have demonstrated solid skills, while also incorporating phrases that inform, encourage, and support employees regarding the areas in which such performance has fallen short. This chapter focuses on the quality and quantity of each employee's work through this broader lens and provides a full spectrum of phrases regarding performance in this critical area.

Accuracy

Exceptional: Consistently exceeds expectations

>> Sets and maintains the highest standards for accuracy in all projects and assignments

>> Produces consistently error-free work

>> Handles and completes projects that are 100 percent accurate, reliable, and verifiable

>> Has zero tolerance for mistakes or sloppy work

Excellent: Frequently exceeds expectations

>> Maintains an ongoing focus on accuracy and clarity

>> Finds and corrects errors prior to submission of any work

>> Emphasizes accuracy to others and helps them when needed

>> Checks and rechecks work for accuracy

Fully competent: Meets expectations

>> Keeps accuracy in mind on all projects from start to finish

>> Expects and maintains accuracy in all aspects of the job

>> Keeps detailed and accurate records

>> Saves time by making sure that work is correct and accurate upon completion

Marginal: Occasionally fails to meet expectations

>> Does not spend sufficient time reviewing work prior to submitting it
>> Produces documentation that is not consistently reliable
>> Is overly tolerant of errors
>> Frequently produces unreliable reports, analyses, and summaries
>> Tends to overlook specifications, details, and documentation

Unsatisfactory: Consistently fails to meet expectations

>> Produces work that cannot be relied upon
>> Provides completed work that needs to be thoroughly reviewed
>> Has made errors that have led to significant problems
>> Rushes through work and ends up with numerous mistakes and omissions
>> Believes that cleaning up work and making it more accurate is a waste of time

Detail-Mindedness

Exceptional: Consistently exceeds expectations

>> Consistently covers all of the significant details
>> Demonstrates thoroughness, completeness, and accuracy on all work
>> Energizes others to be more thorough and careful
>> Catches critical details missed by others
>> Meticulously manages every key detail

- » Manages the details without being managed by them
- » Possesses uncanny insight into the role and relevance of every detail
- » Can discuss details with anyone at any level
- » Remains unsatisfied until all of the relevant details are identified, analyzed, and correctly utilized
- » Accurately analyzes and prioritizes details

Excellent: Frequently exceeds expectations

- » Has an excellent eye for detail
- » Regards the term *minor detail* as an oxymoron, but never gets mired in such details
- » Keeps details in perspective
- » Can get down to a microscopic level if needed
- » Quickly notices when key details are overlooked
- » Digs into the details
- » Has detailed knowledge that is greatly valued by others
- » Supports conclusions with appropriate details
- » Is uncomfortable when details are lacking or treated casually

Fully competent: Meets expectations

- » Includes all relevant details
- » Discerns relevant from irrelevant details
- » Sweats the small stuff
- » Makes sense of masses of detail and generates clarity and focus
- » Steps up to the challenge of handling details
- » Does not miss major or minor details
- » Stays on top of the details at every phase of a given project
- » Is comfortable with the expected level of detail associated with any assignment
- » Pushes extra-hard to handle the details

Marginal: Occasionally fails to meet expectations

>> Has little concern for details
>> Sees the big picture, but overlooks the small picture
>> Leaves the details to others
>> Struggles with details
>> Leaves out points that should be included
>> Randomly omits details
>> Lets the details slide
>> Treats details as unnecessary frills on projects
>> Regards details as a low priority
>> Sees details as an inconvenience
>> Procrastinates when handling details
>> Gets careless with details

Unsatisfactory: Consistently fails to meet expectations

>> Does not get down to details
>> Overlooks essential details
>> Focuses on the minor details and misses the major ones
>> Focuses on the major details and misses most others
>> Tries to bluff when asked about details
>> Omits vital details, but includes insignificant details
>> Regards details as fluff
>> Is easily distracted and sidetracked when working on details
>> Provides details that are sloppy, inaccurate, or incomplete

Meeting Goals

Exceptional: Consistently exceeds expectations

>> Jointly establishes challenging goals and surpasses them

>> Fully understands changing priorities of goals and adjusts accordingly

>> Consistently meets increasingly rigorous performance and development goals

>> Is passionate about meeting goals

>> Gives 110 percent, 100 percent of the time

>> Is the ultimate role model for goal setting and attainment

>> Encourages and guides other employees to surpass their goals

>> Turns obstacles into challenges and then overcomes them

>> Has confidence in being able to meet or exceed challenging goals

>> Is a key source of information about goal setting and goal attainment for employees in many departments

>> Shows high levels of creativity and drive in pursuing performance and development goals

>> Consistently seeks out larger and more challenging goals

>> Demonstrates agility, flexibility, and persistence when encountering unanticipated obstacles while pursing goals

>> Has a passion for goal attainment that spreads across the team

Excellent: Frequently exceeds expectations

>> Can be relied upon to meet or exceed performance and development goals

>> Has a strong goal orientation that is evident in establishing and pursuing goals

>> Will not stop until all the goals are met

- Applies full effort to meet all of the established objectives
- Helps other employees meet their objectives
- Is undaunted by unforeseen disruptions or blockages
- Stays with the plan to reach the established goals, but maintains flexibility to handle the unexpected
- Never loses sight of the target
- Keeps the communication lines open regarding all goal-related matters
- Reaches goals that elude others
- Focuses on high-impact goals, without losing sight of lower-priority goals
- Understands the vision, values, and culture of the company, and develops and pursues goals with them in mind
- Realistically adjusts the priorities of goals as work situations change
- Approaches goals with energy, enthusiasm, drive, and focus

Fully competent: Meets expectations

- Is energized by demanding goals
- Is fully committed to establishing and meeting demanding goals
- Meets both short-term and long-term objectives
- Follows the action plan to achieve goals
- Works around or through obstacles
- Keeps goals in mind throughout the day
- Works diligently to accomplish all the established objectives
- Jointly establishes challenging yet reachable goals
- Is highly motivated to meet every goal
- Is receptive to new and different goals that help the company realize its mission
- Shows initiative and self-direction in setting and pursuing goals
- Clearly explains objectives to others as needed
- Tackles every goal tenaciously

Marginal: Occasionally fails to meet expectations

>> Rarely devotes adequate attention to goals

>> Rushes through the goal-setting process

>> Sets aside the most demanding goals

>> Overlooks the action plan while pursuing goals

>> Devotes questionable effort and energy to meeting goals, while expecting others to meet theirs

>> Spends too much time on second-tier objectives

>> Seeks advice in setting and pursuing goals, but rarely follows it

>> Displays minimal interest, attention, and motivation in establishing and pursuing goals

>> Asks questions about goals and plans, but doesn't always listen

>> Avoids participating in discussions about goals

>> Doesn't place sufficient attention on the company's goals

>> Displays more talk than action when it comes to meeting goals

Unsatisfactory: Consistently fails to meet expectations

>> Fails to meet even the most basic objectives

>> Quickly loses sight of goals

>> Focuses on less-challenging goals and fails to meet them

>> Is easily distracted from goals, rather than attracted to them

>> Has questionable organizational skills, further undermining goal attainment

>> Is overwhelmed by the most basic goals

>> Ignores jointly established and agreed-upon goals

>> Has yet to come up with a truly challenging and productive goal

- » Shows minimal interest and involvement in goal-setting sessions and discussions
- » Fails to fully engage in pursuing objectives
- » Downsizes goals after committing to pursue them as originally designed
- » Puts goals on a back burner and leaves them there
- » Fails to recognize the consequences of missing goals
- » Treats goals as suggestions

Multitasking

Exceptional: Consistently exceeds expectations

- » Deftly carries out several projects simultaneously
- » Is energized by handling multiple assignments
- » Truly enjoys the challenge of multitasking
- » Uses strong organizational skills for multitasking success
- » Understands and prevents issues that can develop with multitasking on highly demanding projects, hence preventing problematic outcomes that can accompany such work
- » Has had multiple successes as a result of multitasking
- » Increases attention and focus to successfully complete several tasks simultaneously
- » Completes the most important tasks and assignments first
- » Actively seeks additional responsibilities
- » Switches seamlessly from one project to another
- » Takes on and completes a wide range of extra work with no loss of quality
- » Is able to effectively manage numerous responsibilities simultaneously
- » Always willing to step up and assume additional work if needed

Excellent: Frequently exceeds expectations

>> Approaches multitasking with multiple skills

>> Can be counted on to say "yes" to additional tasks

>> Maintains excellent focus on all projects

>> Prioritizes work assignments and gets the jobs done

>> Manages time to efficiently complete multiple tasks on schedule

>> Prioritizes work for maximum productivity, output, and results

>> Allocates time effectively to complete a wide range of projects and assignments on time and with excellent quality

>> Is highly regarded and respected for multitasking skills

Fully competent: Meets expectations

>> Readily assumes and completes multiple assignments

>> Regards multitasking as part of the job

>> Accepts additional assignments without hesitation

>> Will not stop until the work is done and the deadlines are met

>> Realistically adjusts and balances priorities when new work is assigned

>> Allocates time effectively on multiple projects

>> Maintains efficiency across a broad range of responsibilities

>> Regards multitasking as a way to add value to the company

>> Keeps quality in mind on all projects and assignments

Marginal: Occasionally fails to meet expectations

>> Has missed deadlines because of questionable multitasking practices

>> Sets sights on the easiest tasks

- >> Agrees to additional assignments, but lets them slide
- >> Jumps from project to project, while completing few
- >> Engages in multitasking, but quality of the work is often marginal
- >> Makes growing numbers of errors as the number of assignments increases
- >> Tends to decline additional work rather than engaging in multitasking

Unsatisfactory: Consistently fails to meet expectations

- >> Is overwhelmed by the expectations of multitasking
- >> Engages in multitasking but does not provide any of the projects with adequate prioritization, attention, or commitment
- >> Inadequately focuses on any single responsibility
- >> Is unable to distinguish major from minor tasks
- >> Stresses out with additional responsibilities
- >> Regards additional tasks as an intrusions and interruptions
- >> Complains when asked to handle additional responsibilities
- >> Can handle only a small number of basic tasks at one time
- >> Looks to others to do the work

Performance Levels

Exceptional: Consistently exceeds expectations

- >> Finds the most effective and productive ways to get the job done
- >> Creates and implements innovative strategies to improve performance

- Directly contributes to performance improvement of fellow employees
- Focuses abundant energy and effort on the job
- Targets efforts for maximum results, and then achieves them
- Is motivated to demonstrate consistently excellent performance
- Demonstrates best practices in virtually all performance areas
- Maintains the highest personal performance standards
- Is clearly outstanding in every measurable area of performance
- Expects and attains excellent results on all projects
- Serves as a highly positive role model in all performance areas
- Took an extraordinarily challenging assignment and turned it into a major success
- Set a new high-water mark on the XYZ project

Excellent: Frequently exceeds expectations

- Comes to work ready to excel on every project
- Sets high personal performance expectations
- Tirelessly pursues goals and generates outstanding outcomes
- Expects and attains high levels of personal performance
- Refuses to settle for status-quo performance
- Does not settle for average performance
- Is energized by the prospect of achieving challenging goals
- Prioritizes work for maximum results
- Has a compelling "can-do" attitude
- Is undaunted by difficult challenges, tough obstacles, or frustrating events
- Plans to succeed and does so

- » Demonstrates excellent resiliency when encountering setbacks
- » Is frequently mentioned by name whenever the topic of outstanding performance comes up
- » Keeps pushing until the desired outcomes are achieved
- » Jump-starts stalled projects
- » Takes great pride not only in meeting goals but in surpassing them

Fully competent: Meets expectations

- » Is open to new strategies to generate greater results
- » Continues to visibly improve personal performance levels
- » Is steadily upgrading every performance area
- » Actively seeks and applies new methods and approaches to improve performance
- » Can be counted on for solid performance
- » Focuses priorities on maximum effectiveness and success
- » Maintains ongoing focus on the main event and is not distracted by secondary issues or matters
- » Takes feedback to heart and strives to improve
- » Focuses on work, not on the clock
- » Is a stable and consistent performer
- » Is very interested in suggestions to build performance and productivity
- » Effectively focuses energy on the job

Marginal: Occasionally fails to meet expectations

- » Is satisfied with current performance, despite the fact that it isn't satisfactory
- » Prefers to slip under the bar instead of leaping over it
- » Can be sidetracked by minor obstacles and challenges
- » Is tolerant of mediocre performance

- >> Regards performance measures as unfair
- >> Has an inflated view of personal output and productivity
- >> Claims that improvements in performance are coming soon, but there have been none to this point
- >> Feels that others are providing inadequate support
- >> Spends more time as a spectator than as a participant
- >> Comes up short on long-term projects
- >> Spends time on low-priority projects
- >> Is primarily interested in matters that have little to do with work
- >> Is rarely around when it's time for heavy lifting
- >> Does C-level work on A-level projects
- >> Misunderstands the priorities of the job

Unsatisfactory: Consistently fails to meet expectations

- >> Blames performance problems on other people
- >> Fails to take responsibility for personal failures
- >> Questionable performance has led to complaints from customers
- >> Has taken no significant action on constructive feedback from management
- >> Has displayed continuously declining performance levels
- >> Talks the performance talk, but does not walk the walk
- >> Has fallen into a habit of substandard performance
- >> Spends more time socializing than working
- >> Shows little interest or motivation in upgrading performance
- >> Places insufficient attention on the high-priority work that needs to be done
- >> Expects others to carry the load
- >> Always seeks the easy way out
- >> Is unwilling to accept feedback and guidance
- >> Steps back when it's time to step up

Productivity

Exceptional: Consistently exceeds expectations

- Produces a remarkable amount of high-quality work
- Inspires others through personal output
- Sets and meets increasingly higher standards for productivity
- Puts the "pro" in *productivity*
- Monitors personal productivity and implements upgrades as needed
- Always seeks opportunities to be even more productive
- Impresses everyone with the quality and quantity of work
- Is productivity minded
- Regards productivity as a top priority
- Generates excellent productivity from others
- Identifies and implements steps and strategies to enhance output
- Is responsible for a major increase in departmental productivity
- Always goes the extra mile to strengthen performance and productivity
- Fully understands the figures behind productivity
- Works hard and works smart
- Streamlines departmental operations for greater output
- Raises the bar for everyone on the team
- Is energized by challenges that would derail others
- Offers outstanding suggestions to increase productivity

Excellent: Frequently exceeds expectations

- Is motivated to be highly productive
- Has steadily increased personal output
- Provides suggestions that enhance productivity

- » Serves as an excellent role model of productive behavior
- » Focuses on people as well as productivity
- » Is productive under less-than-perfect conditions
- » Directly contributes to improving the efficiency, effectiveness, and productivity of other employees
- » Generates and implements creative ideas that lead to improvements in productivity
- » Works directly with others to enhance their productivity
- » Is eager to learn about ways to be more productive
- » Quickly incorporates new knowledge to build productivity
- » Consistently reaches productivity levels that exceed expectations
- » Takes on any task and hits the ground running
- » Took specific actions to increase productivity, ultimately contributing to the success of the XYZ project
- » Is regarded as a productivity guru who fosters productive thinking across the department

Fully competent: Meets expectations

- » Produces an excellent quantity of work that is consistently high quality
- » Helps other members of the team work more productively
- » Shares insight, suggestions, and advice to improve productivity
- » Works with the team to build output
- » Has steadily improved personal productivity
- » Understands how to increase productivity and applies this knowledge to the job
- » Puts in extra hours to reach or exceed the desired results
- » Enhances personal productivity by being well organized
- » Continuously addresses the need to increase productivity
- » Is a storehouse of knowledge regarding productivity and the ways to increase it
- » Does more than talk about productivity

Marginal: Occasionally fails to meet expectations

» Personal productivity levels are often sporadic, inconsistent, and uneven

» Can work hard, but often misdirects attention to matters that are unrelated to productivity

» Productivity suffers due to a lack of adequate focus, energy, and interest

» Tends to set the bar too low

» Does not exert serious or significant effort in carrying out job responsibilities

» Performance frequently falls short in relation to all productivity measures

» Blames productivity problems on others

» Personal performance and productivity suffer as a result of misdirected actions, questionable prioritization, and outmoded processes

» Spends too much time on low-priority tasks

» Works reactively rather than proactively

» Tries to do just enough to get by

» Talks about working productively, but rarely does so

Unsatisfactory: Consistently fails to meet expectations

» Personal productivity is steadily declining

» Is distracted by non-work issues

» Often sidetracked and doesn't focus clearly or directly on the work that needs to be done

» Sets low goals and fails to meet them

» Doesn't regard productivity as a priority

» Sees personal output slipping and does nothing to turn it around

» Interferes with the performance of others

- » Displays disruptive or distracting behaviors
- » Often must rework completed projects and do the same work multiple times to get it right
- » Regards productivity as someone else's concern
- » Takes inappropriate or reckless shortcuts
- » Shows little interest in being more productive
- » Fails to fully engage in projects
- » Disregards suggestions to build productivity

Setting Priorities

Exceptional: Consistently exceeds expectations

- » Understands and resolves A-level matters before B-level and C-level matters
- » Uses sound judgment and insight when rank-ordering projects and tasks
- » Serves as a valuable resource to determine the role and priority of totally different tasks
- » Always knows which projects belong at the top of the list and which play secondary roles
- » Easily and quickly identifies low-priority tasks and handles them appropriately
- » Clarifies priorities for employees at any job level
- » Prevents others from pursuing minor projects that superficially appear to be important
- » Quickly and accurately calibrates project priorities

Excellent: Frequently exceeds expectations

- » Is keenly aware of the subtleties that make one project more important than another
- » Places work priorities over personal priorities

- Effectively adjusts and adapts the workload and priorities to meet workplace demands
- Breaks projects into logical pieces to make sure that top priorities are handled first
- Is able to establish and manage priorities when under pressure
- Tackles high-value projects first
- Targets initial efforts on tasks with the largest payoff
- Uses multitasking to handle lower-priority items

Fully competent: Meets expectations

- Understands priorities and how to establish and manage them
- Discusses priorities when there is confusion
- Is unafraid to ask questions about priorities
- Shifts priorities as needed
- Clarifies and then correctly handles competing priorities
- Is highly aware of priorities and adjusts focus as necessary
- Reviews priorities before starting tasks

Marginal: Occasionally fails to meet expectations

- Confuses priorities with preferences
- Starts working before prioritizing
- Uses inappropriate criteria in determining what to do first
- Leaves major projects until the end
- Frequently argues over priorities
- Decides on priorities and rigidly sticks to them, even when situations call for flexibility, agility, and adjustment
- Regards unessential matters as essential and vice versa
- Lacks insight into the best ways to establish priorities
- Is easily sidetracked by low-value tasks

Unsatisfactory: Consistently fails to meet expectations

>> Ignores the priorities of assigned projects
>> Treats all assignments as having essentially the same priority
>> Places no priority on setting priorities
>> Randomly prioritizes assignments
>> Works on the lowest priorities first
>> Sees only the small picture
>> Spends too much time on low-level priorities and too little time on major priorities
>> Jumps from one project to another with no regard for priorities

Time Management

Exceptional: Consistently exceeds expectations

>> Displays consistently outstanding time management skills on all projects
>> Consistently completes work on time and on target
>> Generates more than an hour's worth of productivity in each hour
>> Is excellent at organizing and prioritizing work to help complete all assignments and tasks on time
>> Helps others manage their time
>> Builds the time-management skills of fellow employees
>> Streamlines tasks and processes for measurably greater efficiencies
>> Has a great sense of time and timing
>> Never misses a deadline
>> Meets deadlines like clockwork

- Creates and implements timesaving strategies without interfering with the quality of the final product
- Consistently makes the best use of time
- Plans the work, and then works the plan
- Has a high degree of expertise in time management, and applies it on every project
- Completes many projects early and all projects on time
- Is sensitive to the time commitments and constraints of others
- Consistently produces on-time, high-quality work
- Knows when and how to delegate

Excellent: Frequently exceeds expectations

- Coordinates projects to meet deadlines
- Develops realistic plans and schedules
- Keeps the entire team on time
- Has a keen sense of what to do and when to do it
- Gives top attention to top priorities
- Manages time instead of being managed by it
- Doesn't procrastinate
- Stays on schedule or ahead of it
- Never loses sight of time constraints
- Is excellent at estimating the time required for projects
- Is punctual in all aspects of the job
- Maintains flexibility to effectively carry out additional tasks
- Completes many projects before the due date
- Has yet to miss a deadline
- Delegates work and follows up as needed

Fully competent: Meets expectations

>> Completes work on time
>> Takes active steps to avoid time-wasting situations
>> Establishes appropriate priorities
>> Develops and adheres to workable schedules
>> Knows what needs to be done and not done
>> Effectively assigns work to others
>> Keeps commitments to get work done
>> Places a premium on planning
>> Keeps projects on schedule
>> Tracks projects carefully
>> Makes productive use of time
>> Follows a proven time-management system
>> Clearly understands and communicates the full range of costs that accompany the misuse of time
>> Makes commitments to deadlines and keeps them
>> Watches the time, not the clock

Marginal: Occasionally fails to meet expectations

>> Treats deadlines as if they are optional
>> Lets second-tier matters interfere with the completion of major projects
>> Rarely completes the assigned tasks on time
>> Constantly feels overwhelmed
>> Works on many assignments that should be delegated
>> Is easily drawn into secondary tasks
>> Is quick to set aside important projects
>> Randomly rank-orders projects
>> Blames others when work runs late
>> Engages in minimal planning when approaching new assignments

- » Is late with major projects but on time with minor ones
- » Surprises others when work is completed on time
- » Occasionally meets deadlines, but frequently with questionable quality

Unsatisfactory: Consistently fails to meet expectations

- » Devotes excessive amounts of time to low-priority tasks
- » Often lets procrastination undercut performance
- » Allows work to pile up, ultimately generating missed timelines and deadlines
- » Typically falls behind from the outset of any given project
- » Has yet to meet a deadline
- » Waits until the last minute on projects large and small
- » Ignores coaching that would help build time management skills
- » Doesn't pay enough attention to the needs of others who are waiting for the work to be completed
- » Consistently fails to make the best use of time
- » Spends too much time crafting excuses
- » Regards time management as a waste of time
- » Is uninterested in time-management tools, training, and software
- » Feels no sense of urgency on any project or assignment
- » Jumps from one project to another with no focus on priorities or deadlines

Working Remotely

Exceptional: Consistently exceeds expectations

- » Consistently maintains high levels of performance, productivity, commitment, and accessibility when working remotely

>> Demonstrates excellent levels of flexibility and responsiveness whenever contacted or needed by other members of the team for updates, help, support, advice, or general communications

>> Carries out work autonomously and successfully while maintaining all necessary contact and communication with key stakeholders whether onsite or remote

>> Handles all aspects of virtual meetings seamlessly, whether as an organizer or attendee

>> Keeps all lines of two-way communication open while working remotely

>> Maintains strong ties to the company and keeps fully abreast of all significant developments related to onsite as well as remote matters

>> Attends onsite meetings whenever needed

>> Demonstrates excellent ability to organize, lead, and facilitate virtual meetings

Excellent: Frequently exceeds expectations

>> Maintains a strong team orientation, sense of affiliation, and collaborative mindset when working remotely

>> Highly competent technically and able to effectively utilize all company digital systems on a remote basis to maintain open communications and carry out individual and team projects successfully

>> Takes extra steps to reach out and re-engage other remote employees who may have become too isolated or removed from the company

>> Joins and contributes to departmental and companywide virtual meetings and programs

>> Directly responsible for introducing several remote work tools that improved the performance, engagement, and success of remote employees

Fully competent: Meets expectations

>> Remotely carries out all job responsibilities with a high degree of diligence, quality, and output

>> Generates ongoing and highly effective teamwork and mutual support with other remote employees as well as with onsite employees

>> Is always well-prepared, thorough, and organized in remote meetings with other members of the team

>> Demonstrates patience, understanding, and support when working with remote employees who are not as proficient in using the technology associated with offsite work

Marginal: Occasionally fails to meet expectations

>> Occasionally unavailable without notice when contacted and needed by other employees during normal business hours

>> Can be disruptive and distracting during virtual meetings due to inadequate familiarly and understanding of virtual meeting platforms and protocols

>> Does not consistently pay attention in virtual meetings and brings up questions and topics that have already been addressed

>> Tends to go into excessive detail whenever making a comment or answering a question during virtual meetings, taking valuable time away from other issues that need coverage

Unsatisfactory: Consistently fails to meet expectations

>> Performance, productivity, output, and results have fallen below par while working remotely

>> Often calendars meetings with other employees and then fails to attend with no advance notice or explanation

>> Frequently turns off the camera function during virtual meetings and essentially disappears, accompanied by a failure to respond when addressed by other attendees

>> Rarely available when working remotely and frequently misses meetings and calls

>> Often ignores protocol in online meetings by joining late, interrupting and talking over others, taking phone calls and doing so without muting, using inappropriate backgrounds, and leaving early without asking or telling anyone

>> Complains, pushes back, and occasionally refuses to come to the office for infrequent but important company or departmental meetings

Chapter **13**
The Best Phrases for Self-Development and Growth

nother key area that contributes directly to employee performance and success on the job, as well as to satisfaction and motivation, is focused on self-development and growth. In light of the significance of these opportunities to so many of today's employees, it's particularly important to include targeted phrases that provide employees with clear information regarding the effectiveness of their actions and behaviors related to their development — specifically in terms of those that were successful and productive as well as those that need improvement.

When structured in this way, your written comments in this area establish a framework that is designed to meet two central objectives. First, these comments help employees experience greater personal growth by better understanding their strengths and areas in need of improvement. Second and equally important, as employees build their skills in these areas, the outcome will not only lead to increased personal growth, but will also lead to increased levels of satisfaction, performance, and productivity as a result of applying new skills, competencies, and proficiencies to the job.

For your feedback regarding employee growth and self-development to generate these positive outcomes, it's important to use phrases that focus on the key underlying and contributory factors, and this includes such topics as enhancing expertise, pursuing additional training, career planning, and building problem-solving skills. An important common thread in this area is that employers as well as employees seek growth and development, and the phrases that are provided in this chapter help both meet this goal.

Adding Value

Exceptional: Consistently exceeds expectations

>> Makes measurable contributions that clearly and consistently exceed expectations

>> Has performed far beyond performance standards and taken actions that have clearly strengthened the company

>> Provides guidance that raises the competence, performance, and output of other employees

>> Has held costs constant while measurably improving personal output as well as the output of other employees

>> Has played a central role in building the effectiveness, productivity, and value of the team through the application of state-of-the-art knowledge and expertise

>> Is able to integrate information from a vast array of sources and then apply highly productive strategies and actions

>> Is clearly an outstanding company asset whose value is steadily increasing

>> Continues to keep personal knowledge base at expert levels

>> Is widely regarded as one of the company's most valuable resources

Excellent: Frequently exceeds expectations

» Is sought out by employees in many departments for advice and guidance on a wide range of business and operational matters

» Possesses a mix of skills and insights that are a major asset for the department and the company at large

» Builds the skills and productivity of other employees

» Has skills that are unique to the department and central to its success

» Has built expertise in areas that directly impact the bottom line

» Takes a wide range of actions that enhance the reputation of the company

» Has played a key role in attracting several outstanding individuals to the company as a result of personal expertise and stature in the industry

» Has made efforts that have contributed to a significant drop in the unit cost of each item

» Generates maximum productivity from company resources

» Is always willing and able to successfully assume and carry out additional projects

» Raises the quality of the decisions that are made in meetings

Fully competent: Meets expectations

» Has a direct and positive impact on the quantity and quality of other employees' work by modeling excellent performance as well as by providing direct help and support when needed

» Continues to make increasingly valuable suggestions

» Develops and applies additional skills that further increase personal and departmental productivity

» Takes steps to build knowledge, skills, and abilities that directly lead to increases in the quality and quantity of work

- Brings a continuously expanding set of unique skills that enhance performance and productivity in the department
- Continues to expand technology skills in areas that are valued by the company
- Has a proactive and productive mindset
- Uses solid planning skills to complete work on time and prevent crises and crunches along the way
- Strives to exceed expectations on all projects

Marginal: Occasionally fails to meet expectations

- Carries out the basics of the job and nothing more
- Contributes to the company in ways that tend to be minimal and of slight value at best
- Has demonstrated decreasing levels of personal productivity and contributions to the company
- Sets goals to increase personal value to the company, but then sets them aside
- Rarely pursues rigorous goals that would truly add value to the company
- Doesn't exert sufficient energy or effort to truly increase personal value to the company
- Claims to add more value to the company than is actually the case
- Focuses energy in areas of minimal importance

Unsatisfactory: Consistently fails to meet expectations

- Has taken no meaningful steps to enhance skills and add value to the company
- Has taken actions that decrease the value of the company
- Takes actions without considering the value that they may add to or subtract from the company

- Demonstrates no significant value-added behaviors due in great part to a lack of interest in self-development and upskilling
- Acts in ways that discourage or diminish value-added behaviors of other employees
- Does the minimum amount of work, leading to the minimum amount of added value
- Makes negative comments about the company
- Shows a lack of concern regarding the impact that personal actions can have on the company's reputation and goodwill
- Rejects all opportunities to assume additional responsibilities
- Fails to seize opportunities to develop skills that would increase personal value to the company

Building Problem-Solving Skills

Exceptional: Consistently exceeds expectations

- Has established and surpassed goals that focus on improving problem-solving skills
- Takes numerous independent steps to strengthen problem-solving skills such as through readings, seminars, and podcasts
- Further enhances personal problem-solving skills by helping other employees build such skills
- Seeks and seizes opportunities to strengthen problem-solving skills
- Models problem-solving skills on those of other highly effective problem-solvers in the company
- Has outstanding problem-solving skills and continues to take steps to make them even stronger
- Has actively pursued training programs that specifically focus on enhanced problem-solving

Excellent: Frequently exceeds expectations

>> Devotes extra time, energy, and effort to building problem-solving skills

>> Is open to new ideas and suggestions to further enhance problem-solving

>> Clearly demonstrated excellent problem-solving skills in handling the XYZ project

>> Has made and kept commitments to upgrade problem-solving skills

>> Has transformed previously questionable problem-solving skills into significant strengths

>> Continues to attend educational programs that focus on strengthening problem-solving abilities

Fully competent: Meets expectations

>> Is steadily showing improvement in solving problems

>> Has solid problem-solving abilities that are continuing to develop

>> Is highly interested in feedback from others to help build problem-solving skills

>> Applies suggestions and strategies from others to help strengthen problem-solving abilities

>> Has demonstrated a marked improvement in problem-solving skills throughout this evaluation period

>> Seeks and accepts feedback on problem-solving skills

Marginal: Occasionally fails to meet expectations

>> Agrees to take steps to improve problem-solving ability, but fails to do so

>> Is satisfied with current problem-solving skills, even though they have consistently fallen short

- Uses problem-solving strategies that no longer apply to workplace issues
- Doesn't take advantage of company-sponsored programs to build problem-solving skills
- Is unresponsive to offers of help from fellow employees who have excellent mentoring skills in several areas including problem-solving

Unsatisfactory: Consistently fails to meet expectations

- Has taken no steps to upgrade problem-solving skills
- Is unwilling to listen to feedback to upgrade problem-solving abilities
- Has shown no improvement in problem-solving skills in spite of feedback and coaching in this area
- Has shown a decline in problem-solving abilities
- Actively avoids opportunities to bolster problem-solving skills
- Has caused smaller issues to turn into major problems as a result of a refusal to build and apply problem-solving skills
- Refuses to acknowledge the problems that have been caused by failing to upgrade current problem-solving skills

Capitalizing on Opportunities to Learn

Exceptional: Consistently exceeds expectations

- Seeks out and attends seminars, podcasts, classes, and training programs on work-related topics
- Is an avid reader of business magazines and journals
- Has outstanding observation skills and absorbs details and nuances that others are likely to miss
- Is consistently acquiring new skills and building existing skills

- » Regards the acquisition of knowledge and building personal expertise as very high priorities
- » Quickly reaches a high level of expertise in new areas
- » Brings a high degree of intellectual curiosity to the job
- » Genuinely enjoys working in challenging situations that require major amounts of learning and upskilling
- » Is highly motivated to maintain cutting-edge expertise

Excellent: Frequently exceeds expectations

- » Puts in extra hours to build skills and abilities
- » Frequently engages in informal discussions that enhance learning
- » Seeks feedback from others in order to continue as well as enhance the learning process
- » Recognizes knowledge gaps and takes active steps to fill them
- » Turns the most challenging work situations into learning opportunities
- » Is always in a learning mode
- » Has continued to expand expertise across a broad range of areas that apply to the job
- » Enjoys work situations in which successful performance requires additional learning and new skills
- » Has positively influenced many others by actively demonstrating a high degree of enthusiasm toward learning
- » Consistently has a fast start-up on highly difficult projects by approaching them with a mindset that is actively focused on learning

Fully competent: Meets expectations

- » Regards performance appraisals and continuous feedback as learning opportunities
- » Takes advantage of the company's mentoring program

- » Strives to actively learn from mistakes
- » Is always taking steps to gain more than a superficial understanding of new information that is relevant to the job
- » Is currently pursuing additional business-related courses at the undergraduate or graduate level
- » Completed all courses in a formal educational program and received the desired certification
- » Asks questions whenever confused or in need of more information or clarification
- » Makes good use of the company's educational benefits
- » Actively participates in the company's educational programs

Marginal: Occasionally fails to meet expectations

- » Rarely takes advantage of the company's educational programs and benefits
- » Begrudgingly attends required educational programs and sessions
- » Infrequently attends in-house or virtual educational sessions or programs
- » Shows no interest in accessing the learning resources available at or through the company
- » Attends educational programs but doesn't actively engage in them
- » Is a vocal critic of company training programs, in spite of rarely attending any of them
- » Doesn't take the time to review the written documentation and supportive information that accompanies new projects
- » Hasn't applied any of the information, techniques, or strategies that were emphasized in company-sponsored training programs
- » Rarely devotes enough time to fully mastering new skills that are required for successful project completion
- » Enters learning programs with the expectation that they offer nothing to be learned — and that expectation is typically fulfilled

- Rarely shows enough interest to ask questions
- Fails to take advantage of widespread learning opportunities that are part of many company assignments and projects

Unsatisfactory: Consistently fails to meet expectations

- Takes no active steps to enhance expertise
- Is invited to many training programs but refuses to attend
- Rejects numerous virtual and onsite educational opportunities
- Regards additional education as unnecessary
- Doesn't accept any personal responsibility for self-development, growth, or education
- Doesn't seek educational opportunities and rejects those that the company offers
- Takes no independent action to pursue learning and upskilling opportunities
- Immediately dismisses information on new techniques, strategies, or approaches
- Continues to rely on outmoded skills and outdated information, even after receiving specific coaching on newer approaches
- Avoids assignments and projects that require the acquisition of new knowledge or skills
- Prefers to do work the old way rather than learning new technologies, processes, or procedures

Engaging in Career Planning

Exceptional: Consistently exceeds expectations

- Is taking all the right steps to meet career goals

- » Applies a strong goal orientation to the career planning process
- » Monitors career plans and makes appropriate adjustments and upgrades
- » Continues to set increasingly higher career goals
- » Accompanies all career goals with solid career planning
- » Has set planning and goals to remain on a fast career track
- » Combines career goals with the energy, drive, and focus to meet them
- » Has built a strong team to facilitate personal advancement as well as increase the opportunities and options for others
- » Adapts career plans appropriately to capitalize on unforeseen opportunities
- » Works collaboratively with management to identify and implement personal career goals and the steps and strategies to achieve them

Excellent: Frequently exceeds expectations

- » Is highly interested in and receptive to career guidance
- » Builds on the career coaching, guidance, and advice that is provided by management
- » Monitors career plans and progress and takes active steps to stay on course
- » Obtains appropriate training and upskilling required for short-term and long-term career goals
- » Treats career goals as seriously as performance goals and works equally diligently to meet them
- » Has serious career goals but never loses sight of the jointly established and agreed-upon performance goals
- » Takes courses and attends seminars to generate additional guidance for self-development and career management
- » Does a good deal of reading in the area of career planning
- » Is serious, thorough, and committed when it comes to career planning

Fully competent: Meets expectations

>> Has clear career plans and goals and takes productive steps to further clarify and pursue them

>> Continues to meet near-term career goals

>> Establishes career plans but does not over-plan

>> Works collaboratively with management to establish and follow career plans

>> Jointly establishes challenging yet realistic career goals and the plans that are needed to pursue them

>> Is undeterred by career setbacks or disappointments

>> Takes advantage of the career-building opportunities available within the company

>> Utilizes the company's resources, support, and advice as key elements in career planning

>> Has learned a great deal in the process of jointly establishing career goals and has used this experience as a basis to help other employees in career planning and goal setting

>> Attends career planning seminars and shares new knowledge, information, and strategies with other employees

Marginal: Occasionally fails to meet expectations

>> Has done no serious career planning

>> Takes a reactive mode when it comes to career planning

>> Sets career goals but lacks career plans

>> Is locked into narrow career plans and instantly rejects potentially fulfilling opportunities

>> Has career plans, but they lack specificity

>> Has set career goals without adequate consideration of the planning required to meet them

>> Puts career plans ahead of performance plans

>> Fails to track the progress that is or is not being made in the pursuit of career goals

>> Focuses more on the format than the content of a career plan

>> Has established a career direction but no career goals

>> Talks a great deal about the importance of career planning, but has taken no significant action in this area

>> Has set career goals but ignores opportunities to move closer to them

>> Takes advantage of none of the company's resources to help develop and solidify a career plan

>> Attends career planning sessions but doesn't apply any of the training

Unsatisfactory: Consistently fails to meet expectations

>> Ignores career plans after they have been established

>> Devotes no time to career planning

>> Assumes no personal responsibility for setting career plans or goals

>> Takes no steps to build knowledge, skills, and abilities required for the next step in the career path

>> Has unrealistic career goals and equally unrealistic career plans

>> Has not engaged in career planning in the past and demonstrates no interest in doing so now

>> Has set career goals but takes steps that directly contradict them

>> Has intentionally missed individual and group meetings to discuss career goals and planning

>> Regards career planning as someone else's responsibility

>> Instantly rejects any advice or coaching that deals with careers

>> Takes no initiative in seeking the training or coaching that would help in the career planning process

>> Expresses regret about career options but takes no action to do anything about them

>> Has landed in the current position without any career planning and has no interest in starting the planning process now

Enhancing Expertise

Exceptional: Consistently exceeds expectations

>> Is consistently among the first to learn new strategies and technologies

>> Actively pursues a broad range of opportunities to build overall expertise

>> Consistently seeks opportunities to learn, both on and off the job

>> Anticipates new business trends and takes steps to build personal knowledge base to capitalize on them

>> Sets challenging goals regarding the acquisition of new knowledge and then takes serious steps to surpass them

>> Reads a vast array of books, business journals, and magazines, and also attends classes, courses, and podcasts, all in an effort to continue to learn, grow, and contribute

Excellent: Frequently exceeds expectations

>> Places a great deal of emphasis on building a personal knowledge base in areas that directly and indirectly enhance job-related skills, abilities, and performance

>> Takes ongoing steps to build a personal knowledge base as well as the knowledge bases of fellow employees

>> Maintains a continuously widening knowledge base

>> Serves as an excellent model for other employees by taking ongoing steps to enhance learning and skill acquisition

>> Maintains an open mind when dealing with information that challenges the current state of knowledge

>> Has taken active and ongoing steps to remain at the cutting-edge of the field

>> Uses ongoing learning as a key element in introducing practices that generate improvements in the department and company at large

Fully competent: Meets expectations

>> Made and kept a commitment to build a broader and deeper knowledge base

>> Frequently attends programs, classes, and seminars to continuously enhance expertise and overall knowledge

>> Uses a wide range of online and offline resources to develop a deeper and wider knowledge base

>> Takes ongoing proactive steps to continue to build a personal knowledge base

>> Wisely uses company resources to continue to build depth and breadth of knowledge and expertise

>> Has continued to expand learning and knowledge base throughout the evaluation period

Marginal: Occasionally fails to meet expectations

>> Sets development goals that are focused on building a wider knowledge base, but fails to meet them

>> Has a base of knowledge that has fallen out of date with the passage of time

>> Continually uses outmoded strategies, highlighting a lack of interest in building a wider knowledge base

>> Waits for others to present opportunities that contribute to knowledge base expansion, but then takes no action to pursue them

>> Demonstrates minimal initiative when it comes to building a broader knowledge base

>> Is uninterested in learning about new strategies and technologies that differ from current practices

Unsatisfactory: Consistently fails to meet expectations

>> Has taken no productive steps to build a wider or deeper knowledge base

>> Actively resists new information that contradicts current practices or ways of thinking

>> Ignores company-sponsored and recommended opportunities that focus on building a wider and deeper knowledge base

>> Ignores suggestions to take specific courses and classes that are essential for knowledge base expansion

>> Has established neither goals nor plans that focus on knowledge base expansion or enhancement

Participating in Training and Upskilling

Exceptional: Consistently exceeds expectations

>> Regards training as a high personal priority

>> Devotes a high degree of energy and effort to getting the most out of all training programs and sessions, whether onsite or virtual

>> Offers insightful comments during and following training sessions that enhance and facilitate learning

>> Is highly enthusiastic about training programs and opportunities

>> Builds a great deal of interest in training across the department

>> Attends training sessions and then informally trains others

>> Actively participates in training programs

Excellent: Frequently exceeds expectations

>> Takes all training seriously
>> Shows immediate interest in new topics for training and upskilling
>> Asks excellent questions and listens carefully to the answers
>> Adjusts easily and quickly to new training technologies
>> Is a valuable participant in all training programs and sessions
>> Quickly applies new knowledge to the job
>> Continues to review training materials after the sessions have ended

Fully competent: Meets expectations

>> Genuinely enjoys the learning process
>> Is an active and eager learner
>> Is never late to training sessions
>> Completes all required preparation prior to training sessions
>> Pays careful attention throughout the training process
>> Is highly appreciative of the training that is provided
>> Strives to apply new skills, processes, and techniques that were covered in training programs

Marginal: Occasionally fails to meet expectations

>> Comes up with numerous excuses to avoid training
>> Rarely participates in discussions during training sessions
>> Is late to most training sessions
>> Attends training sessions but fails to pay attention
>> Claims that additional training isn't needed, although current performance and productivity contradict this assertion
>> Has an inflated view of personal skills and expertise
>> Signs up for training programs but rarely attends

Unsatisfactory: Consistently fails to meet expectations

>> Shows no interest in additional training
>> Is quick to criticize the training that is provided
>> Misses training sessions
>> Engages in disruptive behaviors during training sessions
>> Fails to apply new information to the job
>> Insists on engaging in outdated practices, instead of applying new practices in which training has been provided
>> Can display disruptive and distracting behaviors during training sessions
>> Makes derogatory comments during and about training sessions
>> Fails to attend required classes

Pursuing Development Goals

Exceptional: Consistently exceeds expectations

>> Has a clear vision of the future in terms of career, growth, and development, and works diligently to make it a reality
>> Has a strong and clear focus on personal development goals, and has inspired fellow employees to follow suit
>> Demonstrates a full and unwavering commitment to reach development goals
>> Takes responsibility for personal growth and development
>> Consistently meets development objectives and then collaboratively sets new ones that are even more challenging
>> Jointly establishes clear and challenging short-term and long-term development goals that have led to increased skills, expertise, and opportunities

» Demonstrates high levels of initiative and energy in pursuing development goals, especially in terms of education and upskilling

Excellent: Frequently exceeds expectations

» Effectively collaborates in establishing clear, specific, and measurable development goals

» Continues to pursue and reach development goals, and this has led to markedly improved performance

» Collaboratively sets development goals that are accompanied by well-designed action plans

» Devotes major effort to reach and exceed development goals

» Is able to meet development goals while also meeting performance goals

» Continues to set increasingly challenging and growth-oriented development goals

» Shows confidence, energy, and drive in pursuing development goals

Fully competent: Meets expectations

» Takes all development goals seriously and works diligently to reach them

» Listens carefully to advice, suggestions, and guidance regarding development goals and the best strategies to meet them

» Jointly establishes and pursues challenging yet realistic development goals that include skills, education, and career

» Has a positive and optimistic attitude toward collaboratively establishing development goals and the path to meet them

» Seeks out and obtains the training, education, and guidance that are needed to achieve development goals

>> Helps other employees in determining, pursuing, and achieving their development goals

>> Shows a high degree of tenacity, agility, and resiliency in pursuing development goals

Marginal: Occasionally fails to meet expectations

>> Commits to development goals but places minimal focus and attention on actually reaching them

>> Quickly loses interest in jointly established development goals

>> Ignores action plans, dates, deadlines, and priorities that accompany development goals

>> Only shows interest in unchallenging development goals

>> Hasn't made a serious commitment to meeting development goals

>> Spends considerable time coming up with reasons and rationalizations why development goals weren't met, rather than focusing the same energy on pursuing these goals

>> Demonstrates very little persistence in the pursuit of development goals

Unsatisfactory: Consistently fails to meet expectations

>> Shows no interest or motivation regarding development goals and the enhancement of personal skills, abilities, and expertise

>> Accepts no responsibility for setting development goals

>> Has had the same development goals for an extended period of time and has failed to meet any of them

>> Gives up easily in the pursuit of development goals

>> Jumps from one development goal to another, but reaches none

>> Pursues development goals at the expense of performance goals

Responding to Performance Appraisals and Coaching

Exceptional: Consistently exceeds expectations

» Fully commits to following specific development plans to make improvements noted in performance appraisals

» Accepts constructive feedback positively and is highly oriented toward making improvements in the areas that were discussed

» Has a positive attitude toward feedback and feedforward and takes immediate corrective action based on the coaching that is provided

» Actively seeks coaching and uses it wisely

» Carefully considers every point in performance appraisals and takes specific steps to deal with each

Excellent: Frequently exceeds expectations

» Appreciates coaching and acts on the feedback that is provided

» Uses the feedback and guidance from performance appraisals and coaching to upgrade specific performance and skill levels

» Has been taking highly effective steps to improve performance in areas that were noted during the most recent period and in the last performance appraisal

» Accepts feedback in performance appraisals with an open mind and readiness to take action

» Has measurably improved skills and personal productivity by focusing on the coaching that has been provided

Fully competent: Meets expectations

>> Takes performance appraisal feedback seriously and has made many improvements based on it

>> Pays careful attention to coaching and feedback and has upgraded performance as a result

>> Takes productive steps to act on the feedback and coaching provided during the appraisal process and upgrade performance in the areas that were noted as needing improvement

>> Has taken specific actions as a result of coaching and the most recent performance appraisal, and this has led to marked improvements in performance

>> Is highly receptive to coaching and managerial feedback

Marginal: Occasionally fails to meet expectations

>> Reacts negatively and defensively to performance-related feedback and coaching

>> Appears to listen to coaching and feedback in the performance appraisals, but then makes no changes in behavior

>> Needs frequent prodding before taking any action on the feedback provided in performance appraisals

>> Makes a few quick and easy changes after being coached but ignores the larger issues

>> Asks no questions during the performance appraisal and coaching sessions, and then heads off in the wrong direction

>> Immediately reacts to constructive feedback with denial

>> Commits to taking corrective action after performance appraisals, but then fails to do so

>> Takes some corrective actions immediately after performance appraisals, but then slides back to questionable performance levels

Unsatisfactory: Consistently fails to meet expectations

>> Doesn't listen to any feedback, coaching, or guidance

>> Instantly disagrees with and ignores feedback that is provided in performance appraisals

>> Has taken no action based on the feedback and guidance that has been provided during the current period

>> Has received coaching on the same issue several times and has yet to show any signs of improvement

>> Spends more time arguing than listening in performance appraisal sessions

>> Ignores appointments for coaching sessions

>> Is unreceptive to constructive feedback or coaching

The Part of Tens

Chapter **14**

The Top Ten Words to Include in a Performance Appraisal

As you determine the specific words you'd like to use in providing your employees with feedback and feedforward as part of the performance appraisal process, remember that there is more to words than their definitions. Specifically, many words have an inherent emotional charge that generates conscious as well as unconscious reactions, causing some words to resonate on a deeper and more impactful level than others.

With this in mind, one of the most effective ways to enhance the impact of the appraisals you provide is to select words that have a strong positive emotional charge. For example, one of the positively charged words that is used in this section is *achievement*. Although a common synonym is *feat*, think carefully about both these words and ask yourself which one is more personally meaningful and inspirational for you. Also, you may notice that the word *achievement* has the verb *achieve* embedded in it, practically encouraging you to take action.

This chapter provides you with ten positively charged words that can help take the performance appraisals that you provide to a higher level — and ideally have a similar impact on your employees' performance as well.

Achievement

Sensing achievement at work has been consistently found to be a major source of employee motivation. When employees are specifically recognized for their achievements large and small, their feelings of self-worth, self-satisfaction, and self-confidence all increase. Although these feelings can also be generated internally through the completion of particularly challenging projects or assignments, the positive impact associated with an achievement is multiplied and fortified when employees hear the word *achievement* from their manager.

In addition to the satisfaction that employees experience through recognition for their achievements, a related positive outcome is that these employees are then increasingly motivated and energized to engage in similar types of achievement-oriented behaviors in the future. In addition, as a result of the positive reinforcement and feedback related to their achievements, employees are also likely to experience an increase in their overall levels of engagement and commitment.

By continuing to act in ways that generate significant achievements and recognition, these employees are also likely to serve as influential role models for other members of their team. As they do so, they're likely to enhance the performance of these other employees and generate outcomes that are beneficial to them as individuals, as well as outcomes that are beneficial to the department and company at large.

Advancement

Advancement within the company is another key source of motivation for employees at virtually all job levels. Moving up the company ladder to increasingly important positions is not merely a goal for many employees, but often a key driver that energizes them to continue to work hard, take on additional responsibilities, and continue their learning and upskilling.

When you include the word *advancement* in feedback and feedforward to your employees, regardless of the exact message that you present, you're letting them know that you're thinking positively about them in terms of their potential and promotability going forward. This is typically perceived by employees as a vote of confidence, a reaction that further builds their motivation, commitment, and engagement.

When the word *advancement* is left out of a performance appraisal, employees may think that they've been excluded from any job promotions. By identifying and reinforcing behaviors and actions that can open the door to possible advancement, you set the stage for your employees to continue to do their best, meet their performance and development goals, and to excel. By fostering and supporting this type of mindset among your employees, you also help to further fortify the bench strength of the company, facilitate succession planning, and reinforce a supportive, collaborative, equitable, ethical, and engaging company climate and culture.

Career

Using the word *career* in the performance appraisal process can generate many positive outcomes, as it sends a clear message to your employees that you regard them as having more than a job. With *career* included as part of your feedback and feedforward, you're letting your employees know that you regard them as valuable resources at the present time and also as high-potential assets for the future.

In light of the high degree of interest that many of today's employees have in career development, the use of the word *career* not only shows the company's interest in the employees on a longer-term basis, but also encourages employees to widen their own thinking in terms of their career interests and objectives. This is likely to lead to significantly increased focus on learning, development, and upskilling, again strengthening the team and generating more promotable employees.

As your employees sense that the company is looking at them through a wider lens that includes today and tomorrow, they're also likely to focus on maintaining and enhancing their current levels of performance, productivity, and personal effectiveness in order to demonstrate their readiness for their next career step. By including *career* in the employee appraisals, you send a message of encouragement, support, and positive expectations regarding your employees' current and future performance.

Engagement

The word *engagement* has numerous positive connotations that cover a wide range of employee behaviors and actions, all of which contribute to individual, departmental, and company-wide success. When you include *engagement* in the feedback and feedforward that you provide, your use of this word identifies and emphasizes the value that you place on such performance components as respect and support for the company and its mission, going the extra mile, excellent productivity, solid dedication, and high levels of energy, enthusiasm, commitment, self-development, and collaboration.

By using the word *engagement*, you open the door to identify, recognize, and reinforce a wide range of behaviors that are beneficial to the employee and the company, while also targeting and supporting any related areas in which improvement may be needed. In doing so, you also place your comments in a comforting, familiar, and palatable framework. Rather than having a piece of feedback hang in midair, your use of *engagement* creates a context that makes your feedback and feedforward on any single item within this category clearer and more impactful.

In addition, as employees focus on improving a specific aspect of their engagement, they're also more likely to look beyond that single component and pursue additional ways in which their engagement can be enhanced. As a result, making improvements in any aspect of engagement can also lead to even greater performance across the full range of behaviors in this area.

Ethics

In order to reinforce the importance and centrality that the company places on ethical behavior, in combination with the high degree of interest shared by many of today's employees regarding their desire to work for an ethical employer, another key word for you to include in the performance appraisal process is *ethics*. By using this word, you further communicate and reinforce the company's full commitment to ethical behavior, while also communicating an expectation that employees maintain an unwavering commitment to ethical actions in all aspects of their performance.

As part of the inclusion of *ethics* in this process, it's important to make sure that the word is not used in a vacuum, but rather is tied into specific behaviors that underlie ethics on the job. This means including related feedback and feedforward regarding such factors as fairness, honesty, integrity, diversity, trustworthiness, professionalism, sustainability, and health and wellness.

By focusing on these specific areas, you give your employees additional insight, feedback, and guidance regarding the alignment of their behaviors with the company's mission, goals, and values regarding ethics. This ethical framework also helps employees shape and define many other aspects of their performance on the job, such as in terms of establishing goals, collaborating with others, maintaining high performance standards, continuing their learning and growth, and treating others with openness and respect.

Goals

In light of the central roles played by performance and development goals, it's important to include the word *goals* in the performance appraisal process. The extent to which your employees have met their goals and the key benchmarks associated with them during a given evaluation period are critical indicators of employee success as well as the areas in which their performance needs improvement.

Meaningful goals simultaneously serve several essential purposes that include motivating the employees, aligning the employees' work with the company's mission and objectives, building performance and productivity, and further enhancing the employees' skills, proficiencies, and knowledge base. In this regard, goal attainment provides an array of specific performance-based data that serve as the basis for realistic and relevant feedback and feedforward.

Including *goals* as part of the process is another way of helping your employees further understand the degree of significance that you place on their actions in this area. At the same time, including the word *goals* further demonstrates your solid support behind each employee's performance, success, and development.

Growth

With numerous employees expressing a high degree of interest in learning, upskilling, and development, the word *growth* should also be included as part of your performance appraisals. Many of today's employees specifically want to increase their knowledge base, work-related skills and proficiencies, and overall effectiveness on the job, and your inclusion of *growth* in the appraisal process further demonstrates your interest and commitment in this area.

Specific growth-oriented feedback and feedforward as part of the performance appraisal process can help your employees carry out their current responsibilities more effectively and productively, while also preparing them to handle new projects today and in the future. These types of positive outcomes that are associated with *growth* also lead to higher levels of employee motivation, satisfaction, loyalty, and engagement.

By including *growth* as part of the appraisal process, you also provide encouragement and recognition for employees by identifying the areas in which they experienced significant personal development, while also identifying and providing support in areas in which further growth is needed. Many employees sense considerable positivity when they're part of a growth-oriented business and industry, and they sense an even higher level of positivity when their own growth is valued as well.

Leadership

The word *leadership* plays an important role in the performance appraisal process, not only for your direct reports who are in formal leadership positions, but also for your employees who may informally lead others. By approaching leadership as a process of positively influencing and collaboratively supporting others to reach agreed-upon goals, leadership-related behaviors and feedback clearly extend beyond job titles.

Employees in formal leadership roles should be provided with feedback and feedforward regarding their performance in terms of such outcomes as reaching team goals, building cooperation and collaboration, developing the employees' skills, facilitating communication, managing conflict, and building engagement. Feedback on these topics is expected by employees in these positions, and when it is provided as part of performance appraisals, it can serve as a source of recognition as well as a roadmap for improved leadership skills and effectiveness.

Employees who are not in formal leadership positions can also engage in leadership behaviors when dealing with their peers, such as by clarifying assignments and expectations, providing informal training and guidance, giving direct assistance as the go-to person when on-the-spot questions arise, and assuming leadership responsibilities for ad hoc committees and company events. It's important for these employees to receive feedback and feedforward on the leadership behaviors that they display. Such feedback is motivational and satisfying for them, encourages them to continue to provide help and support for the team, and further enhances their skills, knowledge, and promotability.

Reliability

One of the most important characteristics for employes to display on the job is *reliability*, and hence it is one of the most important words to include in the performance appraisal process. Reliability is typically demonstrated through such actions as keeping commitments, consistently demonstrating high levels of performance, meeting with other employees on time whether virtually or in person, completing work in accordance with agreed-upon deadlines, and being honest and transparent in carrying out all job responsibilities.

When employees are unreliable, their actions and inaction can easily disrupt the team and derail their performance. In addition, the lack of reliability also points to several questionable personal qualities such as minimal respect and consideration for others, a low level of engagement on the job, diminished interest in the quality and quantity of work, negligible concern for deadlines, and a rejection of company values.

Employees who perform reliably should receive recognition for doing so, whereas those who fall short in this area should receive specific feedback and feedforward to get them back on track. By noting, supporting, and reinforcing reliability through performance appraisals, you encourage and incentivize reliable employees to continue their current behaviors in this area. This maintains the positive impact that their reliability has on the team and its operations, while also fostering model behaviors that can help other team members learn how to upgrade their own reliability.

Strengths

A particularly supportive and uplifting word to include in the performance appraisal process is *strengths*. All employees bring various strengths to work, and performance appraisals offer an excellent opportunity to recognize and reinforce them. Regardless of how an employee may be performing, the extra recognition and appreciation that you provide regarding your employees' strengths will be favorably received and have a positive motivational impact.

A related outcome that emanates from this type of managerial feedback is for employees to inherently feel better about themselves, the overall working relationship, and any other feedback and feedforward that they may receive. When employees receive recognition for the specific strengths that they bring and apply to the job, along with the ways in which their strengths have contributed to successful performance, outcomes, and results, they feel encouraged to apply such strengths more regularly and on a wider range of projects and assignments. By doing so, they're able to generate further improvements in their performance, as well as even higher levels of satisfaction and motivation.

When you discuss your employees' strengths with them, you also open the door for additional growth and development opportunities. As employees demonstrate strengths in key areas of their work, this can lead to jointly establishing plans and goals that focus on enhancing these strengths through further training, upskilling, and guidance going forward — a step that makes these employees and the team even stronger.

Chapter **15**

The Top Ten Behaviors Meriting Special Recognition

When you look at your employees' behaviors during a given evaluation period, you find that some stand out beyond others, especially in terms of their impact on individual and team performance as well as alignment with the company's goals, vision, and values. These are the types of behaviors and actions you would like your employees to repeat going forward, not only from the standpoint of their own individual performance, but also from the standpoint of positively influencing their fellow employees to follow their example.

One of the most powerful and effective ways to generate this outcome is for you to use the performance appraisal process to clearly and specifically provide recognition to your employees for engaging in any such behaviors. Recognition associated with particularly excellent behaviors is a highly powerful motivator. By providing it, you not only energize your employees to continue to engage in these positive and productive behaviors, you also increase their overall levels of satisfaction, self-confidence, and attachment to the company — all of which contribute further to their performance.

Although recognizing your employees' excellent behaviors across the full spectrum of roles and responsibilities is important, ten specific behaviors jump off the chart and merit *special recognition*. These behaviors are identified and discussed in this chapter, and the common theme shared by all of them is that they demonstrate particularly high levels of dedication, commitment, energy, and engagement, all of which add significant value to the employees as individuals and the company at large.

TIP

Your employees are learning from you every day, not only as a result of your direct feedback, feedforward, and guidance, but also as a result of your own behaviors. As a result, another effective way to draw out the following top ten behaviors from your employees is to engage in them yourself.

Acting Honestly

Honesty is an essential component in any successful working relationship, and it's a quality widely sought by today's employees. When relationships have even the slightest hint of dishonesty, craftiness, or a lack of credibility, the outcome is that teamwork, cooperation, mutual respect, commitment, engagement, and trust are undermined and undone. At the same time, feelings of dissatisfaction, distress, and disaffection are substantially increased.

When employees demonstrate honesty in approaching their work and carrying out their job responsibilities, the positive measurable outcomes include increased collaboration, shared support, and enhanced overall performance and goal attainment. Employees are far more comfortable and effective when they know that they can count on the words, commitments, and promises of others on the team.

Identifying and reinforcing acts of honesty by a given employee sends a powerful and compelling message to that individual as well as to the entire team. In all truth, one of the most important behaviors to recognize and reinforce at work is employee honesty.

Collaborating with Others

Employees who encourage, support, and engage in ongoing collaboration with others are contributing to individual and organizational success in several ways. Collaborative efforts and actions result in marked increases in employee teamwork, skill levels, performance, innovativeness, satisfaction, and productivity.

In addition, in projects in which collaborative behaviors are clearly in play, employees not only share their expertise with other members of the team, they also learn from these other members. Hence, when employees collaborate, they're furthering their own development as well as the development of their associates.

On a more subtle level, the underlying message in the collaborative process is that all participants' input and ideas are important, and this message helps engender and enhance feelings of personal value, self-worth, inclusion, and achievement. In terms of the bigger picture, another positive outcome associated with collaboration is further enhancement and enrichment of the company's culture and climate.

Communicating Effectively

Effective communication is a key behavior to recognize in great part because it's a major contributor to individual and team performance, productivity, and success on the job. By communicating effectively, employees can develop clear, concise, and comprehensible messages that can be easily understood and acted upon by others. Solid communication skills not only enhance face-to-face interactions, but also upgrade the level of interaction through other media such as virtual meetings, e-mail, texting, and business messaging apps.

An essential element that underlies effective communications is the ability to listen to and empathize with others. Employees who take the time to listen carefully and actively to others, seriously consider what others may be feeling and experiencing, and observe their body language, pitch, tone, and vocabulary, are far more likely to engage in successful communication. By including these types of steps in the communication processes, employees are also helping to prevent future communication-related problems and resolve those that may exist.

Although engaging in one-way communication is quick and easy, employees who consistently use two-way communication generate superior outcomes, especially in terms of engaging others, saving time, and increasing the likelihood of meeting the intent of the messaging in the first place. Effective communications also tend to come with marked increases in teamwork, decision-making, trust, and conflict prevention and resolution.

Exceeding Goals

Employees who regularly exceed their jointly established performance and development goals are demonstrating a vast array of behaviors that are worthy of special recognition. These are the employees who are fully engaged in their work and the company at large, and they demonstrate consistently high levels of energy, drive, focus, and commitment.

Their goal-oriented behaviors also point to solid skills in terms of planning, organizing, managing time, and keeping commitments. Rather than viewing challenging goals as overwhelming and beyond attainment, these employees regard such goals as opportunities to enhance their skills, contribute to the organization, develop their careers, improve personal performance and productivity, and sense the satisfaction that comes from significant achievement and success.

The process of pursuing, achieving, and exceeding challenging goals not only contributes to the individual success of these employees, but also to the success of the department. As their fellow employees see the many positive outcomes that emanate from exceeding goals, their own efforts to do likewise are further energized as well.

TIP

Employees who surpass their goals know that they've done so, and they're likely to sense high levels of personal satisfaction, competence, and effectiveness as a result. You can elevate these positive feelings to even higher levels during the performance appraisal process by specifically recognizing your employees' success in exceeding their challenging goals.

Going the Extra Mile

This visual descriptor of a particularly positive workplace behavior simultaneously connotes several positive actions. It applies to the employees who literally and figuratively take extra steps to generate stellar results, take on additional work, tackle challenging projects, spend extra time helping and guiding coworkers, and actively supporting the company's mission and values.

When employees go the extra mile, they're also demonstrating significant levels of engagement, commitment, and loyalty, as well as genuine concern for the company and their fellow employees. Rather than limiting their roles by rigidly focusing on their job description, or on the bare minimum amounts of required work, or on the clock, these employees are focused on going beyond the generally accepted standards in carrying out their job responsibilities.

By stretching themselves into new areas by going the extra mile, these employees also enhance their own learning and upskilling. As a result, they make themselves more valuable in their current position, while simultaneously increasing their potential to make further contributions to the company in the future. In addition, when employees go the extra mile, those who are beneficiaries of such outreaching behaviors tend to experience and express appreciation as well as satisfaction — and this can include customers and vendors as well as fellow employees.

Handling Work with Agility

Employee agility is an important behavior that merits special recognition, as it's premised on an employee's receptiveness to change, openness to new ideas and strategies, and ability to adapt expeditiously and effectively to today's dynamic work environments, roles, and responsibilities. Through their agile responses and reactions, these employees contribute to the successful implementation of new approaches, strategies, systems, and methods.

Agility also implies forward-looking thinking that is not wedded to past practices and procedures. Agile employees take extra steps to understand the reasoning behind various changes, adjust their behaviors as needed, and approach such changes with positive expectations.

When encountering unanticipated changes and setbacks, these employees respond with resiliency, energy, and drive. As a result of their agile behaviors, they increase the likelihood of other employees reacting similarly, while also reducing the likelihood of widespread and unwarranted resistance and pushback.

Maintaining a Genuinely Positive Attitude

Employees who approach their job with a genuinely positive attitude demonstrate openness, receptivity, optimism, and confidence when faced with the dynamics of work, such as in terms of challenging projects, new or updated assignments, job pressures, organizational changes, or performance-related feedback. Rather than instantly reacting with resistance or rejection in such situations, these employees are far more inclined to step back, listen, think about whatever may be happening, and then step up and focus on what can be done rather than on what can't be done.

The mindset of these employees is to look at work through a positive lens and try to focus on the benefits, pluses, and advantages associated with whatever they may encounter on the job. As they approach the roles, responsibilities, and challenges associated with their work, they experience and express positivity and confidence which they then apply directly to their work.

These positively oriented employees consistently identify and focus on the benefits, pluses, and advantages associated with the vicissitudes of their work, regardless of the magnitude. They expect positive outcomes and results, and these expectations enhance their performance, while often having a similar impact on the performance of their fellow employees as well.

Pursuing Upskilling

By pursuing upskilling, employees are demonstrating a genuine commitment not only to further develop and enhance their personal skills, competencies, and effectiveness, but also to add value to the company and increase the range of measurable contributions that they can make. This type of behavior reflects their motivations to enhance their performance, achieve, advance, and play increasingly important roles in the company.

Employees who pursue upskilling do more than take advantage of company-sponsored training and development programs. Although they certainly participate in such formal and informal programs, sessions, and classes, they also pursue additional skill enhancement by engaging in outside readings, podcasts, conferences, and courses that further build their skill levels.

In addition to contributing to the company by applying their newly acquired skills to the job, they help the development of the team by sharing their newly acquired knowledge with them, such as by providing help, mentoring, and support based on the techniques, methods, and strategies that they have just learned. In addition, by fully committing to upskilling, these employees are also contributing to the future of the company by making themselves more qualified for advancement, as well as strengthening and enhancing their own knowledge base, proficiencies, and career development.

TIP

Although learning is often described as its own reward, the special recognition that you provide to your employees in this area *literally* makes learning more rewarding.

Solving Problems

Employees who show excellence in problem-solving enjoy the challenges that are associated with handling difficult problems at work, especially those that have defied effective solutions in the past. Rather than avoiding or shying away from problems and problematic situations, whether large or small, these employees approach them with a strong sense of confidence, persistence, inquisitiveness, innovative thinking, and optimism.

This does not mean that they instantly jump onto a problem and try to solve it. Rather, their approach is to try to understand the actual problem, the causes, the impacts, and the measurable results that are desired after the problem is solved.

With this problem-solving mindset in place, these employees consistently demonstrate solid analytical skills, outside-the-box thinking, logical strategies, and mental agility. They listen carefully to the input of others who may be directly or indirectly involved in the problem-solving process or impacted by the problem itself, and they know how to generate and implement highly productive solutions by making collaboration part of the process.

Thinking Creatively

When employees come up with creative ideas related to their established roles and beyond, they're also creating additional value for the company as they extend their thinking about work beyond the standard and traditional approaches and topics. By generating and suggesting innovative ideas within the department as well as across the departments, these employees are also demonstrating high levels of motivation, engagement, and drive, along with a genuine desire to make meaningful contributions to the company.

In this regard, when employees come up with new ideas, their behavior also shows a high degree of loyalty and commitment to the company. Rather than just doing their job, these employees are motivated to dig deeper, look carefully at their work and the company at large, and generate new strategies, approaches, methods, and systems that positively impact productivity and performance in targeted areas in the company, wherever they may be.

Another positive outgrowth associated with special recognition for this type of thinking is that it can raise the overall level of creative thinking by other members of the team. As employees see the ways in which creative thinking is valued and utilized in the company, the door is opened for them to engage in such thinking, hence further reinforcing a culture that truly places a premium on creative thinking by everyone.

Index

A

accuracy, phrases related to, 268–269
  excellent, 268
  exceptional, 268
  fully competent, 268
  marginal, 269
  unsatisfactory, 269
achievement
  discussing in feedback and feedforward, 88
  as word to include in appraisals, 320
active listening, 82–83
  being totally present, 82
  letting employees talk, 82
  nonverbal communication, 83
  open-ended questions, 83
  restating, rephrasing, and summarizing, 83
adding value, phrases related to, 294–297
  excellent, 295
  exceptional, 294
  fully competent, 295–296
  marginal, 296
  unsatisfactory, 296–297
administration skills, 245–266
  adjusting to change, 246–248
  applying managerial skills, 248–251
  bottom-line orientation, 251–253
  controlling costs, 253–255
  establishing goals, 255–257
  meeting deadlines, 258–260
  organizing, 260–261

  planning, 261–263
  schedules, 264–266
administrative information and documentation, 44–48
  for diminishing the likelihood of employee claims, 47–48
  for job transfers, 45–46
  for promotions, 44–45
  for succession planning, 46–47
agendas
  joint development of, 66–67, 80
  reviewing before sessions, 80
agility
  as behavior meriting special recognition, 331–332
  phrases related to, 99–101
    excellent, 100
    exceptional, 99
    fully competent, 100
    marginal, 100–101
    unsatisfactory, 101
analytical skills, phrases related to, 213–215
  excellent, 214
  exceptional, 213–214
  fully competent, 214–215
  marginal, 215
  unsatisfactory, 209–210
annual appraisals, 1
  negativity regarding, 7, 9, 24
  new role for, 11, 29–30
  problems associated with, 24–26
    delayed reinforcement, 24–25
    exclusive focus on the past, 25

About the Author

Ken Lloyd, Ph.D., is a nationally recognized management consultant, author, and public speaker who specializes in organizational development, human resources, and management coaching and development. Ken has consulted across the U.S. and Canada in a vast array of industries including healthcare, apparel, financial services, electronics, high-tech, and entertainment. His weekly workplace advice column ran for more than 20 years in numerous newspapers and in their online editions, and for 10 of those years, his column was syndicated by the *New York Times* Syndicate. Over the years, Dr. Lloyd taught numerous management classes in the MBA program at UCLA Anderson School of Management. He has lectured at several universities, and he has been a guest speaker at company meetings, conferences, and business gatherings. He also served as vice president of employee planning and development for more than 18 years at a major manufacturer and distributor of medical apparel and footwear.

Ken has authored and co-authored several successful books. He co-authored a workplace wellness book (with Stacey Laura Lloyd), *Is Your Job Making You Fat? How to Lose the Office 15 . . . and More!* (Skyhorse Press, 2017). He is the author of *Office Idiots: What to Do When Your Workplace Is a Jerkplace* (Career Press, 2013), as well as the first edition of *Performance Appraisals and Phrases for Dummies* (Wiley, 2009). He is also the author of *Jerks at Work: How to Deal with People Problems and Problem People* (Career Press, 1999; revised edition, 2006), *151 Quick Ideas to Recognize and Reward Employees* (Career Press, 2007), *Be the Boss Your Employees Deserve* (Career Press, 2002), and *The K.I.S.S. Guide to Selling* (Dorling Kindersley, 2001). In addition, he co-authored (with Dr. Donald Moine) *Ultimate Selling Power: How to Create and Enjoy a Multimillion Dollar Sales Career* (Career Press, 2002) and the classic *Unlimited Selling Power: How to Master Hypnotic Selling Skills* (Prentice Hall, 1990).

He has made several television and talk-radio appearances that include *Good Morning America*, CNN, *Morning Edition* on NPR, KABC, KTLA, and Fox Morning News, along with numerous podcast appearances on GlobalBusinessNews.

He received his B.A. from UC Berkeley and his Ph.D. in Industrial Relations and Organizational Behavior from UCLA. He is a member of the American Psychological Association, the Society for

Industrial and Organizational Psychology, and the Society for Human Resources Management.

Ken resides in Southern California with his wife and family.

Dedication

To Roberta and our wonderful family!

Acknowledgments

I've greatly enjoyed working on this new edition, and one of the main reasons is that I have had the pleasure of being part of a remarkable team of individuals that helped the project through every phase.

To my friend and professional colleague, Paul Falcone, I offer great thanks for the helpful and insightful thoughts. Paul is the highly regarded author of several bestselling HR books, as well as principal of Paul Falcone Workplace Leadership Consulting, LLC, an organization that specializes in management and leadership training and development, executive coaching, and a wide range of HR advisory services.

I also thank the entire team at Wiley Publishing, Inc. I was very fortunate to receive outstanding guidance and support from Christopher Morris, project editor, along with Alicia Sparrow, associate acquisitions editor, and Jennifer Yee, senior editor. It was a pleasure to work with each of them, and their suggestions, ideas, and comments were consistently first-rate.

I also offer a very special thanks to my fantastic research librarian, friend, and wife, Roberta. Her breadth of knowledge, eye for detail, and input were literally invaluable.

Publisher's Acknowledgments

Acquisitions Editor: Alicia Sparrow
Project Editor: Christopher Morris
Copy Editor: Christopher Morris
Technical Editor: Fayla Schwartz

Production Editor:
Saikarthick Kumarasamy
Cover Image: © PM Images/
Getty Images

Leverage the power

Dummies is the global leader in the reference category and one of the most trusted and highly regarded brands in the world. No longer just focused on books, customers now have access to the dummies content they need in the format they want. Together we'll craft a solution that engages your customers, stands out from the competition, and helps you meet your goals.

Advertising & Sponsorships

Connect with an engaged audience on a powerful multimedia site, and position your message alongside expert how-to content. Dummies.com is a one-stop shop for free, online information and know-how curated by a team of experts.

- Targeted ads
- Video
- Email Marketing
- Microsites
- Sweepstakes sponsorship

20 MILLION
PAGE VIEWS
EVERY SINGLE MONTH

15 MILLION UNIQUE
VISITORS PER MONTH

43%
OF ALL VISITORS
ACCESS THE SITE
VIA THEIR MOBILE DEVICES

700,000 NEWSLET SUBSCRIPT
TO THE INBOXES OF
300,000 UNIQUE INDIVIDUALS EVERY WEEK

# of dummies

Custom Publishing

Reach a global audience in any language by creating a solution that will differentiate you from competitors, amplify your message, and encourage customers to make a buying decision.

- Apps
- Books
- eBooks
- Video
- Audio
- Webinars

Brand Licensing & Content

Leverage the strength of the world's most popular reference brand to reach new audiences and channels of distribution.

For more information, visit dummies.com/biz

PERSONAL ENRICHMENT

Staying Sharp
9781119187790
USA $26.00
CAN $31.99
UK £19.99

Facebook
9781119179030
USA $21.99
CAN $25.99
UK £16.99

Guitar
9781119293354
USA $24.99
CAN $29.99
UK £17.99

Investing
9781119293347
USA $22.99
CAN $27.99
UK £16.99

Beekeeping
9781119310068
USA $22.99
CAN $27.99
UK £16.99

Digital Photography
9781119235606
USA $24.99
CAN $29.99
UK £17.99

Meditation
9781119251163
USA $24.99
CAN $29.99
UK £17.99

Pregnancy
9781119235491
USA $26.99
CAN $31.99
UK £19.99

Samsung Galaxy S7
9781119279952
USA $24.99
CAN $29.99
UK £17.99

iPhone
9781119283133
USA $24.99
CAN $29.99
UK £17.99

Crocheting
9781119287117
USA $24.99
CAN $29.99
UK £16.99

Nutrition
9781119130246
USA $22.99
CAN $27.99
UK £16.99

PROFESSIONAL DEVELOPMENT

Windows 10
9781119311041
USA $24.99
CAN $29.99
UK £17.99

AutoCAD
9781119255796
USA $39.99
CAN $47.99
UK £27.99

Excel 2016
9781119293439
USA $26.99
CAN $31.99
UK £19.99

QuickBooks 2017
9781119281467
USA $26.99
CAN $31.99
UK £19.99

macOS Sierra
9781119280651
USA $29.99
CAN $35.99
UK £21.99

LinkedIn
9781119251132
USA $24.99
CAN $29.99
UK £17.99

Windows 1
9781119310
USA $34.00
CAN $41.99
UK £24.99

SharePoint 2016
9781119181705
USA $29.99
CAN $35.99
UK £21.99

Fundamental Analysis
9781119263593
USA $26.99
CAN $31.99
UK £19.99

Networking
9781119257769
USA $29.99
CAN $35.99
UK £21.99

Office 2016
9781119293477
USA $26.99
CAN $31.99
UK £19.99

Office 365
9781119265313
USA $24.99
CAN $29.99
UK £17.99

Salesforce.com
9781119239314
USA $29.99
CAN $35.99
UK £21.99

Coding
9781119293
USA $29.
CAN $35.
UK £21.9

dummies.com

dummie
A Wile

Learning Made Easy

ACADEMIC

9781119293576
USA $19.99
CAN $23.99
UK £15.99

9781119293637
USA $19.99
CAN $23.99
UK £15.99

9781119293491
USA $19.99
CAN $23.99
UK £15.99

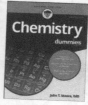

9781119293460
USA $19.99
CAN $23.99
UK £15.99

9781119293590
USA $19.99
CAN $23.99
UK £15.99

9781119215844
USA $26.99
CAN $31.99
UK £19.99

9781119293378
USA $22.99
CAN $27.99
UK £16.99

9781119293521
USA $19.99
CAN $23.99
UK £15.99

9781119239178
USA $18.99
CAN $22.99
UK £14.99

9781119263883
USA $26.99
CAN $31.99
UK £19.99

Available Everywhere Books Are Sold

dummies.com

dummies
A Wiley Brand

Small books for big imaginations